KNOWING YOUR PLACE

BLACK DOG
BOOKS

First published in England 2009
Black Dog Books, 104 Trinity Street, Norwich, Norfolk, NR2 2BJ.
www.blackdogbooks.co.uk

Foreword © Richard Mabey, 2005
Published Extracts © Individual Authors/Authors' Estates

A CIP record of this book is available from the British Library.

ISBN 978-0-9549286-7-4

Typeset in 11.5/15 point Times.

Printed in Great Britain by the MPG Books Group, Bodmin and King's Lynn

KNOWING YOUR PLACE

EAST ANGLIAN
LANDSCAPES AND LITERATURE

FOREWORD BY
RICHARD MABEY

Acknowledgements

In addition to those listed below, this celebration of East Anglia owes much to contributions from fellow East Anglians: D.J.Taylor for his suggestions; Elspeth Barker, Ronald Blythe, Mark Cocker, Ian Collins, Caroline Davison, the late Roger Deakin, Richard Mabey, Edward Storey and William Rivière.

Extracts from copyright material are reproduced by permission of: A.P.Watt Ltd. for *Waterland* by Graham Swift; PDF & the estate of Hilaire Belloc for *Hills and the Sea*; Harper Collins for *The Book of Merlin* by T.H.White; Random House for *Waterlog* by Roger Deakin, *A Passionate Apprentice* by Virginia Woolf, *I'll Stand By You*, *Diaries* and *Letters* of Sylvia Townsend Warner and *The Rings of Saturn* by W.G.Sebald; The Society of Authors for 'Parson Woodforde' by Virginia Woolf and 'George Crabbe and Peter Grimes' by E.M.Forster; C.Sinclair-Stevenson for *A Glastonbury Romance* and *The Dorset Year* by John Cowper Powys; John Murray for *All Done From Memory* by Osbert Lancaster; Gillon Aitken Assocs. and Candida Lycett Green for 'Greatness in Profusion' and 'Perfection Threatened' by John Betjeman; Ed Victor Ltd. for *World Within World* by Stephen Spender; Sheil Land Assocs. for *The Lighting of the Lamps* by Susan Hill and *Country Matters* by Richard Mabey; B.Hamilton and the estate of Sonia Orwell for *Collected Essays, Journalism & Letters of George Orwell*; David Higham Assocs. for *English Excursions* by Geoffrey Grigson.

Peter Tolhurst, Black Dog Books, 2009

CONTENTS

FOREWORD
Richard Mabey

Go East! Who would ever give such advice, and urge the young to take their chances amongst the flints and cheek-paring winds? It would be like encouraging them to run away to sea. Yet, as this anthology shows, writers have repeatedly gone against that supposed instinct to chase the sun and good life and have sought nourishment in the austere air of East Anglia. For many, it has been a kind of spa for the spirit, a place where the excesses and languor of more luxuriant regions can be purged. For J. A. Baker, whose astonishing and matchless book, *The Peregrine*, sees East Anglia's landscapes through, as it were, the eyes of a hawk, the orientation of the compass was an imperative: 'Direction has colour and meaning ... West is a thickening of the earth into trees, a drawing together, the great beef side of England ... East is a quickening in the sky, a beckoning of light, a storming suddenness of sea.'

What does it mean to know a place, to decipher its meaning? The fact that, of East Anglia's two great sandy regions, the one in the west should have been chosen for the Ministry of Defence's Battle Area at Stanford, while the one in the east nourished Benjamin Britten's *War Requiem*, should indicate that the genius loci is always, to some degree, in the mind of the beholder. And can one really group into a coherent area not just these two great deserts – the Breckland and the Sandlings – but the airy grace of Blythburgh church, the wild oaks of Staverton, the front at Great Yarmouth, the Stour Valley and the Portugese quarter of Thetford? Yet some common elements are too

5

persistent to ignore. No-one would use the phrase 'the fat of the land' with reference to East Anglia. The writers who've chosen to pass through, settle, observe, (as well as the indigenous inhabitants, who have had no such choices) see it, almost unanimously, as somewhere spare and spartan. Ronald Blythe calls it the 'candid plain'. The wind, the flatness, the ubiquitous and perilous closeness of water, have nurtured a culture of realism, of making do. I've often felt that the sand country's archetypal joke – 'What county's your farm in?' 'That depends on which way the wind blow. Sometimes thas in Suffolk sometimes in Norfolk' – is East Anglia's creation myth. In a world built on shifting sands – or for that matter on shifting water – you have no choice but to dust yourself down and start again. (Or perhaps move away, as generations have done since the 17th century.)

Which is not to indulge in the foolish and patronising game of trying to define a regional 'character'. Those who still categorise East Anglians as essentially suspicious, friendly, egalitarian, narrow-minded, diffident, extrovert, fatalistic or whatever, need to widen their circle of acquaintances. But a shared culture, especially a shared, ongoing conversation about ourselves, is another matter. Like all essentially rural people, East Anglians tell stories – literary stories, pub stories, tall stories. The narratives are cumulative. They become a kind of regional gossip, a communal self-portrait, a background hum that is part of the landscape. Knowing your place is a reciprocal process: the place also comes to know you, to absorb your voice. To sketch out the linkages between the contributors to this book, as they have talked to, learned from and lived with each other, would be to make an alternative map of East Anglia. And in this ongoing local narrative, tacking is a reflex, a way of navigating through life's uncertainties. 'Well,' begins the customary local response to any involved question, suggesting an infinity of possible answers, qualifications, variations and invitations to rephrase.

I first listened in to this busy myth-making on a childhood holiday in Lincolnshire – even less frequently admitted to the East Anglian club than Essex, but inescapably sharing that North Sea edginess. We went to Skegness for our holidays because my mother thought it was 'bracing', compared to the soporific resorts on the south coast. And 'bracing' is of course the town's own description of its aura, personified in the famous tourist poster of a rotund man, arms akimbo, running along the beach. Bracing. It could be East Anglia's summing up of itself, full as the word is of physicality and ambivalence: 'girding, binding tightly, lacing up, strengthening. The action of assuming a bold or defiant attitude ...', as an adjective 'used chiefly of the air or climate; formerly of tonic medicines'.

I felt pretty bold and defiant myself when, as a naïve and untravelled teenager, I first ventured to East Anglia proper. For the best part of a decade a gang of us spent our weekends and holidays on a converted lifeboat, moored at Blakeney. We ran wild on the marshes, watching birds, picking samphire, cockling, yarning, scribbling, imagining ourselves as scholar gipsies, and in thrall to the way the tides re-made our world twice daily. It gave me, I wrote later, 'a liberating vision of being at the edge of things.' When I took my chances and became a full-time writer in the early 70s, I rented a cottage in Blakeney, not so much to live in, as to continue that dream of being a kind of literary hunter-gatherer. Except that what I was foraging for, I can see now, were not just the wild vegetables I was writing about, but a livelihood, a way of living that was on the cusp between domesticity and wildness. It was a classic piece of Norfolk tacking. For neatly contained spells, I would flit from the Chilterns to the coast, and spend my days prowling the marshes like a noble savage, binoculars over one shoulder and a bundle of sea-kale over the other. Back in the cottage, I'd lay a formal table for one, clean tablecloth included, and eat the weeds of the day, washed down with a bottle from the Wine Society. Going feral was not what I was after.

A sense of squirreling, of making the best of things, of celebrating what is inevitable, shines through in East Anglian writing. In so many of the pieces here there is a reverence for the luminous details of things and places, as if, in a landscape cast as frugal and niggardly, every shard and nugget counts. Edward Thomas, beachcombing at Minsmere in a break from writing his life of Richard Jefferies, makes a collection as telling as the Sutton Hoo treasure: 'champagne corks, sailors' hats, Antwerp beer bottles, fish boxes, oranges, lemons, onions, banana stems, waterworn timber and the most exquisite flat & round pebbles, black, white, dove grey, veined, wheat coloured. Why does Nature make these beautiful things so carelessly & then one wonders whether all beautiful things are not of this careless inevitableness...' T.H. White sees the east wind itself as something solid; 'You could have hooked the crook of your umbrella over it, and it would have hung there'. Sylvia Townsend Warner, relishing the sea-wracked, sharp-shingled landscape of Salthouse after a troubled time in Dorset, sees tank traps uncovered by a storm tide, 'looking like some sort of mineral nettles'. Her cottage was called Great Eye Folly, and was washed away itself in the 1953 floods.

I think that getting to know a place proceeds through much the same developmental stages as one's own life. You begin with a sensual involvement and an instinctive marking out of territory. Objects, secret niches, ritual moments – the smell of gorse, the calls of oystercatchers at night – acquire a totemic power. Then you feel the need for a more intellectual grasp, for more literal maps of place and history, and to trace roots rather than just feel them. Finally, if you are very lucky, imagination and knowledge join, and you begin to inhabit the place, dwell on it. You may even come to live there.

When, flushed with the earnings from my first book, I came to buy my first cottage in East Anglia, I wanted it to be in Suffolk, because I'd moved into that second phase of knowing, and believed (mystifyingly, now) that Suffolk had more history, more depth than Norfolk. I tried to get a forester's cottage in the Breckland, whose extraordinary past as England's inland desert had begun to enthral me. But it was a Forestry Commission house, a property of the state, and all prospective purchasers had to submit to competitive interview. (An interview! – for a hovel in a place of rabbit warrens and sandstorms!) My vague life-plans were not public-spirited or serious enough, I imagine, and I was turned down. I ended up with a small flint house in Wenhaston, just upstream from Blythburgh. On my first night there I lay in bed listening to nightingales, one on the little heath above the house, the other in the churchyard of St Peter, where there is a 16th century painting of the Last Judgement, described by Pevsner as 'distressingly rustic'. I thought of Keat's phrase 'The voice I hear this passing night was heard/ In ancient days ...' That autumn I discovered a toadstool up the lane which hadn't been seen in England for more than 40 years. It was called, rather thrillingly, *Battarraea phalloides*, and was growing in a sandy bank outside Blyford church. It was, needless to say, a bizarre and fickle species. It had a stem like twisted leather, with the spores carried on the outside of the cap, and was apt to disappear for decades at a time. When it was first described by Thomas Woodward from a specimen in Bungay in 1784, he wrote: 'This extraordinary vegetable production arises from a volva, which is buried six or eight inches deep in dry sandy banks; and, consequently, it is extremely difficult to detect in its earliest state.' For a short while it was called Bungea.

History seemed to be thrusting itself on me, which was just what I wanted. Solemn surveys of ancient woods replaced those wild excursions on the north coast marshes. I rambled about now with old maps rather than gathering baskets, noting medieval banks and monkish fish-ponds as if they were the finials and crockets of the landscape. I tracked down ancient records of Suffolk plants and searched for them in their ancestral habitats. Sometimes the sense of continuity stopped me in my tracks. Hopping over to the Aldeburgh Festival one June, I spent the time between concerts botanising on the beach, dimly aware that George Crabbe had done the same two centuries before. I still have the list I made, inscribed inside the fly-leaf of my field-guide. I found many of the sparse and modest plants that he felt such bitter affection for, but many that he wouldn't have seen (and might not have approved of): a luxuriant, prostrate wild apple tree, whose fruits dangled inches above the pebbles; the lovely rangy tree lupin, naturalised from the easy-going coasts of California.

But the greater discontinuity was the difference in our reactions. I felt my heart lifted by these dogged opportunists, springing out of nothing and living so handsomely on this bleak shore. Crabbe saw their meagre proportions and miserly habits as symbolic of the ineluctable poverty of the place and its human inhabitants. As E.M. Forster brilliantly suggests here, he had a love-hate relationship with Aldeburgh: 'The idea of regeneration, so congenial to Wordsworth and the Lake District, does not appeal to this son of the estuary ... Dull, harsh, stony, wiry, soft, slimy – what disobliging epithets, and yet he is in love with the scene ... through the singularity of his taste and associations [it brings] to him'.

There is a long and honourable tradition of social realism in East Anglian writing. Crabbe, Mary Mann and Rider Haggard sent piercing and unsentimental messages about the condition of the rural poor, yet seemed to see them irredeemably pulled down, imprisoned, by the inconstancy of the landscape. Just as old Dunwich had been swallowed by the sea and Santon Downham buried by an inland sandstorm, so the farm workers had lost not just their livelihood during the long agricultural depression, but their human spirit, too. Today we can see much of the very landscape itself destroyed by industrial farming. But not quite. There is the coast and the Broads, and, if one cares to look, signs of tenacity everywhere, amongst both people and nature.

Instability and uncertainty are endemic to East Anglia, yet life goes on. I can't quite remember what I felt when I discovered that the Norfolk Broads were not a series of natural post-glacial lakes, but pretty much a by-product of medieval energy industry. I lost a romantic dream, but gained a story whose true details had the makings of another creation myth – or at least a local parable: the digging of these vast steep-sided pits for peat, much of it for the big Benedictine estates; the great floods of the 13th century that drowned the mines; the Victorians' discovery of the joys of messing about in boats; and now the wildness returning, the great winter gatherings of cranes and raptors. In the understandable fear that global warming will make the sea rise and flood Broadland, we should remember that this is how it was created in the first place. Life goes round, as well as on.

Perhaps it is as important for writers to explore these indomitable cores of life in the landscape and its inhabitants as to reveal the harsher truths. Perhaps that is why so many of those who have written about East Anglia in these pages have been visitors, passage migrants who came voluntarily, and could to some degree choose what they experienced. William Cowper, Angus Wilson and Roger Deakin were incomers; Dorothy Wordworth, Sylvia Townsend Warner and George Orwell, short-term settlers; Virginia Woolf, John Cowper Powys, Edward Thomas, Geoffrey Grigson, Henry James and John Betjeman, just passing through. Graham Swift set his haunting novel *Waterland* in the Fens without, famously, ever having set foot in them. In what some – thinking of that loop of southern rivers – still regard as an island, marooned in the North Sea, migration is a fact of life.

I started as a migrant, and have now come to live here, with the same kind of serendipity as my very first visit. I had got into a rut back in the Chilterns, fallen ill, and drifted by a strange combination of luck and logic towards what I had always thought of as my second home. It was the East country's sense of transitoriness that set me right. I looked out at a field one evening and in the morning it was a lake. Water changes things, but makes renewal a continuous possibility, and is a central feature of the East Anglian narrative. There are more dialect words here for rain than the Inuit have for snow, despite the fact that the rainfall is the amongst the lowest in Europe. But it is not, of course, the water falling from the sky that matters, but that lurking under the earth – the web of springlines and oozing peat and tidal flushes on which East Anglia precariously floats, and which in its many guises is threatening, opportunist, destructive and life-giving. Roger Deakin made the ultimate native odyssey by swimming across Suffolk, through moats and parkland lakes and weedy streams and the underwater maze of drainage channel markers in the Blythe estuary, out to where Suffolk dissolved seamlessly into the sea.

Stories like this make one ponder what meaning 'roots' can have in such a fluid setting. For me – and I shocked myself at how easily I was able to throw off the tethers of a lifetime – they seem to have something in common with the roots of some water-plants, which begin in one place but then spring down, so to speak, in many others. I am now well settled in the Waveney Valley, in a house which has been patched together from a Tudor cottage, a 19th century hemp farm and an American airmen's wartime billet. From my window I can see migrating golden plovers feeding in the fields as they have done, in their many guises, since they were first cleared 3000 years ago. Beyond them the Bangladeshi piece-workers are stooped over the furrows hand-picking coriander for the Midlands cities. I might be tempted to say that the rhythm of both scenes is timeless, but for the fact that they are both rooted so exactly and fascinatingly in time and place.

The one writer who belies all this talk of movement and migration is Ronald Blythe, our paterfamilias, who quite properly begins and concludes this collection. He writes in 'An Inherited Perspective' of how regional writers' 'feeling for nature and the landscape of man deepens when it remains hedged about by familiar considerations.' Ronald Blythe was born in Suffolk and has lived all his life in the Eastern counties. He has lifted the celebration of 'familiar considerations' into a literary form that transcends locality. Yet it has not been strictly by 'staying put'. True to the restless spirit of the place, his imagination swoops about through millennia of writing and thinking. He has taken the East Anglian tradition of 'getting about' across the Atlantic, and been talked to by the Sheriff for walking a little too freely on the freeways. But it is perhaps his account of night-walking at home (in *Word from Wormingford*) with its sense of history and new life and transcendental detail, which might serve as the epigraph for our windblown heartland: 'The church tower is a charcoal stump, just as it was during the summer nights which followed the Conquest ... Gravestones are legible and there are dense scents. Young rabbits are dining off a wreath and other unidentifiable creatures rustle and fidget. Everywhere, it is all so perfectly interesting that one might never go to bed.'

AN INHERITED PERSPECTIVE

Ronald Blythe

(from *From the Headland*, 1982)

'Any landscape is a condition of the spirit,' wrote Henri-Frédéric Amiel in his *Journal In Time*. As a Swiss he could have been reproaching all those British intellectuals and divines who abandoned what their own country had to offer by way of transcendental scenery, the Lake District beginning to lose its efficacy as a spiritual restorative by the mid-nineteenth century, for the Jungfrau and the Matterhorn. *Any* landscape is a condition of the spirit. A few months ago I happened to glance up from my book as the train was rushing towards Lincoln to see, momentarily yet with a sharp definition, first the platform name and then the niggard features of one of the most essential native landscapes in English literature, John Clare's Helpston. I had not realised that the train would pass through it, or that one could. It was all over in seconds, that glimpse of the confined prospect of a great poet, but not before I had been reminded that he had thrived for only as long as he had been contained within those flat village boundaries. When they shifted him out of his parish, although only three miles distant – and for his own good, as they said – he began to disintegrate, his intelligence fading like the scenes which had nourished it. Of all our poets, none had more need to be exactly *placed* than John Clare. His essential requirements in landscape were minimal and frugal, like those of certain plants which do best in a narrow pot of unchanged soil.

I observed this tiny, yet hugely sufficient, world of his dip by under scudding clouds. A church smudge – and his grave an indefinable fraction of it – some darkening hedges, probably those planted after the Enclosure Act had stopped the clock of the old cyclic revolutions of Helpston's agriculture, thus initiating Clare's disorientation, a few low-pitched modern dwellings, and that was all. It was scarcely more impressive in Clare's lifetime. A contemporary clergyman, gazing at it, said that 'its unbroken tracts strained and tortured the sight'. But not the poet's sight, of course. This it nourished and extended with its modest images. He liked to follow the view past the 'lands', which he disliked because of the way they overtaxed the strength of his slight body when he laboured on them, to where the cultivation dropped away into a meeting with heath and fen. From here onwards the alluvial soil swept unbroken to the sea. It was this landscape of the limestone heath, he said, which 'made my being'. And thus it was in this practically featureless country that genius discovered all that it required for its total expression. From it Clare was to suffer a triple expulsion. The first entailed that fracture from his childhood vision of his home scene – something which we all have to endure. The second was when the fields and roads of Helpston were radically redesigned in 1816, evicting him from all its ancient certainties. The third, and quite the most terrible, was when it was arranged for him to live in the *next* village, a well-meaning interference with an inherited perspective which, in his special case, guaranteed the further journey to Northampton lunatic asylum.

To be a native once meant to be a born thrall. Clare's enthralment by Helpston presents the indigenous eye at its purest and most naturally disciplined. By his extraordinary ability to see furthest when the view was strictly limited, he was able to develop a range of perception which outstripped the most accomplished and travelled commentary on landscape and nature, of which in the early nineteenth century there was a great deal. He had no choice. He did not pick on Helpston as a subject. There was no other place. As a boy, like most children, he had once set out from his village to find 'the world's end', and got lost.

So I eagerly wanderd on & rambled along the furze the whole day till I got out of my knowledge when the very wild flowers seemd to forget me & I imagind they were the inhabitants of new countrys the very sun seemd to be a new one & shining on a different quarter of the sky.

is how he described this adventure in his *Autobiography*. And twice more in this book, when he was aged fifteen and when he was aged twenty, he tells of a kind of geographical giddiness, such as that which one has when being spun round blindfold in some game, when he had to leave the balanced centre of his native village to look for work in nearby market towns, and his sense of psychic displacement went far beyond that which could have been brought on by the strain of interviews and so forth. Here is Clare again, as the universe itself careens out of control because he is unable to use his village reference points.

I started for Wisbeach with a timid sort of pleasure & when I got to Glinton turnpike I turned back to look on the old church as if I was going into another country Wisbeach was a foreign land to me for I had never been above eight miles from home in my life I coud not fancy England much larger than the part I knew . . .

I became so ignorant in this far land that I coud not tell which quarter the wind blew from & I even was foolish enough to think the sun's course was alterd & that it rose in the west & set in the east I often puzzled at it to set myself right ...

'I became so ignorant in this far land ...' 'to set myself right' – these are the telling words. Beyond his own parish boundary Clare felt that he was ignorant. He felt his intelligence desert him and that another man's scene – even another man's sun – could nor be understood. When the success of his two collections of published poems brought him into contact with literary London, an event for which many a provincial writer prayed in the hope that their work would provide the

15

exit visa from the limitations which had inspired it, Clare reacted very wisely indeed. 'It seems', says John Barrell in his excellent study, *The Idea of Landscape and the Sense of Place: An Approach to the Poetry of John Clare,* that the more the poet began to understand about literary London, the more tenacious became his desire to write exclusively about Helpston. London's literary landscapes knew no bounds at all. They swept back in immense, formal vistas carrying the educated eye to valleys in Thessaly and to Roman farms. Knowing that he could never be entirely free at home and accepting an element of imprisonment as the major condition for his being a poet, Clare chose the local view.

I believe that, whether with a feeling of relief or despair – or both – the majority of what are called regional poets and novelists come to a similar decision. Their feeling for nature and the landscape of man deepens when it remains hedged about by familiar considerations. Paradoxically, they discover that it is *not* by straying far from the headlands that they are able to transport their readers into the farthest realms of the imagination and its truths, but by staying put.

I find that I have two states of local landscape consciousness. The first I would call instinctive and unlettered, a mindfulness of my own territory which has been artlessly and sensuously imbibed. On top of this I have a country which I have deduced or discovered from scientific, sociological, aesthetic and religious forays into its depths. Of course, like the rest of us, I want to have my cake and eat it too. I do not want the first knowledge, wherein lies all the heart and magic, to give way entirely to the second knowledge, wherein lie all the facts. It is the usual dilemma of intuition versus tuition and how to reconcile the one with the other without patronising either. Because my boyhood East Anglia was by far the major source of all the references which have directed me as a writer, I find myself constantly hankering after primordial statements which still float around in my memory, and which seem to say something more relevant about my own geography than anything my trained intelligence can tell me, yet which tantalisingly avoids definition. All the same, I must say something about the fields and streams and skies, the cottages, gothic churches, lanes and woods of Suffolk as I first recognised them. This could have been the time when I knew the river but did not know its name. Certainly it is a verifiable fact that much which can be seen now could be seen then – when I was ten or twelve. Or two or three. When does one begin to look? Or does landscape enter the bloodstream with the milk?

'Local' – a limited region, says the dictionary. And 'location', the marking out or suryeying of a tract of land. Also a position in space. So, early on, we begin to take stock of our limited regions, marking them out, and with never a suspicion that they at this period could be marking *us* out. I took stock of flowers first, then paths and then architecture. I do not know that I ever at this time took stock of weather or of inhabitants. The latter were thin then, pared down to the high cheek-bone by the long agricultural depression and with skins polished by the winds. But however great the omissions, I saw enough to lay in a lasting stock of feeling and emotion, for as Lord Holland said, 'There is not a living creature ... but hath the sense of feeling, although it hath none else.' We, of course, are taking feeling beyond such an elementary sensation and into human sensibility. It is this proto-sensibility created by the impact of nature on our earliest awareness that intrigues us later on. We know that climates create cultures and cultures create types, but an individual voice within us says that there is more to it than this, conceit notwithstanding.

'Those scenes made me a painter', wrote John Constable, acknowledging the river valley in which I now live and just above which I was born. It has been said that from these scenes he fashioned the best-loved landscapes of every English mind. Thomas Gainsborough too, another local boy pushed into art by scenery, was born in this valley and was sketching along the same footpaths in the eighteenth century as I, when a child, was wandering in the twentieth. Indeed, my old farmhouse is roughly perched at the frontier of these two artists' territorial river inspirations. Gainsborough's landscape was upstream and flowing back in golden-brown vistas to the Dutch masters; Constable's was down-stream and flowing forward to the French Impressionists. When I was an adolescent, these two local painters dominated my equally native landscape to an alarming extent, often making it impossible to see a field for myself. And I was further alarmed when I heard that Sickert had called the entire district a sucked orange. Would there be anything left for a writer to feed on, or would I be like someone attempting to take an original view of Haworth or Egdon Heath? Ancestry decided it. Not that I knew much about the centuries of farming fathers stretching away from me, perhaps into Saxon days, but the realisation that our eyes had repeatedly seen the same sights began to promote a way of looking at life which was vigorous and questioning, and which did nor depend on past conclusions.

And so what was my inherited perspective? What, particularly, was I recognising before I was educated in history and ecology and, most potently, in literature? Or even in local loyalty, for in all the provinces, in every hamlet, one might say, there is this beaming self-congratulation of those who have been born there and who indicate that it would be superfluous to ask more of life. Although not quite as restricted as Clare in mileage terms, as a boy in those immediate pre-World War Two days from a rural family apparently existing on air, I saw a very little world indeed. Until I was twelve or so, East Anglia was for me no more than a small circle of villages round a small town, plus an annually visited beach, or rather a slipping, clinking wall of cold shingle, monotonously piled up and pulled down by the North Sea. The landscape of Crabbe, in fact, who had made the definitive statement about it. Benjamin Britten was able to say something else about it in another medium. I saw this beach as the edge to my interior landscape, disregarding the distance in between. From the beginning I was laying claim to a broader scenic inheritance than some writers. ...

My own powerful landscape inheritance was not walled off from me until I grew up. There was no pittance to start with in the shape of an elementary soil brought home in paper-bags, no rationing of the sky, no ignoring of the native scene's prophets, one of whom was no less than the foremost artist of the English romantic movement, John Constable. And yet, like all children, how little of it I comprehended as a boy! Looking back, I am as much intrigued by my blindness to the obvious, as by the way I sometimes instantly grasped some central truth. There seems to be a considerable osmotic action in landscape, particularly one's native landscape, which causes it to be breathed in as it thrusts against our earliest senses. Being there, right under our noses, we inhale it as well as comprehending it with our intellects. For some it is a fatal air, for others a kind of inescapable nourishment which expands the soul. Quite where the emotional – I will not say mindless – absorption and the instructed viewpoint began to fuse in myself, I find it impossible to say. Nor can I tell if I have continued all these years, living as I have among the first earthly patterns and colours I ever saw, to absorb them instinctively as well as intellectually. But I do recall some of those instances in which the obvious says nothing to the child. For example, I climbed a road called Gallows Hill every day and never once did it say something agonising, macabre and morbid to me. What it said was freedom, running loose. Gallows Hill was the path to the white violet and cowslip sites – for plants remained undisturbed in their locations for generations then, and village people of all ages saw them as a form of permanent geography by which the distance of Sunday walks could be measured, or where tea or love could be made, or, in my case, where books could be read. These special flowers in their hereditary places were solidly picked, I might add, but there were always just as many next year. Had the victims of Gallows Hill picked them in the years before they picked pockets? I expect so.

Gallows Hill also led to Froissart and Malory for me, for just above stood a little moated manor with a castellated tower and swans on the dark water, and even now I see this as an annexed scene, as a house which does not belong to its residents, but to my most personal countryside. So do the aged village relations who sat four-square in their lush gardens like monuments, as if growing out of the Suffolk clay itself, their bodies wooden and still, their eyes glittering and endlessly scanning leaves and birds and crops, their work done and their end near. I remember very distinctly how these old country people were not so much figures in a landscape, as local men and women who, in their senescence, were browning and hardening back into its simple basic elements.

As a rule, children draw back from the illimitable, except when they catch such suggestions of it in the experience of running down grassy slopes with open arms on a windy day, and prefer the secret, the clandestine and the enclosed. I had to grow up to see that East Anglia was not a snug den but a candid plain, an exposed and exposing place. Once it was all manageable privacies and concealments, each memorably furnished with its particular stones, flora, water and smells. In this secret range I included the North Sea, for although it was all of thirty miles off and seen so rarely, perhaps only once a year, I felt the same parochial tenderness about it as I did about the meadows – fields, really, gone to weed due to the agricultural depression – which led to my grandmother's house. As I sighted this quite unimaginably immense liquid wall at the end of the coast road, with the Rotterdam shipping riding its horizon, I can remember how it revoked all the feelings I had for the interior. The sea makes us treacherous; it captures our senses and makes us faithless to the land. I found myself in a different state by the sea; not freed, but in another kind of captivity. I lived by it briefly when I first became a writer and felt myself both in my own deeply-rooted country and on the edge of things. The entire ecology changes long before one even suspects the presence of the Suffolk sea. A twelve-mile belt of light soil, which we call the sandlings, produces heath and coniferous forests, and pale airy villages, dyked meadows and vast stretching skies, and by the time one has reached the rattling beach, still guarded by forts built to repel Bonaparte and Hitler, the interior seems remote. This is the land of our seventh-century Swedish kings who lie buried in their great ships at Sutton Hoo and whose palace is under a Nato bomber base. Screaming sea-birds and screaming planes on practice runs, and often profound silences, this is the indigenous periphery. Also a cuffing wind and an intriguing marine flora which between them force the gaze to the ground. This is Benjamin Britten's rim of country. When, at the end of his life, he worked for a brief spell in a cottage sunk in the cornlands of Suffolk, he told me how utterly d i fferent the imaginative stimulus was, and I realised that we had shared similar experiences of territorial disorientation within the home area, but from opposite directions.

What half-entranced, half-shocked me about the coast was its prodigious wastefulness. Here nature was humanly unmanageable, and I was not deceived by breakwater and drain or the sly peace of the marshes. There was another kind of wastefulness in the central clay country which, to my child's eye, was transmuted into a private harvest of benefits. Every hollow held water, and in the ancient horse-ponds and moats, under coverlets of viridescent slime starred with water ranunculus, lay the wicked pike, fish of legendary size, cunning and appetite which we believed were a century old, and which grew fat on suicides. The small heavy land fields had not then been opened up to suit modern machinery, and most of them possessed what the farmers called 'muddles', or uncultivated scraps which were crammed with birds, insects, flowers, shrubs, grasses and animals. Towering quickset hedges from enclosure days survived as well as mixed shrub hedges from Saxon, Norman and Tudor times, all still containing the oak trees which Shakespearean ploughmen must have used to set their first furrow. The surface of the land was littered with flint, and no matter however much was picked up for making churches and roads, no field was ever cleared, even when it had been hand-quarried for a millennium. It was a kind of catch-crop which worked itself up to the surface from its silican depths to provide assured hard labour for each succeeding generation of country people. Its permanency was like that of the mountains to field-workers in the north. 'So light a foot will ne'er wear our the everlasting flint,' says the priest as Juliet approaches to marry Romeo. We expended a massive amount of energy splitting these weighty stones to find the toad which was said to live inside them. We also spent hours in vast old gravel-pits searching for 'dawn stones' (eoliths, as I was to learn in my gradual enlightenment), but which then I was convinced meant the first stones warmed by the sun in the first chapter of Genesis. We would spend whole days in these workings, many feet below the peripheral corn, scraping away at the partly-known and the unrealised, but really at our ultimate ancestry, the Scandinavian Maglemose forest folk who, ten thousand years ago, before the sea washed us away from the continental mainland to which we were tenuously attached by salty lagoons, walked to Suffolk and began agricultural pattern-making on its fertile clays. We learned that they were followed by the Windmill Hill folk and the Beaker people, and these homely appellations would cut through time as the blade cut through June grass, making hay of its density. Distant past has moments of tangibility to a native, particularly to one who has not yet encountered the written history of his area. I can remember the need or compulsion I had to touch stones. I suppose I felt them for their eloquence and because an adjacent artifact told me that a Windmill boy might have done the same. Later, I came to love the stoniness of the symbolism in the poetry of Sidney Keyes, one of the best poets of the last war, who died in African sand, aged twenty-one.

It must be added that, seascape or richly dilapidated clayscape, the natural history of my childhood was marvellously impacted with mystery. There were swaying rookeries and barns like dust-choked temples almost within the precincts of our market town, behind the main streets of which ran a maze of courts and yards fidgety with sullen life. Naphtha flares blazed over the banana stalls and cheapjacks in the square, whilst mediaeval bells burled their sound for miles along the river valley when the wind was right. Having the wind right for this or that was something one heard a lot about. It was the bitter wind of a dry country and you had to stand up to it, they said. Vagrants and itinerants brewing up in the shelter of marl-pits fought a losing battle against it, and the silk factory operatives, sweeping in and out of their villages on bicycles, were swept along by it like pedalling birds. The scene was one of stagnant animation. One would catch the eye of a solitary worker among the sugar-beet, and it would be strangely hard and transparent, like glass. Extremes were normal. I once saw twenty men joyfully and silently clubbing scores of rats to death in a stackyard. No words, only rat-screams. Only a few yards from this spot Gainsborough had posed Mr and Mrs Robert Andrews against a spectacle made up of trees and towers and bending stream, and painted what Sir Sacheverell Sitwell has called the finest English domestic portrait. The young husband is seated between his gun and his wife. And once on this hill I heard the rarest, most exquisite aeolian music when the wind was right. It was a sound that made one weightless and emancipated, and I had that momentary sensation of *being* nature – nothing less or else.

Richard Jefferies used a nineteenth-century language to describe this transition of man into landscape and landscape into man in *The Story of My Heart*. We may have a later language or no language at all to put this feeling into words, but we have shared the experience. This is his way of puffing it:

Moving up the sweet short turf, at every step my heart seemed to obtain a wider horizon of feeling; with every inhalation of rich pure air, a deeper desire. The very light of the sun was whiter and more brilliant here. By the time I had reached the summit I had entirely forgotten the petty circumstances and the annoyances of existence. I felt myself, myself. There was an intrenchment on the summit, and going down into the fosse I walked round it slowly to recover breath ... There the view was over a broad plain, beautiful with wheat and inclosed by a perfect amphitheatre of green hills. Through these hills there was one narrow groove, or pass, southwards, where the white clouds seemed to close in the horizon. Woods hid the scattered hamlets and farmhouses, so that I was quite alone. I was utterly alone with the sun and the earth. Lying down on the grass, I spoke in my soul to the earth, the sun, the air, and the distant sea far beyond sight. I thought of the earth's firmness – I felt it bear me up ...

Recognisable in this post-Darwinian, pre-Freudian landscape confession is that confusion of the newly articulate response and incommunicable sensation which all of us have known. Jefferies was often exasperated by not being able to find a natural way to talk about nature. He saw that men operated on the assumption that nature was something which surrounded them but which did not enter them. That, glorious though it was, and inspiring, they were outside its jurisdiction. When they spoke of the influence of environment on a person, they meant some aspect of men's social environment, not climate and scenery. The man who, for some reason or other, remains on his home ground, becomes more controlled by the controlling forces he sees around him than he could wish or realise. Jefferies sought such a control in a quasi-religious and poetic pilgrimage to the grassy heights above his Wiltshire farm, and Thomas Hardy and Emily Bronte created immense dramas by allowing their characters to be activated as much by weather and place as by society. These, and many other writers and artists, shock us by showing us the malignancy of the native scene, how it imprisons us as well as releases us. Jefferies and Hardy, of course, were cynically amused that we should imagine it would be interested in doing either.

However, because we have had such a considerable hand in the actual arrangement of the local view, we must be allowed some subjectivity. Over the centuries we introduced the non-indigenous trees and flowers and crops, we made the roads, fields and buildings, and we filled in the heath with forests and levelled the woods for corn. What we see is not what nature, left to its own devices, would let us see. To be born and to die in an untouchable scene, in the wild mountains, for example, is quite a different matter. Comparatively few people do this. And so what the majority of us celebrate as natives is native improvements. The shapes, colours and scents have an ancestral significance, and what moves us is that the vista does not radiate from some proto-creation like a dawn-stone but that it is a series of constructions made by our labouring fathers. Within these, the normal partisan provincial will insist, must lie all that the inner and outward life requires.

Landscape and human sensibility can come to shallow terms in villages, which are notorious for the resentment they display when some indigenous guide, poet or painter, presents them with the wider view. The field workers who saw Cézanne and Van Gogh painting, and John Clare writing, believed that they were in the company of blasphemers. In a letter to his publishers Clare complains how isolating it is to be in possession of a literate landscape.

I wish I livd nearer you at least I wish London woud creep within 20 miles of Helpstone I don't wish Helpstone to shift its station I live here among the ignorant like a lost man in fact like a man whom the rest seem careless of having anything to do with – they hardly dare talk in my company for fear I should mention them in my writings & I find more pleasure in wandering the fields than mixing among my silent neighbours who are insensible of everything but toiling and talking of it & that to no purpose.

And yet, ironically, it was only by keeping their faces to the earth could these neighbours and their forebears carve out the sites where the poet's intelligence could dwell. The average home landscape entailed more looking down than looking around. As for the agreeability of a used countryside, as the poet and critic Geoffrey Grigson said, 'When I see men, and women, bent over the crops, I realise it isn't so agreeable for them. *'C'est dur l'agriculture'* (read Zola in *La Terre*). I like seeing machines which keep the human back from bending, as in the last five thousand years.'

When I was writing *Akenfield*, and thinking of the old and new farming generations, it struck me that I was seeing the last of those who made landscapes with their faces hanging down, like those of beasts, over the soil. Grigson also notes how artists and poets push landscape forward, thrust it into view and make contact with it unavoidable. In the past the figures which inhabited it were both gods and mortals, Venus and the village girl, Apollo and the shepherd. The scene was both natural and supernatural. And the indigenous man will occasionally look up from his disturbance of the surface of his territory as he earns his living, to draw into himself all that lies around him in a subconscious search for transcendence. From childhood on, what he sees, he is. Flesh becomes place. Although it was said of my East Anglian countryman, George Borrow, that he could look at nature without looking at himself. What an achievement!

WATERLAND

The Fens

ABOUT THE FENS
Graham Swift
(from *Waterland*, 1983)

Which are a low-lying region of eastern England, over 1,200 square miles in area, bounded to the west by the limestone hills of the Midlands, to the south and east by the chalk hills of Cambridgeshire, Suffolk and Norfolk. To the north, the Fens advance, on a twelve-mile front, to meet the North Sea at the Wash. Or perhaps it is more apt to say that the Wash summons the forces of the North Sea to its aid in a constant bid to recapture its former territory. For, the chief fact about the Fens is that they are reclaimed land, land that was once water, and which, even today, is not quite solid.

Once the shallow, shifting waters of the Wash did not stop at Boston and King's Lynn but licked southwards as far as Cambridge, Huntingdon, Peterborough and Bedford. What caused them to retreat? The answer can be given in a single syllable: Silt. The Fens were formed by silt. Silt: a word which when you utter it, letting the air slip thinly between your teeth, invokes a slow, sly, insinuating agency. Silt: which shapes and undermines continents; which demolishes as it builds; which is simultaneous accretion and erosion; neither progress nor decay.

It came first from the coast of Yorkshire and Lincolnshire, borne on the inshore currents which flowed southwards into the ancient Wash. In the blue-black clay which lies under the soil of Cambridgeshire are deposits of silt containing traces of shells of a type occurring on the beaches and cliff-beds of north-east England. Thus the first silts came from the sea. But to these marine silts were added the land silts carried by the rivers, the Ouse, the Cam, the Welland, which drained, and still drain, into the ever-diminishing Wash.

The silt accumulated, salt-marsh plants took hold, then other plants. And with the plants began the formation of peat. And peat is the second vital constituent of the Fens and the source of their remarkable fertility. Once it supported great forests which collapsed and sank when climatic changes caused water to re-immerse the region. Today, it forms the rich, black beet- and potato-bearing soil which is second to none in the country. But without silt, there could have been no peat.

All this was still happening not so long ago. In 870 the Viking fleets sailed with ease as far as Ely, through a region which was still predominantly water. Two hundred years later Hereward, defending the same high ground of Ely, watched his Norman besiegers flounder and drown in the treacherous peat-bogs. The landscape was still largely liquid.

For consider the equivocal operation of silt. Just as it raises the land, drives back the sea and allows peat to mature, so it impedes the flow of rivers, restricts their outfall, renders the newly formed land constantly liable to flooding and blocks the escape of floodwater. For centuries the Fens were a network of swamps and brackish lagoons. The problem of the Fens has always been the problem of drainage.

What silt began, man continued. Land reclamation. Drainage. But you do not reclaim a land overnight. You do not reclaim a land without difficulty and without ceaseless effort and vigilance. The Fens are still being reclaimed even to this day. Strictly speaking, they are never reclaimed, only being reclaimed. Without the pumps, the dykes and embankments, without the dredging programmes ... And you do not need to remind a Fenman of the effects of heavy inland rainfall, or of the combination of a spring tide and a strong nor'easter.

So forget, indeed, your revolutions, your turning-points, your grand metamorphoses of history. Consider, instead, the slow and arduous process, the interminable and ambiguous process – the process of human siltation – of land reclamation.

Is it desirable, in the first place, that land should be reclaimed? Not to those who exist by water; not to those who have no need of firm ground beneath their feet. Not to the fishermen, fowlers and reed-cutters who made their sodden homes in those stubborn swamps, took to stilts in time of flood and lived like water-rats. Not to the men who broke down the medieval embankments and if caught were buried alive in the very breach they had made. Not to the men who cut the throats of King Charles's Dutch drainers and threw their bodies into the water they were hired to expel.

I am speaking of my ancestors; of my father's forefathers. Because my name of Crick, which in Charles's day was spelt sometimes 'Coricke' or 'Cricke', can be found (a day's delving into local archives) amongst the lists of those summarily dealt with for sabotaging drainage works. My ancestors were water people. They speared fish and netted ducks. When I was small I possessed a living image of my ancestors in the form of Bill Clay, a shrunken, leathery carcass of a man, whose age was unknown but was never put at less than eighty, a one-time punt-gunner and turf-cutter, who had witnessed in his lifetime the passing of all but the dregs of the old wild fens in our area; who stank, even with his livelihood half gone, of goose fat and fish slime, mud and peat smoke; who wore an otter-skin cap, eel-skin gaiters and whose brain was permanently crazed by the poppy-head tea he drank to ward off winter agues. Old Bill lived with his wife Martha in a damp crack-walled cottage not far from the Ouse and on the edge of the shrinking reed-filled marsh known, after the watery expanse it had once been, as Wash Fen Mere. But some said that Martha Clay, who was some twenty years younger than Bill, was never Bill's wife at all. Some said that Martha Clay was a witch ...

But let's keep clear of fairy-tales.

The Dutch came, under their engineer Cornelius Vermuyden, hired first by King Charles, then by His Lordship, Francis, Earl of Bedford. Honouring their employer's name, they cut the Bedford River, and then the New Bedford River alongside it, to divert the main strength of the Ouse from its recalcitrant and sluggish course by Ely, into a straight channel to the sea. They built the Denver Sluice at the junction of the northern end of the new river with the old Ouse, and the Hermitage Sluice at the southern junction. They dug subsidiary cuts, drains, lodes, dykes, eaus and ditches and converted 95,000 acres into summer, if not winter, grazing. Practical and forward-looking people, the Dutch. And my father's forebears opposed them; and two of them were hanged for it.

Vermuyden left (he should have been rich but the Dutch Wars robbed him of his English fortune) in 1655. And nature, more effectively than my ancestors, began to sabotage his work. Because silt obstructs as it builds; unmakes as it makes. Vermuyden did not foresee that in cutting new courses for the rivers he reduced, not quickened, their flow; since a divided river conducts at any one point a decreased volume of water, and the less water a river conducts the less not only its velocity but also its capacity to scour its channel. The Earl of Bedford's noble waterways gathered mud. Silt collected in the estuaries, where the current of the rivers was no match for the tide, and built up against the sluices.

And Vermuyden did not foresee one other thing. That reclaimed land shrinks – as anything must shrink that has the water squeezed out of it. And peat, above all, which absorbs water like a sponge, shrinks when it dries. The Fens are shrinking. They are still shrinking – and sinking. Land which was above sea-level in Vermuyden's day is now below it. Tens of feet below it. There is no exaggerating the dangers. The invitation to flooding; the diminution of the gradient of the rivers; the pressure on the raised banks; the faster flow of upland water into the deepening lowland basin. All this, and silt.

In the 1690s the Bedford River burst a sixty-foot gap in its banks. In 1713 the Denver Sluice gave way and so great was the silting below it that the water from the Bedford River was forced landwards, upstream, up the old Ouse to Ely, instead of discharging into the sea. Thousands of acres of farmland were submerged. Cottagers waded to their beds.

And at some time in all this, strangely enough, my paternal ancestors threw in their lot with the drainers and land-reclaimers.

Perhaps they had no choice. Perhaps they took their hire where they were forced to. Perhaps they responded, out of the good of their hearts, to the misery of inundated crops and water-logged homes. In 1748, among the records of wages paid to those employed in rebuilding the Denver Sluice, are the names of the brothers James and Samuel Cricke. And in the parish annals of the Crick homeland, which in those days was north of the small town of Gildsey and east of the New Bedford River, are to be found for the next century and a half, and in the same tenacious connection, the names of Cricks. 'John Crick: for repairing the west bank ...'; 'Peter Crick: for scouring the Jackwater Drain and cutting the new Middle Drain ...'; 'Jacob Crick, to work and maintain the windmills at Stump Corner ...'

They ceased to be water people and became land people; they ceased to fish and fowl and became plumbers of the land. They joined in the destiny of the Fens, which was to strive not for but against water. For a century and a half they dug, drained and pumped the land between the Bedford River and the Great Ouse, boots perpetually mud-caked, ignorant of how their efforts were, little by little, changing the map of England.

Or perhaps they did not cease to be water people. Perhaps they became amphibians. Because if you drain land you are intimately concerned with water; you have to know its ways. Perhaps at heart they always knew, in spite of their land-preserving efforts, that they belonged to the old, prehistoric flood. And so my father, who kept the lock on the Leem, still caught eels and leant against the lock-gates at night, staring into the water – for water and meditation, they say, go together. And so my father, who was a superstitious man, always believed that old Bill Clay, the marsh-man, whose brains were quite cracked, was really, none the less, and if the truth be known, a sort of Wise Man.

When you work with water, you have to know and respect it. When you labour to subdue it, you have to understand that one day it may rise up and turn all your labours to nothing. For what is water, which seeks to make all things level, which has no taste or colour of its own, but a liquid form of Nothing? And what are the Fens, which so imitate in their levelness the natural disposition of water, but a landscape which, of all landscapes, most approximates to Nothing? Every Fenman secretly concedes this; every Fenman suffers now and then the illusion that the land he walks over is *not there*, is floating ... And every Fen-child, who is given picture-books to read in which the sun bounces over mountain tops and the road of life winds through heaps of green cushions, and is taught nursery rhymes in which persons go up and down hills, is apt to demand of its elders: Why are the Fens flat?

To which my father replied, first letting his face take on a wondering and vexed expression and letting his lips form for a moment the shape of an 'O': 'Why are the Fens flat? So God has a clear view ...'

When the land sinks below the water-level you have to pump. There is nothing else for it: water will not flow upwards. The pumps came to the Fens in the eighteenth century, in the form of black-sailed windmills, over seven hundred of which once creaked, whirred and thrummed in the wind between Lincoln and Cambridge. And my ancestor, Jacob Crick, operated two of them at Stump Corner. When the redcoats were storming Quebec, and the citizens of New England were rising up against their British masters (and offering a model for the discontented citizens of Paris), Jacob Crick was putting his cheek and ear to the air to feel the direction and force of the breezes. He was leaning and pushing against the tail-poles of his twin mills to set the sails in the right position. He was inspecting his paddle-wheels and scoops. But in times when there was no wind or the wind blew steadily in the same quarter, requiring no resetting of the sails, he would catch eels (because he was still a water-man at heart), not only with wicker traps but with a long, many-bladed spear called a glaive; and he would cut sedge and snare fowl.

Jacob Crick manned the mills at Stump Corner from 1748 to 1789.

He never married. In all those years he probably moved no further than a mile or two from his mills, which at all times he had to guard and tend. With Jacob Crick another characteristic of my paternal family emerges. They are fixed people. They have tied around their legs an invisible tether, and have enjoined upon them the stationary vigilance of sentinels. The biggest migration the Cricks ever made – before I, a twentieth-century Crick, made my home in London – was to move from the land west to the land east of the Ouse – a distance of six miles.

So Jacob Crick, mill-man and apprentice hermit, never sees the wide world. Though some would say the Fenland skies are wide enough. He never learns what is happening in Quebec or Boston. He eyes the horizon, sniffs the wind, looks at flatness. He has time to sit and ponder, to become suicidal or sagely calm. He acquires the virtue, if virtue it is, of which the Cricks have always had good supply: Phlegm. A muddy, silty humour.

And in the momentous and far from phlegmatical year 1789, whose significance you know, children, though Jacob Crick never did, Jacob Crick died.

Wifeless, childless. But the Cricks are not extinct. In 1820 it is a grand-nephew of Jacob – William – who is foreman of a gang employed in digging the southern end of the Eau Brink Cut, a new, deep channel to carry the waters of the lower Ouse by the shortest route to King's Lynn. For they are still trying to straighten out the slithery, wriggly, eel-like Ouse. In 1822, Francis Crick, perhaps another grand-nephew of Jacob, is entrusted with the operation of the new steam-pump on Stott's Drain, near the village of Hockwell. For the wind-pump is already obsolete. A windmill's use is limited. It cannot be used when there is no wind or when a gale is blowing; but a steam-pump will chug through all weathers.

So steam-power replaces wind-power in the Fens, and the Cricks adapt themselves, as we might say, to technology. To technology, and to ambition. For in this once wallowing backwater, in this sink of England, there are suddenly reputations to be made. Not only are

Smeaton, Telford, Rennie and numerous other renowned engineers discovering that in the problems of drainage lies a test for their talents, but a host of speculators, contemplating the rich dark soil that drainage produces, have already seen the wisdom of investing in land reclamation.

One of them is called Atkinson. He is not a Fenman. He is a prosperous Norfolk farmer and maltster from the hills where the Leem rises and flows westwards to the Ouse. But, in the 1780s, for reasons both self-interested and public-spirited, he forms the plan of opening up for navigation the River Leem, as a means of transport for his produce between Norfolk and the expanding market of the Fens. While Jacob Crick spears his last eels by Stump Corner and listens not just to the creaking of his mill sails but to the creaking of his ageing bones, Thomas Atkinson buys, little by little and at rock-bottom prices, acres of marsh and peat-bog along the margins of the Leem. He hires surveyors, drainage and dredging experts. A confident and far-seeing man, a man of hearty and sanguine, rather than phlegmatic, temperament, he offers work and a future to a whole region.

And the Cricks come to work for Atkinson. They make their great journey across the Ouse, leaving old Jacob at his solitary outpost; and while one branch of the family goes north to dig the Eau Brink Cut, another goes south, to the village of Apton, where Thomas Atkinson's agents are recruiting labour.

And that is how, children, my ancestors came to live by the River Leem. That is how when the cauldron of revolution was simmering in Paris, so that you, one day, should have a subject for your lessons, they were busy, as usual, with their scouring, pumping and embanking. That is how, when foundations were being rocked in France, a land was being formed which would one day yield fifteen tons of potatoes or nineteen sacks of wheat an acre and on which your history teacher-to-be would one day have his home.

It was Atkinson who put Francis Crick in charge of the new steam-pump on Stott's Drain. When I was a boy a pump still worked on Stott's Drain – though it was no longer steam – but diesel-driven and manned not by a Crick but by Harry Bulman, in the pay of the Great Ouse Catchment Board – adding its pulse-beat to that of many others on the night I learnt what the stars really were. It was Atkinson who in 1815 built the lock and sluice two miles from the junction of the Leem and Ouse, christening it the Atkinson Lock. And it was another Atkinson, Thomas's grandson, who, in 1874, after violent flooding had destroyed lock, sluice and lock-keeper's cottage, rebuilt the lock and named it the New Atkinson. A Crick did not then become lock-keeper – but a Crick would.

Yet why, you may ask, did the Cricks rise no further? Why were they content to be, at best, pump-operators, lock-keepers, humble servants of their masters? Why did they never produce a renowned engineer, or turn to farming that rich soil they themselves had helped to form?

Perhaps because of that old watery phlegm which cooled and made sluggish their spirits, despite the quantities of it they spat out, over their shovels and buckets, in workmanlike gobbets. Because they did not forget, in their muddy labours, their swampy origins; that, however much you resist them, the waters will return; that the land sinks; silt collects; that something in nature wants to go back.

Realism; fatalism; phlegm. To live in the Fens is to receive strong doses of reality. The great flat monotony of reality; the wide empty space of reality. Melancholia and self-murder are not unknown in the Fens. Heavy drinking, madness and sudden acts of violence are not uncommon. How do you surmount reality, children? How do you acquire, in a flat country, the tonic of elevated feelings? If you are an Atkinson it is not difficult. If you have become prosperous by selling fine quality barley, if you can look down from your Norfolk uplands and see in these level Fens – this nothing-landscape – an Idea, a drawing-board for your plans, you can outwit reality. But if you are born in the middle of that flatness, fixed in it, glued to it even by the mud in which it abounds ...?

How did the Cricks outwit reality? By telling stories. Down to the last generation, they were not only phlegmatic but superstitious and credulous creatures. Suckers for stories. While the Atkinsons made history, the Cricks spun yarns.

And it is strange – or perhaps not strange, not strange at all, only logical – how the bare and empty Fens yield so readily to the imaginary – and the supernatural. How the villages along the Leem were peopled with ghosts and earnestly recounted legends. The Singing Swans of Wash Fen Mere; the Monk of Sudchurch; the Headless Ferryman of Staithe – not to mention the Brewer's Daughter of Gildsey. How in the past the Fens attracted visionaries and fanatics: Saint Gunnhilda, our local patroness, who in 695, or thereabouts, built a wattle hut for herself on a mud-hump in the middle of a marsh, and resisting the assaults and blandishments of demons and surviving on nothing but her prayers, heard the voice of God, founded a church and gave her name (Gunnhildsea – Gildsey: Gunnhilda's Isle) to a town. How even in the no-nonsense and pragmatic twentieth century, this future schoolmaster quaked in his bed at night for fear of something – something vast and void – and had to be told stories and counter-stories to soothe his provoked imagination. How he piously observed, because others observed them too, a catechism of obscure rites. When you see the new moon, turn your money in your pocket; help someone to salt and help them to sorrow; never put new shoes on a table or cut your nails on a Sunday. An eel-skin cures rheumatism; a roast mouse cures whooping cough; and a live fish in a woman's lap will make her barren.

A fairy-tale land.

And the Cricks, for all their dull phlegm, believed in fairy-tales. They saw marsh-sprites; they saw will-o'-the-wisps. My father saw one in 1922. And when echoes from the wide world began to penetrate to the Cricks, when news reached them at last, though they never went looking for it, that the Colonies had rebelled, that there had been a Waterloo, a Crimea, they listened and repeated what they heard with wide-eyed awe, as if such things were not the stuff of fact but the fabric of a wondrous tale.

For centuries the Cricks remain untouched by the wide world. No ambition lures them to the cities. No recruiting party or press-gang, foraging up the Ouse from Lynn, whisks them off to fight for King or Queen. Until history reaches that pitch – our age, children, our common inheritance – where the wide world impinges whether you wish it or not. Till history performs one of its backward somersaults and courts destruction. The waters return. In 1916, '17 and '18 there is much flooding of fields, much damage done to embankments and excessive silting in the estuaries, because of the unavailability of those normally employed in the peaceable tasks of drainage and reclamation. In 1917 paper summonses call George and Henry Crick, of Hockwell, Cambs., employees of the River Leem Drainage and Navigation Board, to be fitted out with uniforms and equipped with rifles.

And where do they find themselves, that autumn, separately but as part of the same beleaguered army? In a flat, rain-swept, water-logged land. A land not unlike their own native Fenland. A land of the kind where the great Vermuyden earned his reputation and developed those ingenious methods which none the less proved inappropriate to the terrain of eastern England. A land where, in 1917, there is still much digging, ditching and entrenching and a pressing problem of drainage, not to say problems of other kinds. The Crick brothers see the wide world – which is not a wondrous fable. The Cricks see – but is this only some nightmare, some evil memory they have always had? – that the wide world is sinking, the waters are returning, the wide world is drowning in mud. Who will not know of the mud of Flanders? Who will not feel in this twentieth century of ours, when even a teenage schoolboy will propose as a topic for a history lesson the End of History, the mud of Flanders sucking at his feet?

In January 1918 Henry Crick is shipped home, an obliging shrapnel wound in his knee. By that time plans are already afoot in Hockwell to raise the war memorial that will bear, amongst others, the name of his brother. Henry Crick becomes a hospital case. Henry Crick limps and blinks and falls flat on his face at sudden noises. For a long time he finds it hard to separate in his mind the familiar-but-foreign fields of the Fens and the foreign-but-familiar mudscapes he has come from. He expects the ground to quake and heave under his feet and become a morass. He is sent to a home for chronic neurasthenics. He thinks: there is only reality, there are no stories left. About his war experiences he says: 'I remember nothing.' He does not believe he will one day tell salty Tales of the Trenches: 'In some of the big old shell-holes – there were eels ...' He does not believe he will ever talk to his son about mother's milk and hearts.

But much will happen to Henry Crick. He recovers. He meets his future wife – there indeed is another story. In 1922 he marries. And in the same year Ernest Atkinson brings indirect influence to bear on his future employment. Indirect because the Atkinson word is no longer law; the Atkinson empire, like many another empire, is in decline, and since before the war, when he sold most of his share in the Leem Navigation, Ernest Atkinson has been living like a recluse, and some would say a mad one at that. But in 1922 my father is appointed keeper of the New Atkinson Lock.

OLD FURROWS NEWLY PLOUGHED
Edward Storey
(from *Places: An Anthology of Britain*, 1981)

I wish I had known the poetry of John Clare when I was ten, or fifteen, or even at twenty, for I know of no other poet who teaches us how to *see* the world in which we live and grow.

I had, admittedly, just discovered the poetry of Clare by the time I was twenty, but it has taken another twenty years or more fully to appreciate his individual gift of 'making a miracle out of the ordinary'. And now I am even more excited by his remarkable ability to focus *my* vision on the particular, making me see the familiar as if for the first time.

Clare had a poet's eye long before he began scribbling his poems on the backs of his mother's grocery bags. Perhaps we all have a poet's eye as children but lose it as we grow older and become influenced by what other people see, or expect us to see. Clare never lost the child's fresh view of the world in which he lived, and I needed his writings to remind myself of the many wonders I had seen as a child – wonders I took for granted and nearly buried forever in that dark pyramid of the memory, where they might have mummified or decayed.

Clare grew up in Helpston, in that northern corner of Northamptonshire, an area rich in woodlands and wild flowers. At a crucial period of his life, when he was thirty-nine and almost forgotten, he moved three miles east into the lower, flatter, bleaker landscape on the edge of the Lincolnshire fens.

I was brought up in the western half of the Cambridgeshire fens, only a few miles from Clare's country, and know the villages and walks he wrote about as more than places on a map. I now live in a cathedral's precincts on an invisible boundary between the present and the past, poised conveniently between two worlds.

It is, however, the safer world and landscape of my childhood to which I return again and again for my own writing. As a child I assumed that all the world was as flat, spacious, huge and bright as the world at the end of our street. I had never seen a mountain and probably did not know such things existed. No patchwork-coloured globe spinning in the crowded classroom of my primary school could convince me that the earth was round. Experience taught me otherwise. Day and night there was the land and the sky – two generous opposites. You saw the sun rise from the eastern horizon and move like mercury up heaven's wall until at midday it shone above your head. Then you watched it slide down to the western horizon as the temperature dropped, and it was night again.

It was as simple as that. You did not need geography lessons to teach you about the shape of the earth. If there were mountains, forests, cities, lakes and jungles, they belonged to another world that was not my world. My world was flat, big, warm, solitary and almost treeless. It was a world of space and light. It belonged to the wind and skylark, to the heron and reed-mace, pea-fields and harvest, dandelions and poppies – and, of course, childhood.

In those innocent days of discovering that I belonged to such a world I knew nothing of the floods, drainage, riots, resentment and hunger that had made the fen country a bitter place in which to live. I knew nothing of the iron winters that locked the land in a grip of frost and snow making men idle for weeks at a time without work or money. I lived through such times with my family but, as a child, forgot. I knew only of those summers where wheat ripened to mahogany brown; where frayed tassels of barley rustled like silk or moved like shoals of shrimps over the low-tide fields; where harvesters came with clumsy machines to cut and stook the crops, leaving their wigwams of sheaves to dry under an Apache sun. A few days later, when the harvest had been ceremoniously carted home, we were allowed into the fields for gleaning. Towards evening I would pretend to have an abundance of energy just to stay out there long enough to see the cart-wheel moon rise out of that mysterious space beyond the horizon. To see a full moon rising over the fens on any night of the year is to watch a spectacle that must have struck awe into our first fathers. It arrives like a god from secret waters. It rides on the mist and ascends into the sky and, at harvest time, displays its ancient majesty so that even now, with the knowledge that men have walked there, it still makes my spine tingle. As a child my eyes glowed wide with wonder and I went home believing that I had witnessed a divine happening. Although I assumed that everyone on earth shared a similar landscape, with their own vast sky, I believed that only a chosen few were allowed to stay out late enough to watch the arrival of a full moon.

Night has always been a fascination, especially if it is star-lit. The expanse of sky enjoyed during the day is still there when dark but pinned now with a million stars. To stand on a river-bank, away from town, and to look up at the sky's extravagance, is an excitement worth going miles to experience. Stand for a few moments. Forget who you are, and where. Then listen. The fields have taken on a deeper stillness. The only sound might be of sheep snatching at grass, or an owl talking to itself in a willow tree. Slowly you feel yourself becoming part of the night. Your feet strike roots into the soil. Your head reaches towards the stars. The blood beats with a very ancient rhythm as the heart hears echoes too distant to record. I would not want the world round, or crowded with cities at such a time. I listen for forgotten voices, for the dark music that must have trembled over these fens from shadowy faces a thousand years ago.

But, you may be asking, what has all this got to do with John Clare? Simply this, that I needed him to show me what a minute-by-minute thrill of a world it was in which I lived; that everything was significant if only I used my eyes to *see*, to focus closely on the small things as well as the large, and to respect their own timeless history. Clare had a great reverence for life and he taught me how to celebrate. So, although I have always lived within a seven-mile radius of where I was born, I feel now that I have a world full of miracles on my doorstep because each day is re-created with a thousand secrets to discover. Everything once took for granted I now look at with new eyes. Old furrows are newly ploughed. Skylarks have just been given a new song. The heron is trying out his heavy wings for the first time, and the sky's pattern of clouds has never once been repeated since the earth was made – flat or round.

I even needed Clare to make me see the sky. Throughout his work he refers to it over three hundred times. He describes it as an 'exhaustless sky'; an 'unfrequented sky'; a 'cloud-betravelled sky' and a 'tender-watching sky'. It is also a 'troubled' – 'mackerel' – 'miser' sky and, when summer goes we are left with 'the desert of a winter sky'. No one has written better about these fenland spaces where 'black clouds mimicked mountains' and the landscape 'spreads from the eye its circle far away'. He frequently referred to the clouds as mountains – they're the only ones we'll have: 'The sun those mornings used to find/Its clouds were other-country mountains ...' On other days he tells us how 'the crampt horizon now leans on the ground' or that 'The arch of light around us bowed/Stretches for days its cloudless sky/Save freckling shadows of a cloud/That lose to nothing passing by'.

Slowly I discovered that Clare was describing my landscape in his own individual and unforgettable way, and that if I could train my imagination to see through a similar eye I would find myself looking at a different world each day. When he wrote 'the sheep unfolded with the rising sun' or the heron 'flaps his melancholy wing'; when he described the cart-rut 'rippled with the burden of the rain' or spoke of dandelions that 'closed like painters' brushes when even was', he was talking to me about things I had seen hundreds of times but never with such sharp vision or imagination. So I began to look more closely, to particularize and employ metaphor. I tried to become part of creation, giving names to things that needed renaming. Every season, every day and every hour became important and I began to understand what it meant to be a 'writer of place', to have not only roots in the soil but eyes in my fingertips. I began not only to *see* but to *feel*, to respond with my whole being to wherever I happened to be, and I decided that the people and places I had known all my life were to be the subjects of my books. I had to reappraise the land of my fathers and make it mine. I had to re-enter the child's private world and give it identity. Fortunately, at the age of nineteen, I realized this could be done through poetry, especially when I discovered a year later that John Clare had shown the way. I have carried this belief into my prose – the topography and local history.

When I first visited Clare's birthplace the street still had its village pump and the nightingales still built their nests in Royce Wood. Now they have gone, with many other favourite places he wrote about. I remember it was an early spring day and the sky was overcast. I went with a friend and we picked a few primroses to place at the foot of the poet's grave, then overgrown with long grass and in need of a clean. Afterwards we sat in the church for a while and later walked to the flour mill at Maxey, then on to Glinton and Northborough. Mary Joyce and Patty Clare became as real as the poet himself. The daisies we trod on, the larks above our heads, the grasshoppers and sheep were all direct descendants of the ones he'd celebrated. And, although ugly pylons and railway tracks now disfigured his countryside, the sky and the clouds, the fens' 'faint shadow of immensity', that 'arch of light around us bowed', were just as he had seen them over a hundred years ago. From that moment I believed we had a relationship. It was not idol-worship – we have cursed each other too often for it to be that – but we became neighbours and I, for one, was glad to compare notes and listen to his voice. If Clare found his Eden in the gentler rises of Northamptonshire on the edge of the fens, before Enclosure came to change his world, so I found my Eden in the open spaces of the Cambridgeshire fens before mechanization and urban sprawl changed my world.

After recurring illnesses in infancy I remember my mother taking me for walks in the afternoon – they were not even walks for me at that time because I was still in a push-chair. But the size of the fields, the far distant horizons, the bunches of wild flowers we gathered and the inexhaustible song of the larks stayed with me more vividly than nursery rhymes. Hedgerows were heaped with the cream of may blossom; rivers were silver with fish or oozy with eels; rabbits, kingfishers, pheasants and lapwing were all part of my daily recovery, Even the nearby brickyard chimneys were living things, squeezing their smoke slowly on to the sky's palette, giving shades to an autumn sundown not seen anywhere else. And then school, and the years of being locked away in Victorian classrooms with high windows out of which I could only see the sky. The sky began to mean freedom. I daydreamt those years away longing for space and fields and the colour of hedgerows. At the age of five I might have been a poet if I'd had words to describe what my body felt. At ten I might have written about the silent avalanche of clouds at the end of our street, or the fields of jet-black corduroy. But I was afraid to put my thoughts into such words. We were not expected to use language like that. A spade was a spade and a cloud was a cloud, and corduroy trousers were worn by farm-labourers not fields. And then, at twenty, my first visit to Helpston and the discovery of Clare's poetry – thousands of poems all about the places and people and things I knew. People? Yes, I knew the woman in his sonnet 'Scandal', and 'The Mole-catcher', 'The Thresher', 'The Braggart', and 'The Foddering Boy'. They were of another generation but were, like the daisies and birds, direct descendants of the ones Clare had known. The realism with which he wrote about these subjects excited me:

> *She hastens out and scarcely pins her clothes*
> *To hear the news and tell the news she knows*
> *She talks of sluts marks each unmended gown*
> *Herself the dirtiest slut in all the town . . .*

> *Tattered and ragg'd with greatcoat tied in strings*
> *And collared up to keep his chin from cold*
> *The old mole-catcher on his journey sings*
> *Followed by shaggy dog infirm and old . . .*

> *With hand in waistcoat thrust the thresher goes*
> *Early at morn to follow his employ*
> *He nothing wants to know and nothing knows*
> *And wearies life along with little joy . . .*

Nor was Clare afraid to write about a rainy day either, when the land looks anything but golden:

> *So moping flat and low our valleys lie*
> *So dull and muggy is our winter sky*

46

Drizzling from day to day with threats of rain
And when that falls still threatening on again
From one wet week so great an ocean flows
That every village to an island grows . . .

He knew each mood of the year. The seasons have not changed. Crows still 'tumble up and down/At the first sight of Spring/And in old trees around the town/Brush winter from its wing.' And still in summer 'the ballad-singing larks now troop/By dozens from the hay/And dozens down as soon as up/Leaves one the time to play.' The sun which Clare mentions over five hundred times is still a very significant part of our land and remains, as it did for him, 'the unfettered sun' or 'hot, relentless sun', everything from 'the spoiling sun' to the 'pale splendour of a winter sun' constantly controlling our days. The sun was for Clare the beginning of life, the magician of seed and flower, the 'eternal ray' of hope. The harvest scenes may have changed but the tradition of harvest remains. And when summer is over the autumn returns with its own healing: 'There's nothing calms the unquiet mind/Like to the soothing of an autumn wind.' It is a season when the eye 'revels in wild delights', when 'every leaf of bush and weed/Is tipt with autumn's pencil now', where 'every object wears a changing hue' and 'naked fields hang lonely on the view.'

But it is, perhaps, in writing of winter that Clare excels. When he says ''Tis winter and I love to read indoors', I share the joy of settling down before a fire with a favourite book while outside 'The small wind whispers through the leafless hedge/Most sharp and chill.' From his cottage he would have looked out on a world that has a habit of withdrawing itself in December and January. The sky becomes hard and sullen as a frozen pond. The pheasant's cry bounces over it like a pebble on ice. The call of the wildfowl from a distant mere comes also from a secret past. Reeds shuffle along the dykes, their frosted banners all that remain of forgotten warriors. Flood water stutters its cold syllables against the hedge-roots. The vast sky goes into mourning and

47

the snow begins to fall on 100,000 acres of sleeping farmland, slowly changing our world from black to white. And the excitement starts all over again.

I wrote in my first book *Portrait of the Fen Country* – 'No part of the country can be isolated into a weekend or judged by a season, least of all the Fen country. After weeks of rain during sugar-beet lifting even the most ardent fen-lover will find his world damp and miserable. In winter the winds from the north-east can be so fierce and pitiless that you feel as if needles of ice are being thrown at your eyes. But in May when white mist hovers over young spring wheat the fens will feel as calm as a cathedral, and in summertime when the air is rich with the smells of meadowsweet and the first gold-rush of harvest it can be as perfect as Eden ever was.'

Clare taught me how to enjoy the seasons and the everyday things of life. Now, several books later, I can still say with him 'There is a breath – indeed there is/Of Eden left – I feel it now.'

KINGSLEY'S 'HEREWARD THE WAKE'
Peter Tolhurst

During his last years at Eversley in Hampshire the Revd. Charles Kingsley managed to combine his pastoral duties with those of Professor of Modern History at his old Cambridge college (Magdalene). His reputation as a writer of historical fiction had been established some years earlier with the publication of his first novel *Westward Ho!* (1855). Encouraged by its success and the more recent popularity of his classic children's story *The Water Babies* (1863), Kingsley embarked on a new historical novel based on the legendary exploits of the fenland hero Hereward the Wake.

Kingsley's knowledge of the *Anglo Saxon Chronicle* enabled him to create a vivid picture of life during the Norman Conquest but his information about Hereward was taken from a more dubious source. The *Gesta Hereward* by the 10th century monk Ingulf of Croyland, which contains the earliest account of the English outlaw, is considered by some historians to be a 15th century forgery. It did however provide a starting point and, like all good storytellers, what Kingsley couldn't verify he made up using a mixture of local folklore, elements of medieval romance and Norse sagas. His descriptions of this vast watery landscape teeming with wildlife were drawn from childhood memories of wildfowling expeditions with his father from their home at Barnack near Peterborough and his later excursions into the fens whilst a Cambridge academic.

The result is a powerful evocation of a wild, inaccessible region; the pagan beliefs of its people still so widespread that Christianity clings precariously to a few ague-ridden monastic outposts. Although *Hereward* is an uneven work, little more than a series of adventures, Kingsley overcomes its limitations as a novel by transforming fragmentary evidence into a memorable tale of resistance in which his semi-mythical hero fights an epic rearguard action against the Norman warlords.

Rather like Robin Hood, that other folk hero of the forest whom he often resembles, Hereward is an outlaw of noble blood, the son of Earl Leofric and Lady Godiva and heir to the Lordship of Bourne on the edge of the Lincolnshire Fens. His campaign of guerilla warfare begins here when he returns to the ancestral hall from Flanders to find it full of French soldiers in drunken revelry. Putting them to flight Hereward delivers his mother to the safety of Croyland Abbey where, on discovering his brother has been beheaded, he vows never to rest until the French are driven from his lands.

The fens are full of people like Wulfric the Hero, men dispossessed of their lands and driven to take refuge in the reed beds where they are ready to die in defence of their l i b e r t y. Having freed four brothers condemned to be hanged in Norfolk on Wrokesham Bridge, Wulfric roams the countryside luring his pursuers deeper into its more treacherous reaches, striking with deadly purpose when they flounder in the mud, then vanishing into the mist with the aid of a leaping pole which carries him out of danger across the dykes.

Hereward knows he can call on men like Wulfric and, having split the war arrow, it is carried into every corner of the fens and beyond into the forest of Brunewald, passing from one free man to another with the whisper 'The Wake is come again'. Receiving the call, armed outlaws rally to Bourne and place themselves at his command. Soon Hereward has enough support to raise an army and strike at the heart of the enemy. After one skirmish, clothed in his magic armour, Hereward slays the brother of Earl Warrene of Norfolk and his knights at King's Lynn before disappearing in a great cloud of sea birds.

And after that then fen-men said to each other that all the birds upon the meres cried nothing save 'The wake is come again'. And so, already surrounded with myth and mystery, Hereward flashed into the Fens and out again, like the lighting brand, destroying as he passed. And the hearts of all the French were turned to water, and the land had peace from its tyrants for many days.

The story reaches its dramatic climax when William the Conqueror decides to march on Ely with the largest army he can muster in one final thrust to dislodge Hereward. News has already reached him that the Danes have abandoned the city and sailed for home leaving its defence to The Wake, but first the French have to cross 'a black abyss of mud and peat and reeds ... with the deep sullen westwater or Alderiche of the Ouse winding between them'. A floating causeway is hurriedly constructed, but in their eagerness to gain the opposite bank and plunder the treasures of Ely Cathedral, soldiers trample each other underfoot and the bridge collapses engulfing 'in that foul stream the flower of Norman chivalry'.

Having failed in his attempt to take the Isle, William withdraws to Weeting Castle to consider his next move. The Isle has enough fresh food to withstand a long siege but fearing a renewed attack, Hereward, disguised as a potter, leaves Ely on his horse Swallow, intent on discovering the king's plans. Before entering the Castle he stays the night in a hut on the edge of Brandon Heath where he overhears two old crones foretell the time and place of William's next attack. The following day Hereward enters the king's court where he becomes involved in a kitchen brawl. He is spared by William and escapes on Swallow before his identity can be discovered, skirting the fens in a great arc before throwing off his pursuers and re-entering the Isle beyond Cambridge.

Unlike many episodes in Kingsley's saga there is no record of the event in the medieval manuscripts he used to construct his own story of Hereward's resistance. The incident was set in Weeting purely on the basis of its ruined Norman castle, even though the archaeological evidence suggests that it was built a century later. Moated, but without a curtain wall and consisting of a hall and substantial tower, it was more like an early fortified manor house than a castle, but there on the edge of the fens it served Kingsley's purpose.

William is persuaded by the witch of Brandon's promise to conjour up a violent storm in the face of the English army and returns to Aldreth where preparations begin for a second assault on the Isle. Despite Hereward's success in destroying French landing craft, a bigger, stronger causeway is eventually ready, complete with a high tower from which the old crone will hurl down vile curses on the enemy.

Hereward's wife Torfrida, having renounced the black arts and embraced the new religion, agrees to counter the witch's incantations with the power of prayer – *Hereward* is after all the work of a Victorian clergyman. She leads the women of Ely in procession to the well of their patron saint, Etheldreda, where on receiving her blessing, Torfrida begins a silent vigil of prayer and penance. Working herself into a religious frenzy she leads Hereward's men into battle riding 'at their head on a white charger, robed from throat to ankle in sackcloth, her fetters clanking on her limbs' to confront the old hag of Brandon. From her tower on the opposite bank, the old witch 'howled and gibbered with filthy gestures, calling for the thunderstorm which did not come'. And then, inspired by visions of Etheldreda, as the French advance across the causeway Torfrida begins to sing 'like an angel', her voice rising above the noise of battle, at the same time pointing to the reed beds from which smoke is already pouring. The flames, spread quickly by the evening breeze, are 'leaping and cackling, laughing and shrieking like a fiend' as they sweep over the causeway leaving

... a long black smouldering, writhing line; the morass to right and left, which a minute before had been deep red, an open smutty pool, dotted with boatfuls of shrieking and cursing men; and at the causeway end the tower with the flame climbing up its posts, and the witch of Brandon throwing herself desperately from the top and falling dead upon the embers, a motionless heap of rags.

So the day ends with good triumphant and William's men put to flight. Although Hereward knows he cannot hold out indefinately it is an act of treachery that eventually secures Ely for the French. In retreat Hereward lays waste the land for miles around, denying the enemy cover, but in doing so he is forced deeper into the fens in search of food. On one occasion whilst he and his men are away foraging, William sends word to the monks of Ely that their lands will be confiscated unless they surrender. Terms are hastily agreed with Abbot Thurstan, the French occupy the town and as Hereward returns he can only watch helplessly from the river as Ely burns.

Harried through the fens, the English outlaws take refuge deep in Brunewald Forest until at last, weary of the struggle and with his followers reduced to a handful of men, Hereward surrenders to William and returns to Bourne where he is set upon by French knights. With the name of Torfrida on his lips he fights like a madman but without his sword Brainbiter and without his magic armour he is finally hacked down. Torfrida sails from Croyland to claim his body and lays it to rest in the abbey.

And past the Deeping, down the Welland Stream,
By winding reaches on, and shining meres
Between gray reed-ronds, and green alder beds,
And the brown horror of the homeless fen,
A dirge of monks and wail of women rose
In vain to heaven for the last Englishman;
Then died far off within the boundless mist
And left the Frenchman master of the land.

According to Kingsley, Hereward's deeds were celebrated in song and folktales long after his death whenever people gathered together in remote Fenland cottages or riverside ale houses; and so they kept alive his memory and awaited his return. Kingsley argued that the spirit of liberty which Hereward embodied was immortal, had moulded the English into a great nation and would give birth to 'still greater nations in lands as yet unknown'. At this point his inevitable belief in the 'civilising' effect of a budding colonial policy in which missionary zeal allied to ruthless commercial exploitation had already begun to destroy tribal cultures throughtout the Empire, simply underlined his failure to recognise the effect of those forces at work in the medieval fens. As a writer concerned with the suffering of working class people in his own country but who despised negroes, Kingsley embodied some of the central paradoxes of his time.

By casting Hereward in the role of freedom fighter, Kingsley failed to appreciate the true nature of his central character who assumes heroic status not just because he died fighting an oppresive regime but because he embodied the very spirit of the fens, a pagan will o' the wisp figure haunting the reed beds. The last chapter 'How Deeping Fen was Drained' is a rather unconvincing postscript in which Kingsley extols the benefits of land drainage. Prosperity is achieved at the price of freedom as the destruction of the last great wilderness in lowland England gathers pace.

Where there had been lonely meres, foul water courses, stagnant slime, there were now great dykes, rich and fair corn and grasslands, rows of white cottages.

No sooner has Kingsley lamented the death of 'the last of the English' than he acclaims Richard de Rubs as 'the first of the new English, who with the inspiration of God, began to drain the Fens', ridding its people of superstitious beliefs in the process. Seeing him as the first of 'the English noble class of agricultural squires' Kingsley chooses to ignore the repessive series of enclosures, emparking and other agricultural improvements instigated by de Rubs' successors which enabled the landed gentry to create huge estates and a whole new class of landless peasants.

Rural unrest, which became widespread in the eastern counties, found its expression among fenmen as early as the 17th century. Dutch engineers, brought over to create a massive new network of dykes and drainage channels, threatened their traditional livelihood as wildfowlers and fishermen and reawaked the rebellious spirit of Kingsley's hero. Their fierce resistance earned them the knickname 'Fen Tigers', a name which persists to this day even though the transformation of the fens into the most fertile and intensively cultivated region in the country is now complete. The spirit of the fens, reduced to one remaining area of natural reedbed at Wicken Fen, may rise again as part of the National Trust's ambitious plan to recreate a vast new wetland stretching from its reserve at Wicken south west to Angelsey Abbey.

If Kingsley were alive and his ideas less clouded by a religious dogma which insisted on man's authority over the natural world, the following eulogy for the fens taken from his *Prose Idylls* suggests he might have argued more strongly the concepts of diversity and wilderness conservation propounded by ecologists today.

The fancy may linger without blame, over the shining meres, the golden reed beds, the countless water-fowl, the strange and gaudy insects, the wild nature, the mystery, the majesty – for mystery and majesty there were – which haunted the deep fens for many hundred years ... dark green alders and pale green reeds stretched for miles round the broad lagoon, where the coot clanked and the bittern boomed ... while high overhead hung motionless, hawk beyond hawk, buzzard beyond buzzard, kite beyond kite, as far as the eye could see ... while clear above all sounded the wild whistle of the curlew and the trumpet note of the great wild swan. They are all gone now. Gone are the ruffs and reeves, spoon bills, bitterns, avocets; the very snipe, one hears, disdain to breed. Gone too, not only from the Fens but from the whole world, is that most exquisite of butterflies – Lycaena dispar – the great copper, and many a curious insect more.

WHITE-FRONTED GEESE
T.H.White
(from *The Book of Merlin*, 1978)

The place where he was, was absolutely flat. In the human world we seldom see flatness, for the trees and houses and hedges give a serrated edge to the landscape: even the grass sticks up with its myriad blades. But here, in the belly of the night, the illimitable, flat, wet mud was as featureless as a dark junket. If it had been wet sand, even, it would have had those little wave marks, like the palate of one's mouth.

And, in this enormous flatness, there lived one element: the wind. For it was an element; it was a dimension, a power of darkness. In the human world, the wind comes from somewhere, and goes somewhere, and, as it goes, it passes through somewhere: through trees or streets or hedgerows. This wind came from nowhere. It was going through the flatness of nowhere, to no place. Horizontal, soundless except for a peculiar boom, tangible, infinite, the astounding dimensional weight of it streamed across the mud. You could have ruled it with a straight-edge. The titanic grey line of it was unwavering and solid. You could have hooked the crook of your umbrella over it, and it would have hung there.

The king, facing into this wind, felt that he was uncreated. Except for the wet solidity under his webbed feet, he was living in nothing: a solid nothing, like chaos. His were the feelings of a point in geometry, existing mysteriously on the shortest distance between two points: or of a line, drawn on a plane surface which had length, breadth but no magnitude. No magnitude! It was the very self of magnitude. It was power, current, force, direction, a pulseless world-stream steady in limbo.

Bounds had been set to this unhallowed purgatory. Far away to the east, perhaps a mile distant, there was an unbroken wall of sound. It surged a little, seeming to expand and contract, but it was solid. It was menacing, being desirous for victims: for it was the huge, the remorseless sea.

Two miles to the west, there were three spots of light in a triangle. They were the weak wicks from fishermen's cottages, who had risen early to catch a tide in the complicated creeks of the salt marsh. Its waters sometimes ran contrary to the ocean. These were the total features of his world, the sea sound and the three small lights: darkness, flatness, vastness, wetness: and, in the gulf of night, the gulf-stream of the wind.

When daylight began to come, by premonition, he found that he was standing among a crowd of people like himself. They were seated on the mud, which now began to be disturbed by the angry, thin, returning sea, or else were already riding on the water, wakened by it, outside the annoyance of the surf. The seated ones were large teapots, their spouts tucked under their wings. The swimming ones occasionally ducked their heads and shook them. Some, waking on the mud, stood up and wagged their wings vigourously. Their profound silence became broken by a conversationable gabble. There were about four hundred of them in the grey vicinity: very beautiful creatures, the wild White-Fronted Geese, whom, once a man has seen them, he will never forget.

Long before the sun came, they were making ready for their flight. Family parties of the previous year's breeding were coming together in batches, and these batches were themselves inclined to join up with other ones, possibly under the command of a grandfather, or of a great-grandfather, or else of some noted leader in the host. When the drafts were complete, there came a faint tone of excitement into their speech. They began moving their heads from side to side in jerks. And then, turning into the wind, suddenly they would all be in the air together, fourteen or forty at a time, with wide wings scooping the blackness and a cry of triumph in their throats. They would wheel round, climbing rapidly, and be gone from sight. Twenty yards up, they were invisible in the dark. The earlier departures were not vocal: they were inclined to be taciturn before the sun came, only making occasional remarks, or crying their single warning-note if danger threatened. Then, at the warning, they would all rise vertically to the sky.

He began to feel an uneasiness in himself. The dim squadrons about him, setting out minute by minute, infected him with a tendency. He became restless to embrace their example, but he was shy. Perhaps their family groups, he thought, would resent his intrusion: yet he wanted not to be lonely: he wanted to join in, and to enjoy the exercise of morning flight, which was so evidently a pleasure to them. They had a comradeship, a free discipline and joie-de-vivre.

When the goose next to him spread her wings and leaped, he did so automatically. Some eight of those nearby had been jerking their bills, which he had imitated as if the act were catching, and now, with these same eight, he found himself on pinion in the horizontal air. The moment he had left the earth, the wind had vanished: its restlessness and brutality had dropped away as if cut off by a knife: he was in it, and at peace.

The eight geese spread out in line astern, evenly spaced, with him behind. They made for the east, where the poor lights had been, and now, before them, the bold sun began to rise. A crack of orange broke the black cloud-bank far beyond the land; the glory spread, the salt marsh growing visible below. He saw it like a featureless moor or bogland, which had become maritime by accident; its heather, still looking like heather, having mated with the seaweed until it was a salt wet heather, with slippery fronds. The burns which should have run through the moorland were of sea-water on blueish mud. There were long nets here and there, erected on poles, into which unwary geese might fly. These, he now guessed, had been the occasions of those warning-notes. Two or three widgeon hung in one of them, and, far away to the eastward, a fly-like man was plodding over the slob in tiny persistence, to collect his bag.

The sun, as it rose, tinged the quicksilver of the creeks and the gleaming slime itself with flame. The curlew, who had been piping their mournful plaints since long before the light, flew now from weed-bank to weed-bank: the widgeon, who had slept on water, came whistling their double notes, like whistles from a Christmas cracker: the mallard toiled from land, against the wind: the redshanks scuttled and prodded like mice: a cloud of tiny dunlin, more compact than starlings, turned in the air with the noise of a train: the blackguard of crows rose from the pine trees on the dunes with merry cheers: shore birds of every sort populated the tide line, filling it with business and beauty.

The dawn, the sea-dawn and the mastery of ordered flight, were of such intense beauty that he was almost moved to sing. All the sorrow of his thoughts about man, the miserable wishes for peace which had beset him in the Combination Room so lately, these fell from him for the moment in the glory of his wings. He would have liked to cry a chorus to life, and, since a thousand geese were on the wing about him, he had not long to wait. The lines of these creatures, wavering like smoke upon the sky as they breasted the sunrise, were all at once in music and in laughter. Each squadron of them was in different voice, some larking, some triumphant, some in sentiment or glee. The vault of daybreak filled itself with heralds, and this is what they sang:

> *Oh, turning world, pouring beneath our pinions,*
> *Hoist the hoar sun to welcome morning's minions.*

See, on each breast the scarlet and vermillion,
Hear, from each throat the clarion and carillion.

Mark, the wild wandering lines in black battalions,
Heaven's horns and hunters, dawn-bright hounds and stallions.

Free, free: far, far: and fair on wavering wings
Comes Anser albifrons, and sounds, and sings.

WALKING THE WASH
Hilaire Belloc
(from *Hills And The Sea*, 1906)

The town of Wisbeach is very like the town of Boston. It stands upon a river which is very narrow and which curves, and in which there rises and falls a most considerable tide, and which is bounded by slimy wooden sides. Here, as at Boston, the boats cannot turn round; if they come in frontways they have to go out backwards, like Mevagissey bees: an awkward harbour.

As I sat there in the White Hart, waiting for steak and onions, I read in a book descriptive of the place that a whale had come to Wisbeach once, and I considered that a whale coming up to Wisbeach on a tide would certainly stay there; not indeed for the delights of the town (of which I say nothing), but because there would be no room to turn round; and a whale cannot swim backwards. The only fish that can swim backwards is an eel. This I have proved by observation, and I challenge any fisherman to deny it.

So much for Wisbeach, which stands upon the River Nene or Nen, which is the last of the towns defended by the old sea-wall – which is the third of the Fen ports – the other two being Boston and Lynn, which is served by two lines of railway and which has two stations.

Very early next morning, and by one of these stations, another man and I took a train to a bridge called Sutton Bridge, where one can cross the River Nen, and where (according to the map) one can see both the sea-walls, the old and the new. It was my plan to walk along the shore of the Wash right across the flats to Lynn, and so at last perhaps comprehend the nature of this curious land.

When I got to Sutton Bridge I discovered it to be a monstrous thing of iron standing poised upon a huge pivot in mid-stream. It bore the railway and the road together. It was that kind of triumphant engineering which once you saw only in England, but which now you will see all over the world. It was designed to swing open on its central pivot to let boats go up the River Nen, and then to come back exactly to its place with a clang; but when we got to it we found it neither one thing nor the other. It was twisted just so much that the two parts of the roads (the road on the bridge and the road on land) did not join.

Was a boat about to pass? No. Why was it open thus? A man was cleaning it. The bridge is not as big as the Tower Bridge, but it is very big, and the man was cleaning it with a little rag. He was cleaning the under part, the mechanisms and contraptions that can only be got at when the bridge is thus ajar. He cleaned without haste and without exertion, and as I watched him I considered the mightiness of the works of Man contrasted with His Puny Frame. I also asked him when I should pass, but he answered nothing.

As we thus waited men gathered upon either side – men of all characters and kinds, men holding bicycles, men in carts, afoot, on horseback, vigorous men and feeble, old men, women also and little children, and youths witless of life, and innocent young girls; they gathered and increased, they became as numerous as leaves, they stretched out their hands in a desire for the further shore: but the river ran between.

Then, as being next the gate, I again called out: When might we pass? A Fenland man who was on duty there doing nothing said, I could pass when the bridge was shut again. I said: When would that be? He said: Could I not see that the man was cleaning the bridge? I said that, contrasting the bridge with him and his little rag, he might go on from now to the Disestablishment of the English Church before he had done; but as for me, I desired to cross, and so did all that multitude.

Without grace they shut the bridge for us, the gate opened of itself, and in a great clamorous flood, like an army released from a siege, we poured over, all of us, rejoicing into Wringland; for so is called this flat, reclaimed land, which stands isolated between the Nen and the Ouse.

Was I not right in saying when I wrote about Ely that the corner of a corner of England is infinite, and can never be exhausted?

Along the cut which takes the Nen out to sea, then across some level fields, and jumping a ditch or two, one gets to the straight, steep, and high dyke which protects the dry land and cuts off the plough from the sea marshes. When I had climbed it and looked out over endless flats to the sails under the brume of the horizon I understood the Fens.

Nowhere that I have been to in the world does the land fade into the sea so inconspicuously.

The coasts of western England are like the death of a western man in battle – violent and heroic. The land dares all, and plunges into a noisy sea. This coast of eastern England is like the death of one of these eastern merchants here – lethargic, ill-contented, drugged with ease. The dry land slips, and wallows into a quiet, very shallow water, confused with a yellow thickness and brackish with the weight of inland water behind.

I have heard of the great lakes, especially of the marshes at the mouth of the Volga, in the Caspian, where the two elements are for miles indistinguishable, and where no one can speak of a shore; but here the thing is more marvellous, because it is the true sea. You have,

61

I say, the true sea, with great tides, and bearing ships, and sea ports to which the ships can go; and on the other side you have, inhabited, an ancient land. There should be a demarcation between them, a tide mark or limit. There is nothing. You cannot say where one begins and the other ends. One does not understand the Fens until one has seen that shore.

The sand and the mud co-mingle. The mud takes on little tufts of salt grass barely growing under the harsh wind. The marsh is cut and wasted into little islands covered at every high tide, except, perhaps, the extreme of the neaps. Down on that level, out from the dyke to the uncertain line of the water, you cannot walk a hundred yards without having to cross a channel more or less deep, a channel which the working of the muddy tides has scoured up into the silt and ooze of the sodden land. These channels are yards deep in slime, and they ramify like the twisted shoots of an old vine. Were you to make a map of them as they engrave this desolate waste it would look like the fine tortuous cracks that show upon antique enamel, or the wandering of threads blown at random on a woman's work-table by the wind.

There are miles and miles of it right up to the EMBANKMENT, the great and old SEA-WALL which protects the houses of men. You have but to eliminate that embankment to imagine what the whole countryside must have been like before it was raised, and the meaning of the Fens becomes clear to you. The Fens were long ago but the continuation inland of this sea-morass. The tide channels of the marsh were all of one kind, though they differed so much in size. Some of these channels were small without name; some a little larger, and these had a local name; others were a little larger again, and worthy to be called rivers – the Ouse, the Nen, the Welland, the Glen, the Witham. But, large or small, they were nothing, all of them, but the scouring of tide-channels in the light and sodden slime. It was the high tide that drowned all this land, the low tide that drained it; and wherever a patch could be found just above the influence of the tide or near enough to some main channel for the rush and swirl of the water to drain the island, there the villages grew. Wherever such a patch could be found men built their first homes. Sometimes, before men civic, came the holy hermits. But man, religious, or greedy, or just wandering, crept in after each inundation and began to tame the water and spread out even here his slow, interminable conquest. So Wisbeach, so March, so Boston grew, and so – the oldest of them all – the Isle of Ely. ...

We returned from a long wandering upon the desolate edges of the sea to the bank which we proposed to follow right round to the mouth of the Ouse: a bank that runs not straight, but in great broken lines, as in old-fashioned fortification, and from which far off upon the right one sees the famous churches of the Wringland, far off upon the left a hint beyond the marshes and the sands of the very distant open sea.

A gale had risen with the morning, and while it invigorated the travellers in these wastes it seemed to increase their loneliness, for it broke upon nothing, and it removed the interest of the eye from the monotonous sad land to the charge and change of the torn sky above, but in a sense also it impelled us, as though we were sailing before it as it swept along the edge of the bank and helped us to forget the interminable hours.

The birds for whom this estuary is a kind of sanctuary and a place of secure food in all weathers, the birds swept out in great flocks over the flats towards the sea. They were the only companionship afforded to us upon this long day, and they had, or I fancied they had, in their demeanour a kind of contempt for the rare human beings they might see, as though knowing how little man could do upon those sands. They fed all together upon the edge of the water, upon the edge of the falling tide, very far off, making long bands of white that mixed with the tiny breaking wavelets. Now and then they rose in bodies, and so rising disappeared; but as they would turn and wheel against the wind, seeking some other ground, they sent from moment to moment flashes of delicate and rare light from the great multitude of their wings. I know of nothing to which one may compare these glimpses of evanescent shining but these two things – the flash of a sword edge and the rapid turning in human hands of a diaphanous veil held in the light. It shone or glinted for a moment, then they would all wheel together and it disappeared.

So, watching them as a kind of marvel, we saw distant across the sea a faint blue tower, and recognized it for Boston Stump, so many, many miles away.

But for the birds and this landmark, which never left us, all the length of the dyke was empty of any sight save the mixing of the sea and the land. Then gradually the heights in Norfolk beyond grew clearer, a further shore narrowed the expanse of waters, and we came to the river mouth of the Ouse, and caught sight, up the stream, of the houses of a town.

Every man that lands in Lynn feels all through him the antiquity and the call of the town; but especially if he comes, as I came in with another man in springtime, from the miles and miles of emptiness and miles of bending grass and the shouting of the wind. After that morning, in which one had been a little point on an immense plane, with the gale not only above one, as it commonly is, but all around one as it is at sea; and after having steeped one's mind in the peculiar loneliness which haunts a stretch of ill-defined and wasted shore, the narrow, varied, and unordered streets of the port enhance the creations of man and emphasize his presence.

Words so few are necessarily obscure. Let me expand them. I mean that the unexpected turning of the ways in such a port is perpetually revealing something new; that the little spaces frame, as it were, each unexpected sight: thus at the end of a street one will catch a patch of the Fens beyond the river, a great moving sail, a cloud, or the sculptured corner of an excellent house.

The same history also that permitted continual encroachment upon the public thoroughfares and that built up a gradual High Street upon the line of some cow-track leading from the fields to the ferry, the spirit that everywhere permitted the powerful or the cunning to withstand authority – that history (which is the history of all our little English towns) has endowed Lynn with an endless diversity. ...

You can see the past effect of ownership and individuality in Lynn as clearly as you can catch affection or menace in a human voice. The outward expression is most manifest, and to pass in and out along the lanes in front of the old houses inspires in one precisely those emotions which are aroused by a human crowd.

All the roofs of Lynn and all its pavements are worthy (as though they were living beings) of individual names.

Along the river shore, from the race of the ebb that had so nearly drowned me many years before, I watched the walls that mark the edge of the town against the Ouse, and especially that group towards which the ferry-boat was struggling against the eddy and tumble of the tide.

They were walls of every age, not high, brick of a dozen harmonious tones, with the accidents, corners, and breaches of perhaps seven hundred years. Beyond, to the left, down the river, stood the masts in the new docks that were built to preserve the trade of this difficult port. Up-river, great new works of I know not what kind stood like a bastion against the plain; and in between ran these oldest bits of Lynn, somnolescent and refreshing – permanent.

The lanes up from the Ouse when I landed I found to be of a slow and natural growth, with that slight bend to them that comes, I believe, from the drying of fishing-nets. For it is said that courts of this kind grew up in our sea-towns all round our eastern and the southern coast in such a manner. It happened thus:

The town would begin upon the highest of the bank, for it was flatter for building, drier and easier to defend than that part next to the water. Down from the town to the shore the fishermen would lay out their nets to dry. How nets look when they are so laid, their narrowness and the curve they take, everybody knows. Then on the spaces between the nets shanties would be built, or old boats turned upside down for shelter, so that the curing of fish and the boiling of tar and the serving and parcelling of ropes could be done under cover. Then as the number of people grew, the squatters' land got value, and houses were raised (you will find many small freeholds in such rows to this day), but the lines of the net remained in the alley-ways between the houses. ...

The open square of the town, which one looks at from the Globe, gives one a mingled pleasure of reminiscence and discovery. It breaks on one abruptly. It is as wide as a pasture field, and all the houses are ample and largely founded. Indeed, throughout this country, elbow-room – the sense that there is space enough and to spare in such flats and under an open sky – has filled the minds of builders. You may see it in all the inland towns of the Fens; and one found it again here upon the further bank, upon the edge of the Fens; for though Lynn is just off the Fens, yet it looks upon their horizon and their sky, and belongs to them in spirit.

In this large and comfortable square a very steadfast and most considerable English bank is to be discovered. It is of honest brown brick; its architecture is of the plainest; its appearance is such that its credit could never fail, and that the house alone by its presence could conduct a dignified business for ever. The rooms in it are so many and so great that the owners of such a bank (having become princes by its success) could inhabit them with a majesty worthy of their new title. But who lives above his shop since Richardson died? And did old Richardson? Lord knows! ... Anyhow, the bank is glorious, and it is but one of the fifty houses that I saw in Lynn.

Thus, in the same street as the Globe, was a facade of stone. If it was Georgian, it was very early Georgian, for it was relieved with ornaments of a delicate and accurate sort, and the proportions were exactly satisfying to the eye that looked on it. The stone also was of that kind (Portland stone, I think) which goes black and white with age, and which is better suited than any other to the English climate.

In another house near the church I saw a roof that might have been a roof for a town. It covered the living part and the stables, and the outhouse and the brewhouse, and the barns, and for all I know the pig-pens and the pigeons' as well. It was a benediction of a roof – a roof traditional, a roof patriarchal, a roof customary, a roof of permanence and unity, a roof that physically sheltered and spiritually sustained, a roof majestic, a roof eternal. In a word, it was a roof catholic. And what, thought I, is paid yearly in this town for such a roof as that? I do not know; but I know of another roof at Goudhurst, in Kent, which would have cost me less than £100 a year, only I could not get it for love or money.

There is also in Lynn a Custom House not very English, but very beautiful. The faces carved upon it were so vivid that I could not but believe them to have been carved in the Netherlands, and from this Custom House looks down the pinched, unhappy face of that narrow gentleman whom the great families destroyed – James II.

There is also in Lynn what I did not know was to be seen out of Sussex – a Tudor building of chipped flints, and on it the mouldering arms of Elizabeth.

The last Gothic of this Bishop's borough which the King seized from the Church clings to chance houses in little carven masks and occasional ogives: there is everywhere a feast for whatever in the mind is curious, searching, and reverent, and over the town, as over all the failing ports of our silting eastern seaboard, hangs the air of a great past time, the influence of the Baltic and the Lowlands.

A TEST OF FRIENDSHIP
Virginia Woolf in the Fens
Peter Tolhurst

At the beginning of August 1899 Virginia Stephen and family found themselves standing on the platform of an isolated Fenland station awaiting the omnibus that would take them to the rectory at the far end of the village. They had come to this desolate spot some six miles north east of Huntingdon at the behest of cousin Dorothea Stephen, a frequent and unwelcome visitor to the family's London residence at Hyde Park Gate. Earlier that year she had written to Virginia and Vanessa: '"We shall be very glad if you will spend the summer near us at Warboys – only we think you will have to change the name to Peace Girls." !!!!' The flurry of exclamation marks came later in a letter from Virginia to her cousin Emma Vaughan.

Arriving on a day overcast and wet, Virginia's initial response to this landscape of endless horizons was decidedly unenthusiastic: '... the country through which our train passed was dull in the extreme.' Situated on a spur of higher ground thrust out into the heart of the fen, the village of Warboys appeared equally unattractive. Strung out along the main street this mixture of Victorian chapels, institute buildings and grey brick houses, was a rather dreary product of the railway era, but just as Virginia's spirits began to flag the weather brightened dramatically:

> ... the sun shot a shaft of light down; & we beheld a glorious expanse of sky – this golden gauze streamer lit everything in its light; & far away over the flat fields a spire caught the beam & glittered like a gem in the darkness & wetness ...

Buoyed up by this dazzling spectacle on the short journey from the station, during which time they passed no less than nine public houses, Virginia felt moved to declare 'Room for Dorothea's band of Hope here!' a sly reference to her evangelical cousin's membership of the London Temperance Society.

The few buildings of any distinction lie at the far end of the street beyond that ubiquitous feature of Fenland villages, the Jubilee clock tower (1887). Here the stately parish church of St Mary Magdalen rises from the fields, its medieval broach spire a landmark for miles around. The 17th century manor house immediately north of the churchyard with its large shaped gables and its red brickwork already laid in Flemish bond, is a clear reminder that it was Dutch engineers who first drained the Bedfordshire Levels. Opposite, and hidden from view by a generous belt of trees, stands the old rectory, now Moat House, the large gault brick residence that was to be home to the Stephen family for the next six weeks.

The following day dawned bright and sunny and Virginia spent the morning drifting listlessly in a punt on the moat in 'this eternal throbbing heat' unable to throw off the mood induced by the strange, flat country where 'Such melting gray of sky, land & water is the very spirit of monotony.' A stroll in the churchyard seemed appropriate to her melancholy:

... full of sombre tombstones, with queer carvings & angels heads sprawling over date & name and all. There are many graves that are nameless; & I was startled to think that I was walking over some ancient dust forgotten & undistinguished from the hillocks of the field. The graves rise in swelling mounds side by side all along the bottom of the churchyard.

Days later Virginia discovered for herself the architectural delights of St Mary Magdalen, most notably its impressive Norman chancel arch, its 13th century font with stiff-leaf decoration and its Perpendicular windows 'whose long brass latches are picturesque though doubtless inefficient'. She was accompanied on this occasion by the curate in charge, 'the first live specimen I have ever shaken hands with ...'. Although resident in the village for nearly a year, he knew surprisingly little about his church but at dinner that evening managed to redeem himself with amusing snippets of village gossip. Mr Blake Milward was by inclination High Anglican and seemed ill at ease among the predominantly Baptist population of Warboys who practiced total immersion every Easter in a pond near the station. The only things that made life tolerable in this isolated outpost were a healthy contempt for the rector's wife, a Mrs Proudie figure with whom he was in open hostility, and the opportunity to shoot rabbits. Acceptance into the community was for Virginia a remote possibility:

The people about here are a peculiar race. So embedded are they in their own delving pursuits, living lonely self contained lives, with a few strong religious opinions that only serve to narrow their minds, that a stranger is in their eyes a most contemptible creature.

As the temperature soared Virginia and her brother Adrian decided to postpone their daily exercise until after tea. With no 'disturbing Hills' to slow their progress this was perfect cycling country and the two often rode for miles along narrow straight tracks beside the dykes in the cool of the evening. Surveying a landscape alive with the sound of harvest she felt more disposed to the Fens and its inhabitants. Having persevered with a rather scratchy pen her inability to describe the scene to her satisfaction was matched only by her wretched handwriting.

This is the midst of the old Fen country. This solid ground on which we stood was, not many years ago, all swamp & reed; now indeed there is a pathway, & on either side grow potatoes & corn, but the Fen character remains indelible. A broad ditch crosses the Fen, in which there is cold brown water even in this hot summer. Tall rushes & water plants grow from it; & small white moths, the inhabitants of the Fens, were fluttering among them in scores ... how this country impresses me – how great I feel the stony-hard flatness [?] & monotony of the plain.

Just four miles north of Warboys, stands the small market town of Ramsey where, a few days before, the train carrying the Stephen entourage had stopped briefly on its journey from London. Having consulted her guide book and discovered the ease with which she could traverse the countryside, Virginia decided it might be worth cycling the short distance in search of monastic remains. Situated on a low rise Ramsey Abbey had once been one of the great religious houses in the Fens to rival Croyland and Ely. This outpost of Christianity, surrounded by a huge expanse of 'dense & melancholy marshes' teeming with fish and wild fowl, was well placed to nurture the contemplative life until, at the Dissolution, the great Benedictine church was pulled down and pillaged for its building materials. Some of the more ornate pieces of Barnack stone have been used as garden sculpture including the section of elaborately moulded column from the nave arcade that found its way to Warboys rectory. Here, beneath a large chestnut tree, it is still used as a chopping block.

Today Ramsey is an unremarkable place, redeemed at the far end of the High Street by an attractive group of buildings arranged around a spacious green. Here the series of pretty estate cottages is offset on one side by the parish church and opposite by a richly ornamented fragment of the abbey gatehouse, inside which is the marble effigy (c.1230) of Aelwin, founder of the Abbey in 969. Ramsey appears to have left little impression on its young visitor who copied out the bare historical facts from the relevant volume of Kelly's 1885 Directory without further comment, but years later when casting around for ideas it may have provided Virginia with a name for the Ramsay family in *To The Lighthouse*.

The town of St Ives, unlike its Cornish namesake, receives only a passing reference in Virginia's journal. In her entry for August 18th,1899, entitled 'Warboys Distractions', the stone bridge with its medieval chapel built by the Abbots of Ramsey warrants a mention and by the end of the day there are additional notes on the town's history. The weekly market granted a charter by Edward I, the disastrous fire of 1680 and St Ives' most famous resident, Oliver Cromwell, are all dutifully transcribed from Kelly's Directory in the manner of her Ramsey notes. The sudden interest in the town had been prompted by an unscheduled ride through its cobble streets on her way to a 'terrible oppressive gathering of Stephens' beside the river at Godmanchester. The outing, planned well in advance with the help of Bradshaw's Railway Guide, had begun ominously enough. Having almost missed the train at Warboys the Stephen family eased themselves with some relief into a third class carriage and gazed out of the window: 'All around were gray flat fields with rain swishing over them & the pollard trees sobbing in the wind.'

The protracted journey involving several changes had terminated at St Ives station where, due to a misunderstanding over platforms, they had missed their connection to Huntingdon and were being driven through a succession of picturesque villages in a hastily arranged pony trap – 'such antiquity grows depressing after a time' – to a belated luncheon with a daunting collection of relatives who 'bring with them the atmosphere of the lecture room; they are severe, caustic & absolutely independent & immoveable [sic]'. The company and the weather conspired to produce what Virginia concluded was a 'somewhat grim day of pleasure'. A boat trip was followed by a dreary walk along the river bank before the guests eventually decided on a place to spread their picnic:

Picture us uncomfortably seated on a towing path; half the party in a ditch, the other half in long grass – a cold wind blowing, with occasional drops of rain – no glow in east or west – but a grey melancholy vista of sky. Sir Herbert fought wasps & eat bread & jam – then we slowly packed our basket & started back for Godmanchester. I sat in one boat with Lady Stephen ... The rain fell now with a vengeance.

There can be little doubt that the Stephen children were relieved to return to the comfort and seclusion of Warboys where they could resume their passion for bugging. The first stage of their sugar campaign, described in great detail, involved smearing a selection of trees in the grounds with a lethal mixture of rum and thick black treacle. Later that evening, under cover of darkness, the intrepid explorers set about their deadly business. Julian, dressed like a brigand and clutching his jar of poison, was followed by Vanessa in evening dress and shawl carrying a net, Virginia holding a bicycle lamp 'of brilliant but uncertain powers of illumination' and Adrian 'a supernumerary amateur of no calling ... proficient in the art of obscuring the lamp at critical moments.' Gurth, the family pet, who proved adept at catching moths 'for no entomological purpose whatever', completed the expedition. At each tree the more interesting specimens, already intoxicated by the sticky liquor, were swiftly despatched by the leader with a single drop from his uncorked bottle.

As the lantern bearer argued in her own defence: 'Death might come more painfully.'

For Virginia the best form of relaxation available at Warboys was to lie in the punt with a good selection of reading material. Here, drifting through the duck weed, she developed the idea for an outrageous piece of spoof journalism written for the amusement of her cousin Emma Vaughan in which the author is sent by a local paper as its special correspondent to report a fatal accident at Warboys rectory. The article that appeared in the Huntingdonshire Gazette beneath the headline 'TERRIBLE TRAGEDY IN A DUCK POND' recounts the harrowing tale of three young people drowned when their punt capsized during a moonlight excursion on the lake. Written in a style more suitable to a Victorian melodrama a few days after her 'grim day of pleasure', Virginia showed commendable restraint when she might well have felt like choosing relatives other than Emma and Adrian to accompany her to a watery grave:

The angry waters of the duck pond rose in their wrath to swallow their prey – & the green caverns of the depths opened – & closed – The cold moonlight silvered the path to death – & perhaps tinged the last thoughts of the unfortunate sufferers with something of its own majestic serenity. We know not if their end was promptly consummated, or if terrible shrieks & agonized struggles for air preceded the merciful rest that soon was theirs. Alone, untended, unsoothed, with no spectator but the silver moon, with no eye to weep, no hand to caress, three young souls were overwhelmed by the waters of the duck Pond.

Throughout her Warboys Journal, Virginia's frequent use of the word 'melancholy' to describe the Fens and her interest in the many unmarked graves beyond the rectory gates suggest an unhealthy affinity with this strange, watery landscape. Despite its self-mocking tone her 'duck pond tragedy' – death by drowning – foretells her own suicide years later in the Sussex Ouse with unnerving accuracy. Her account of a Fenland funeral procession is in stark contrast to this light-hearted exercise in tabloid journalism. The traders' carts full of mourners creep like huge black beetles along a bone white track that stretches away to the far horizon. These people, who in their poverty and their grief are inescapably bound to the black fen and utterly exposed to the elements, resemble characters from one of Hardy's tragic novels, but as the experience becomes internalised so the images take on a more sinister, nightmarish quality.

They came from the east along the absolutely straight white road. We saw them crawling towards us with the sky heaping clouds & the wind blowing blue spaces around them. As we passed them, a boy looked down at us very sullenly & with the peculiar sodden depressed look that Fen men & women have; they were absolutely silent; & the procession went on to the heart of the Fen. I dreamt most vividly of this last night; how I looked into the womens faces; & the carts passed on and into the [night?] they were going back to some strange dark land, & they said the only time they saw the light of day was when they came to Warboys to bury their dead.

As she became more familiar with the surrounding countryside its distinctive ethereal appeal soon dispelled any reservations Virginia still had for the Fens: 'There is a curious feeling in this land of infinite sky: so that you can become a weather prophet lying on yr. back.' By September 3rd the whole of her entry for that day is devoted to a description of the most glorious Turneresque sunset, but after just a few days at Warboys she is already celebrating her new found enthusiasm for the great cloudscapes and wide horizons. Cycling back from Huntingdon with a string bag of melons bumping against her knees, Virginia was in rapturous mood; a mood conveyed to Emma Vaughan the following day:

You dont see the sky until you live here. We have ceased to be dwellers on the earth. We are really made of clouds. We are mystical and dreamy and perform Fugues on the Harmonium ... I shall think it a test of friends for the future whether they can appreciate the Fen country. I want to read books about it, and to write sonnets about it all day long. It is the only place for rest of mind and body, and for contentment and creamy potatoes and all the joys of life. I am growing like a meditative Alderney cow. And there are people who think it dull and uninteresting!!!!

Virginia was always alert to the most subtle change of atmosphere and on her last day at Warboys (20th September), her mood of melancholy had acquired a distinctly autumnal flavour: 'a sharp wind comes racing across the plain, and brown coveys of partridges rise from the stubble ...' The hedges were now laden with berries, the colours more subdued, but the most distinctive sign was always a 'mellow clearness in the air' that brought with it '... odours of burning wood & weeds; and delicious moisture from the shaven earth; it is cleaner & more virile; it is autumn in its youth, before decayed woods & weeping vapours have come to end its substance.' The sight of weeds burning on a hill when they had last cycled to Ramsey seemed to epitomize the changing season and by way of illustration she refers her reader to Millais' picture 'Autumn Leaves'.

Later that year brother Thoby went up to Trinity and Virginia soon came to know his close undergraduate circle, but whether Lytton Strachey, Saxon Sydney-Turner or the rest were ever dragged out into the Fens and subjected to her test of friendship remains uncertain. What *is* clear is that she enjoyed her holiday in the Fens more than any other apart from those in her beloved Cornwall. Evident too in her letter to Emma Vaughan is a precocious literary style which, according to Quentin Bell, with its 'pace, its mockery, its exaggeration, its flights of fancy' came to characterize her more mature correspondence. Here and in her Warboys Journal Virginia Stephen first discovered her unique literary talent.

SWIMMING WITH EELS

Roger Deakin

(from *Waterlog*, 2000)

The Fens, 14 May

The approach to Ely is always dramatic. The city and its cathedral
loom at first faintly through the blue haze of the Fens, distinguishable
as a whiter shade of pale. As you draw closer the whole island
shimmers like a mirage or a UFO that has just landed, and as the
cathedral spire comes into focus, the place seems poised to take off
again. Even the moated allotments, with their lowly huts like outside
privies, derive an air of grandeur from their own row of boundary
poplars reaching for the heavens and striping them with long shadows.
This is a holy island no less striking than Mont St Michel, and no less
holy, set off by the graphic flat horizon, rising out of the deep brown
earth beneath a sea-blue sky. It dominates the most mysterious
landscape in Britain, full of water and odd corners that can still be hard
to reach, let alone find. As Daniel Defoe put it when he surveyed the
Fens from a safe distance at the top of the Gogmagog Hills in 1724:
'All the water of the middle part of England that does not run into the
Thames or the Trent, comes down into these fens.'

I was on my way over to join Sid Merry, the last eel trapper in a city
where the monks once paid their tithes to the cathedral with 30,000
eels a year. Sid Merry was born by the waters of Babylon, an island
separated from the city by the Great Ouse, opposite the slipway by the
Ship Inn. Cut off from the rest of the city, and often flooded, it must
have been christened by some wit in one of the monasteries or at the
cathedral. The Merrys' house on Babylon is now long gone, like the
other seven that once stood there, but Sid still owns the land. He grows
vegetables on it and keeps ducks and geese in pens surrounded by
fences of eel-netting. A variety of old boats in various states of repair

stand around propped up by wooden stilts.

We boarded his punt from a wooden landing-stage. I sat on an upturned crate feeling curious and apprehensive at the prospect of meeting my totemic ancestors. Sid untied several keep-nets full of puzzled-looking eels that hung underneath the boat and attached them to the landing-stage. The light was softening, and by the time our evening's work was done, it would be dark. Sid goes out every day just before dusk to lay his eel-traps in the river, and the lines of complex nets and hoops, weights and steel chain lay in neat piles like laundry in the bottom of the boat. Everything had a distinctive whiff of mud, water-mint and fish. As we went down the wide, lazy river the only sound was the punt's outboard engine and the slapping of the bow-waves against the banks.

Sid is a wiry, weather-beaten man of medium build who knows the Great Ouse as well as anyone. He and his father used to trap eels in baskets or eel-hives. 'They would sink naturally to the bottom once they were soaked enough. What we'd do was get a little tobacco tin and prick holes in it and fill it full of worms, and the eels would go in the basket after it.'

Like many people who lived by the water, Sid and his dad also used to put out a night line for eels. It would be about thirty yards long with a dozen hooks baited with small fish, sparrows; anything dead and preferably rotting. They would throw it out last thing at night and harvest the eels off it before first light. Eels will try anything to avoid the light, and will tangle the lines if left until daybreak. There was always a market for eels in the Fens. People would sell them in buckets and baskets in Ely market until just a few years ago. But unless you sold out, you were left with eels on your hands, because you can only sell them alive. Once killed, an eel must be cooked straight away, and in warm weather they will die within five minutes of leaving the water.

Sid steered the boat off the river into a narrow channel that leads under a railway bridge whose bricks are scored by the passage of barges from the old clay-pits, now themselves sheets of reedy open water. The cargoes of clay were for mending and building the raised banks of the fenland rivers and dykes. We slid past a great crested grebe on her floating nest and Sid began laying the nets straight off the stern along the edge of the reed-bed. This is where the eels would go to feed at night. A kind of anchor went in first, followed by a length of chain, and then the 'leader' nets that guide the unsuspecting creatures towards the mouths of the traps, which each have a series of funnels and chambers along the lines of a lobster pot. Sid laid twenty nets in two rows but didn't seem to mark their position. Why? 'Because I don't want to lose them to anyone. I just say, "All right, there's a tree there, or a bunch of nettles," and make a mental note.' As we chugged back in the sunset, and the eels began their night-life below us, Sid mapped the shape of his year.

All winter he makes new traps in his attic and in the workshop at the end of his garden from yards of special sheep-netting. He starts trapping in April when the weather warms up. An eel trapper likes a sultry night with a reasonable flow on the river. The flow spurs the eels to move about and hunt for food. He keeps going all summer until September, when the silvers go away. Silvers are the mature eels that are ready to make the fabled journey across the Atlantic to the Sargasso Sea where they breed. Eels emerge from the Fens in three distinct runs to the sea in September, October and November, and they usually go on the new moon. The rougher the river the better they like it. They are caught in wing-nets, stretched right across the river. You see them dimly sometimes, swimming in processions about three feet down, always in midstream. Eels are clearly in close touch with the moon, moving with it like the tides and shunning the sun. It is no wonder, when you consider that they spend the first three years of their lives as elvers drifting on the ocean currents towards our shores. They are sea creatures living inland.

The elvers arrive in May, after hitch-hiking along the Gulf Stream from the Sargasso, preyed upon by just about every living creature in the Atlantic. They swim up the river at night in dark brown shoals like tadpoles, although nowhere near so many now as there used to be. They are still caught in big landing nets on the Severn where they fetch prices that are inflated by their recent scarcity, and are sent off to the gourmets of France and Japan.

I spent that night in Freckenham, dreaming of my mother teaching me to swim, cradling my head as I kicked my legs in the water. I returned through the Fens in mist at a quarter to six next morning to meet Sid and collect the night's catch. His friend John was on board too, also dressed in yellow oilskin trousers but lacking the old tweed fishing hat Sid seemed to live in. John's job was to help haul in the tackle and untie the netting at the bottom end of each trap to release the eels.

As we approached last night's reed-bed, Sid's eye was on whatever subtle landmarks he had chosen to help him locate the row of sunken traps. He throttled down the engine and John swung a grappling iron over the side, waited for it to sink, then heaved. 'I think it's the nets,' he said. 'I hope it's not a body.' In came the chain, then the first of the traps with the dark brown glistening shapes and flashes of white belly. Nothing could be more streamlined or agile than this. An eel's head, with its eyes set close together and high in the skull, and the sharp snout, bears a remarkable similarity to Concorde. Nothing could be so outlandish. An eel is so mottled and green and varnished in mucus it could be an uprooted plant, a mandrake root come to life.

John untied each trap at the bottom and tipped the creatures deftly into the plastic tub, where they subsided into a glutinous tangle, making little kissing sounds. Their electric energy was astonishing. They reared straight up in the tub on the tips of their tails like snakes, waving their little heads about looking for a way out, swaying like puppets, naked as bedsprings. Every now and again an eel spilled on to the bottom of the boat and slithered in reverse, then forward, curling itself into a question mark as if to say: 'What the hell is going on here?'

79

I noticed they picked it up with a towel, or a pair of kinked tongs, and Sid explained: 'You keep your fingers away from them. If they did happen to get hold of you, you'd know about it. The trouble is they suck everything in, and the teeth go inwards and . . .' He pursed his lips and made a sucking sound. 'I did get nabbed once; they got this finger. But I got it out. Same as pike, you've got to be careful.' Sid sorted the eels as they came in, flicking the smaller ones back. Some nets had as many as half a dozen eels in them. John had to keep disentangling young 3- or 4-inch bream out of the leader nets. 'No ruff,' he says, 'thank God.' Ruff are horrible little spiky fish that get tangled in the net like bits of thistle.

It was a respectable catch: about 25 pounds altogether. Sid's biggest eel to date weighed $7^{1/4}$ pounds and measured nearly 4 feet. It was not as big as the 10 eels he saw recently that had come out of the lake at Holkham Hall in north Norfolk when they drained and dredged it. They weighed between 8 and 12 pounds and were up to 6 feet long. Nobody seems to know why some eels get the urge to breed and become silvers and others just stay where they are and grow. Some, like the Holkham eels, may just find themselves cut off from the sea. Sid says they're usually between 10 and 20 when they go back to the sea, weighing between 1 and 4 pounds. They grow about an inch a year, so the 7-pounder he caught was probably a 45- or 50-year-old. Once they have gone back to spawn in the Sargasso, the silvers never return. Like spawning salmon, they simply die.

On the way back Sid spoke of his best-ever catch. 'It was May Day – the first Spring Bank Holiday on a May Day – and I was down here at the clay pits in a place I had netted several times before. That night I just thought "I'll drop them here again." There was a row of willow trees all along the bank with their roots in the water, and I know what had happened. The fish had gone in the previous day, because it was a nice day, and spawned. The eels had followed them in at night, but they couldn't get at the spawn because they hit the nets first. I got 285 pounds out of 10 nets; about 250 eels, probably more.

He said the best conditions for catching eels would often be rough weather. 'We used to say a good thunderstorm would get them started.' Eels will travel overland during rain. Sid remembered a thunderstorm one afternoon about the time the silvers were making their way back towards the sea. They came out of a pond and across a field on Highflyer's Farm just outside Ely, but the storm didn't last long and the sun came out. Sid had the farmer on the telephone asking him why there were dead eels all over his field and where on earth did they come from.

I asked what eels eat. 'Everything,' said Sid airily. 'Fish, fish spawn, worms, frogs, snails, all rubbish, bodies, anything. They'll eat one another. They're proper scavengers.'

'Bodies?'

'Oh yes. When people drown themselves, if you pull the bodies out you pull eels out with 'em.'

Sid knew what he was talking about, too.

'There used to be a pub down here called the Ship. They would come out of the pub and walk straight into the bloomin' river.'

Sid and his brothers and sisters all swam in the Great Ouse as children. 'Father used to have a long pole and put a bit of rope round your waist and that was how we learnt. There was what we called the Ely Bathing Place near the station. It had a nice gravel bottom and you could nearly walk right across the river. There was an old crane there we used to swing off by the bonding house wharf. We would swim off the slipway, and by the Black Horse at Littleport. People have had their feet bit by pike. They can be vicious, especially if they're hungry and you happen to go by kicking your feet. They're out in a flash.'

Sid's grandfather, James, was famous for his life-saving on the Ouse. He was a crane driver on the Great Eastern Railway wharf in the days when most people still travelled around the Fens by water. At a civic ceremony in Ely in 1906, Mr Merry was presented with a variety of elaborate gifts that included a walnut chiffonier, a dining table, a 'purse of gold' and a framed testimonial inscribed: 'Presented to Mr

James Merry by his fellow citizens as a token of their appreciation of the bravery shown by him in rescuing twenty people from the River Ouse during a period of twenty years.' He had been received with much cheering, and said in his modest reply that 'the rescues he had effected were only what any ordinary Englishman would have done had they been placed in the same circumstances'.

Back at the landing-stage on Babylon, Sid poured the eels out of the tub into a plastic fish-tray in the punt and began sorting them by size with the tongs. The bigger ones went into a keep-net under the boat with others reserved for a 'special customer'. The rest went into another net, also stored in the cool shadow of the punt, to await the weekly visit of Bill, the wholesale merchant. He would take the eels back to London, jelly them, and sell them on. With added gelatine.

Sid is a purist when it comes to jellying. 'The actual jelly's in the skin. A lot of people do wrong and they'll skin an eel, but I never skin mine. All the goodness is in that liquor, and it will set like a jelly. Bring them to the boil, let them simmer ten to twenty minutes according to size, and stick a couple of shallots in too. If you're having them stewed, make some white sauce and have them hot. They're very good fried in butter with shallots and a glass of white wine, or dipped in batter and fried at my brother's fish shop.' As a man who eats an awful lot of eels, Sid should know.

It was still only breakfast time when I left Sid and went off to swim in Adventurer's Fen in a pool at the junction of Burwell Lode and Reach Lode. (A lode in the Fens is a small river, between five and twenty yards wide.) I went in across a raft of reeds and subsided rather than dived into the half-clear green water. It was surprisingly shallow: only three to five feet, with a soft, black, mud bottom. Reach Lode and Burwell Lode stretched away from the confluence in straight lines for as far as I could see, like two enormous swimming pools, banked and raised some twenty feet above the surrounding fen. Floating at this level, I felt half-suspended in the reflected sky and very remote from anywhere.

I swam down the middle of the wide stillness of Burwell Lode to where it joins Wicken Lode, and, further on, the River Cam. I had a powerful sense of eels in the reeds and in the invisible mire below. Divers who go down in the Fens see holes in the river bottom where big eels lie up, growing their annual inch and waiting for nightfall. A fish rose before me in a lazy flick. The morning was already warm, with little white clouds bringing the sun in and out, and the shallow water felt mild enough too, in spite of a breeze that combed the surface in flurries. I breaststroked a few hundred yards along the deserted lode and began to appreciate the sense of space. The banks, contoured and softened by reeds, didn't look nearly so uniformly straight once I was in the water. A marsh harrier came over, its quiet, loping wings darkening the sky for a moment.

The rich, black silty earth along the banks of the Cam around here has been farmed by the same families for years. Because the river was the main artery of transport, the farmhouses and buildings were all sited along its banks. Two miles away, I had met a family who have farmed at the remote junction of Swaffham Lode and the Cam for over a hundred years, and have always swum in the river. In summer they have ten or twelve children swimming from the farm, and building elaborate carpeted rope walks as diving platforms in the trees. Thirty years ago, the whole village used to come out to the farm to picnic and swim in the river in summer. At harvest time, the farmers, farm workers and children would all be covered in the black peaty dust off the land at the end of each day. They would each be given a piece of soap to take into the river as they bathed, washing off the grime, larking about, and sending bubbles of lather floating off down the river. Even the grandmother, who was over eighty, used to swim in the Cam in a hat with her pearls and glasses on. Alver Badcock and his River Board gang would come along on a barge once a year to dredge the lode, with their own hut and stove on board. As recently as the 1960s, the sugar beet was taken away from the farm on barges, which would line up in a row to be loaded with thirty tons each.

As I turned off to swim under a wooden bridge and up Wicken Lode, the sound of warblers was everywhere in the green clouds of sallow bushes on the opposite bank. A water pump was audible somewhere in the distance, a reminder of the energy-intensive measures which the draining of the Fens has made necessary. Like any other unnatural system of land management, it doesn't quite add up. The Fens today will work only with the massive invisible input of electricity to run the pumps that keep the system working.

The water in the lode was becoming brilliantly clear – 'gin clear' as they say here. The banks were thick with reeds. Roach were clearly visible under the lily pads. It was obvious that I was swimming beside a nature reserve, but since Wicken Lode is open to navigation, and, more to the point, none of the wild life seemed to be taking the slightest notice of me, I could see no objection to this. I could certainly think of no objection to the delicious water except W.C.Fields's famous quibble about what fish do in it. I swam right up to a frog, which eyed me, but didn't dive or even blink. As every member of the Special Boat Unit knows, you are pretty well hidden when you swim, and aquatic animals are relatively unconcerned about you once you too are submerged. You have become, after all, one of them.

Just then, a group of birdwatchers appeared in the top of a wooden tower hide on the other bank and began scanning the fen with binoculars. Was this a search party? The moment was suddenly reminiscent of a scene in Geoffrey Household's *Rogue Male*, in which the fugitive hero, half-dead from torture and in need of clothes, purloins the trousers of four bathers off a river bank and hides from them in the water, then steals downstream with his soggy raft of breeches. A group of us, sharing a Paddington flat in the sixties, used to know the book almost by heart and derived from it a coded cult language. One of our inventions was the verb 'to quive', meaning to move by stealth, covertly, as when stalking a wild animal, or up to no good. It derives from the name of the anonymous hero's ruthless and relentless pursuer, Major Quive-Smith, a master of tactics and fieldcraft who runs our man to ground in a hidden Dorset lane, like a wild animal.

I *quived* silently into the reeds and floated there up to my nose like a crocodile until they had gone, taking a good deal of boyish pleasure from their failure to notice me. The moment it becomes a subversive activity, swimming is that much more interesting. I swam upriver to a crystal pool where the New River flows in to join the lode and there is a mooring. Why was the water so very clear? I had two theories: first, that this was water pumped up from underground by the Environment Agency to prevent Wicken Fen from drying out and losing its essential character as a wet fen; and second, that it was springwater from around Snailwell, which is also the source of that quintessential fenland river, the Snail. Perhaps, because the fen is managed in such a benign way, with no agricultural chemicals, this was just how water could be anywhere, if we would only look after it with more care.

I scrambled out with the help of the reeds but still managed to daub myself in a woad of black silt, so that I had to face the walk back along the bank in my swimming trunks, looking like some neolithic erstwhile inhabitant. I passed a digger, fortunately unmanned, that had unearthed a huge tree of bog oak six feet down in the peat. This remnant of the ancient woods that grew here over 4,000 years ago was now almost pure black, with the peat that preserved it still fresh. Such trees were not necessarily oak; they may have been pine or yew and were often very tall, eventually killed by rising water levels and felled by storms. A boat came along the lode; some sort of pleasure launch. But the couple on board in yachting caps just waved a cheery hallo as though quite accustomed to meeting half-naked tribesmen at large in the Fens.

Now fully clothed, I returned through the village of Wicken where the churchyard headstones sang a requiem of fenland names: Dorcas Bishop, Jabez Taylor, Violet Bailey, Albert Delph, Sophia Kettle, Joseph Tebbitt, Joshua Hatch, Steadman Aspland. I also met Mr and Mrs Bullman in the best bungalow front garden in England. They had built a model village complete with a working water mill, pub, village hall, manor house, cottage hospital, fish and chip shop, church, vicarage, barn, chapel, forge, fire station, hotel, bakery, butcher, post office, florist, hairdresser, various cottages with outside privies, a station, signalbox and railway. There was even a car-boot sale and a tourist information centre. Only one thing was missing: a swimming pool. Still, there is something generous and public-spirited about a beautiful front garden. It is quite different from the back garden, which is a private pleasure. Occasionally in a city you will see from the top of a bus a bright waterfall of windowbox flowers down the front of a house or flat in an otherwise dull street. The Bullmans' garden was like the spontaneous gestures of welcome you encounter when you travel in the Arabian countryside, bringing the pleasure of surprise to passing strangers.

That night I met Ernie Hall playing darts in the Three Tuns at Welney, where three grey and white cats curled up in the window, and a washing line on the river bank danced with long johns, flowered frocks and pairs of woollen gloves. He told me how, after work on hot days, he and his friends used to dive off the bridge there into the muddy Hundred Foot Drain, swim down on the ebb-tide to the Crown, three miles away, sink three pints while the tide turned, then swim back up on the rising tide to Bank Farm, where he lived. 'Nobody worried,' he said. 'There was no law against it.' Bank Farm lies just below the massive bank of the Hundred Foot Drain, some twenty feet below the surface of the river. 'We used to drink that water in the Hundred Foot,' said Ernie, sipping his pint thoughtfully. 'There was nothing else to drink. We used to siphon it out and take turns to do the pumping. It was bloody hard work.' They would stand the water overnight to let the silt settle, decant it, and boil it. They had water butts too, so not a drop of rain was ever wasted. 'If you ever drink rainwater you'll never drink nothing else.'

When it froze they would take to their skates and travel the dykes and rivers like roads for miles all over the Fens. A favourite would be to skate from Littleport for three miles up the Great Ouse to Brandon

Creek, where it meets the Little Ouse, for a drink at the Ship. On a Sunday afternoon at Welney in cold weather there would be 2,000 people skating on the Ouse Washes, and even more for the Fenland Skating Championships on Bury Fen if it froze hard enough. Welney has produced more first-class skaters than any other fenland village, breeding whole families of champions.

I was struck by the fierce loyalty amongst these people. Everyone in the Three Tuns agreed with Ernie when he said they were all salt of the earth in the Fens and would 'give you a sack of potatoes as soon as look at you'. Once you got beyond Cambridge, however, 'They wouldn't give you the drippings off the end of their nose.' They were still talking about a dog otter that had been found killed on the road at Welney three weeks before, and they all remembered the last coypu captured in the river there. It weighed 35 pounds and was probably eaten by the lock keeper upstream at Earith, who used to trap the amiable rodents for the stewing pot.

Another of the fenmen, Don Dewsbury, described standing on the banks of the big Hundred Foot Drain in stormy weather and feeling the banks shaking with the sheer weight of water. He had worked for the Great Ouse River Board for fifty years, and was once on a barge in the river with his friend Budgie from Soham when the banks burst and they were washed through on a great wave of brown surf and beached in the middle of a potato field. Mick Willets, who lives by the sluice at Denver, said he once picked potatoes from aboard a punt on a farm at Willingham with his auntie during the 1947 floods.

Each village would have its own favourite natural lido. Across the Fens in Cottenham, the people would walk north along a track over Smithey Fen to swim where the sandy bank slopes gently into the Old West River. Pop Day was one of the swimmers, and he had seen as many as a hundred bathing there together and basking on the banks. He undid his shirt buttons to show me the scar he got from diving into the river over the hedge at Stretton Pumping Station and cutting his chest open on the shallow gravel. He said most of his friends still have scars from diving accidents in the river. Kamikaze running dives from the far side of the hedge were a favourite sport. No fen boy was truly initiated without a set of scars from the lacerating thorns or unknown hazards under the surface. At that time there was a lot more traffic on the water, and the swimmers would splash people in the boats, holding on to the gunwales, and getting into trouble.

Pop learnt to swim in the Old West River, by the steam-powered Stretham Pumping Station. He and his friends clung on to an old oil drum, gradually learning to let go and keep swimming. Later, they graduated to underwater swimming, and bets and dares. But the favourite bathing hole in that part of the Fens was near Wilburton where the Old West River runs past Australia Farm, so called because it was so remote. Just as everyone on the Fens seemed to go by their nickname – 'Fish', 'Turkey', 'Boxer', 'Scadger', 'Pop' – so did fens, farms, dykes and rivers. Names from the colonies or remote wars were often used to denote a far-away field or farm. Hence Sebastopol Farm, or Botany Bay, where the Twelve Foot Drain joins the Little Ouse at one end of Stallode Wash, miles from anywhere.

THE BLASTED HEATH

Breckland

THE CALL OF THE HEATH

W. G. Clarke

(from *In Breckland Wilds*, 1925)

Night on the heathland is an experience that appeals to all our primitive instincts. Here one seems in tune with the infinite, capable of communicating with the spirits in the stars, of hearing 'as the roar of a rain-fed ford, the roar of the Milky Way,' or of peering at the earth like 'a feather floating in the gulf.' The waste, as Thomas Hardy said of Egdon Heath, is majestic without severity, impressive without showiness, emphatic in its admonition, and grand in its simplicity. It is possible to think clearly, with no distracting influence save the call of the wild creatures – the hoo-oo-oo-too-wit of the tawny owl, the shrill whistle of the stone-curlew, the wail of the lapwing like the cry of a lone spirit seeking a companion, the short plaintive note of a ringed plover, or the reel of a nightjar on some windbent pine. Calls of pheasants resound through the woodland silences; as a low undercurrent comes the far-off dreamy cadence of the wind in the ever-singing pines. The world is audible, but not visible. Rarely is a stone-curlew outlined against the apple-green afterglow in the western sky, occasionally the form of a spectral shadow-shape, a barn owl, appears against the darkness of the plantings, or the rustle of rabbits among the bracken is followed by a glimpse of a white scut dodging hither and thither. Or the sounds may have a deeper significance – the cry of a hare caught in a noose, a rabbit in the clutches of a blood-thirsty stoat, or the squeaking of a vole gripped by the talons of an owl. Partridges maintain a continuous clucking among the bents; a song thrush tries a few hesitating disconnected bars of melody; evidence of distant civilisation is furnished by the baying of a dog and murmurs in the sheepfold.

Dawn certainly brings joy. Clear comes the blackbird's trill from the far-off woods, a sound that makes the calmness seem more deep; a thrush bursts forth into song from the clump of pines that crowns the tumulus where some warrior was laid to rest in the youth of mankind – voices calling from the outer world, imperious and profound. The edges of the trackway are covered with grey lichen cups, tufts of fine grass, and moss on which the sunshine glints. Lapwings flash white against a stony 'breck,' or the empurpled distant woodlands touched with green. On a bare expanse a pair of stock-doves chase each other round and round the deserted rabbit-hole which they have made their temporary home. From a spectacular point of view the heathland is not at its best in spring. The swells seem bare, as the bracken which in early winter is still stiff and sturdy, is beaten down by the sweeping blasts until in the spring it lies battered and tangled and torn. In the golden days of summer, when the green bracken fronds are restful to the eye, the smell of the gorse and the wild thyme, of the sweetbriar and the pine unite to form a pleasant opiate, the harbinger of a desire

To live and lie reclined
On the hills like gods together, careless of mankind.

From an ancient boundary bank carpeted with moss of velvet sheen, purple blooms of the aromatic thyme, and grass kept short as on a lawn by the nibbling rabbits, the rolling wastes of heathland lie before us. With such wide expanses of earth and sky merging together amidst the shimmering heat waves at the far horizon, the details of the landscape are difficult to detect. But near at hand trivial objects have vast significance. The tender green of a curled frond, the soft ooziness of a marshy hollow, the hawthorns, and elderbushes, the startled hare or bolting rabbit, all add their quota to the wonder and incomprehensibility of it all. Wheatears take short flights on the sandy patches; stone-curlews rise close at hand, showing the white tips of their wings; lapwings run hither and thither on the bare breck half-way up the opposite slope, and the call of the whinchat, like flint striking flint, carries our thoughts back to the day when these heaths were the homes of prehistoric man, and the grass-grown tracks his main roads. Days like this remain in the memory not so much on account of their incident as their perfect serenity.

Not that there is always peace. There come times when the winds begin to wail, and the angry stormclouds cover the sky from horizon to horizon. Then there is the joyousness of battling with the breeze until almost breathless with the struggle, of knowing that the wild south-west wind which whistles in your ear was an hour ago 60 miles distant, of seeing everything but yourself bending to the fury of the blast. Some of the Viking blood whirls through the arteries; the deep diapason of the storm in the distant woodlands sounds like a saga of the days of old, now inciting to further struggle with the elements, now recalling dim ancestral memories, and at length providing soothing satisfaction for a task accomplished.

The aspect of the heathland is always changing. It changes with the seasons, with sunshine and shadow, with snow and frost and rain. Whatever spring beauty the heaths lack in some aspects, when compared with the heavy lands, is atoned for by the contrasts between the spring garb of beech and larch and the sombreness of the Scots pines and, as for blossom, nowhere else in Norfolk or Suffolk do the crab-apple trees approach in size and mass of bloom those in Breckland. Some of the trees are 30 feet in height, with wide-spreading branches almost touching the ground, and billowing out from top to bottom with pinky-white flowers. The heathland is very slow to show signs of spring and when the bracken in the plantations is over a foot in height, that on the open heath is scarcely visible. Sere bracken fronds and rusty heather still give tone to the vegetation, and though some of the minute heath plants are in bloom, the chief beauty of the heathland is not yet obvious. Compared with the heavy land districts it seems devoid of flowers, for primrose-covered banks and cowslip-covered pastures are unknown. Yet in spring there are compensations, unexpected brilliances – the clustered masses of lesser celandine in the valleys, the rosy plumelets of the larch, the large patches of ground ivy, and acre after acre covered with the tiny blossoms of the vernal whitlow-grass, intermingled with the beautiful blue of the spring forget-me-not, the red-foliaged rue-leaved saxifrage, and the dingy spikes of the field wood-rush.

No human eye sees millions of the flowers that bloom; no human ear hears the song of thousands of birds. Yet each flower gives something of its fragrance to the passing wind; each bird adds to the flood of melody which surges through the land – a throbbing of life, a chorus of joy, an uprising of the elemental forces. New beauties are perceptible with each succeeding dawn, – a tinge of green here, a richer purple there, sun and cloud weaving the warp and woof of the panorama of colour in the landscape, flashing on the silver trunk of a birch or the ruddy richness of a Scots pine or plunging the distant woodland into a haze of blue.

The colouring of the heathland in summer is more varied if less gorgeous than in autumn, yet the segregation of many plants gives brilliant patches, of brick-red sorrel, of blue common bugloss, of purple viper's bugloss, or red and purple hound's tongue. Heather and wild thyme are in blossom where the gorse and the bracken do not hold sway and shimmering heat-waves often lie trembling just above the earth, making the horizon vague and indistinct. There are days when in the small hours the sun rises into a sky of carmine and gold, tinging the cloud-billows floating in the azure with shades whose fleeting beauties the artist tries in vain to depict; reigning unchallenged at midday high up in the rondure of the empyreal blue; and then at eventide sinking to rest in a blaze of splendour, with the western sky a sea of molten gold, and the eastern a vast lake of liquid ultramarine, every minute changing in depth and extent as the sun recedes from view below the horizon. On such days the pine woods set in the heathland have cool recesses where the sun does not penetrate. There is a solemn stillness and grandeur in the gaunt pines – a charm such as no other tree possesses. Lofty arboreal archways and columns form dim aisles stretching far away till lost in the haze of distance, where the wood appears a confused mass of green and brown. Bracken, like tree-ferns, stretches high above the head, with glades in the green whence the outside world is as naught, whilst rabbits rush headlong hither and thither. Through the foliage above, the sky appears in splashes and patches of blue and white, as the vapour-flecks scud from west to eastern horizon.

> *The solemn firs*
> *Stand like sentinels dark and high,*
> *And the wind continually moves and stirs*
> *In their topmost boughs, a gentle sigh.*

In a pine wood there is much less rustling than in other woods – a silence that can be felt, a silence which is almost oppressive on such a day. There is less surface on the leaves in a pine wood than in a plantation of almost any other tree, therefore the wind does not so much possess the power of making music save only in minor keys. On the ridges the wind sweeps along with nothing to check its onward course, over miles upon miles of heathland through the spreading cloisters of the pine woods; laden with the fragrance of gorse and heather and wild thyme, and with the more pungent smell of the young bracken, it seems to contain vitalising properties. The wind blows the loose sand about with terrific force, and during a gale the atmosphere is often as thick as a London fog, the driving sand entirely obscuring belts close at hand, providing an unpleasant but realistic reproduction of the sand-storm of the desert.

When night falls on the heath there is never a light visible. Darkness is audible, perceptible, palpable, and the darkness of the heathland is intensified in the woods. At night the heath becomes colossal and mysterious. Familiar things put on a fantastic appearance. Great clumps of heather are like a flock of recumbent sheep. Rabbit-holes become black tunnels to an imagined underworld, the home of goblins, sprites, gnomes and fairies. They are also traps for the unwary. The foliage of the pines is like a cloud against the sky. What light exists is apparently strengthened by the waters of the stream which flows at the

95

foot of the long heathland slope. It even reflects the shadows of the alders and reeds on the further shore. The soughing of the wind in the pines, its whisper among the aspens, the deep diapason of the far-stretching woodlands, are broken only by the cries of the creature of the wilds – a rabbit caught by a stoat, or in its death agony in a noose of copper wire or mallard in the reedbeds, or the varied twitterings of smaller birds unsettled for a short period. Paths, familiar and apparently fairly level, in the night darkness develop unexpected protuberances and depressions. Walking is therefore in the nature of an experiment. To wander a foot from the beaten track is to court disaster. Rabbit-holes, mole-hills, tree-roots, heather-tufts, grass-grown ant hills, ancient workings for stone, all conspire to alter the pedestrian's position from the perpendicular to the horizontal.

The heathland is, however, indubitably at its best in autumn. Though much wider stretches of heather are obtainable on the Yorkshire and Scottish moors, the colouring there is no more brilliant, and perhaps loses something in intensity by the absence of contrasting vegetation such as is always to be found in Breckland, either in the great wastes of bracken, the waving tresses of yellow beats, the greys of the lichens, or the belts of Scots pines. The heaths consist of ridges, valleys, knolls and hollows, and the effects of sunlight and shadow and tones conferred by a distance are therefore the more diversified. Often there is a tawny slope of breck or primeval heathland, perhaps diversified with patches of heather glorious in all the purple majesty of autumn. On one heath the heather is nearly all green and closely cropped by rabbits; on another the giant tufts make progress extremely difficult, their thick woody branches pulling up the unwary pedestrian with a sudden jerk, while on another the brilliance of the purple blossoms is toned to a delicious softness by the tall white bents which overtop and dim, but do not obscure, the more lowly heather. Sweeping over the big heather tracts the wind brings a dainty fragrance; in some of the hollows among the uplands, almost shut off from the outer world, there seems a concentrated essence of its characteristic smell. Big bracken patches are on some areas yet green, but on others they are gorgeous with all the golden autumnal tints. Many of the mixed plantations are a blaze of varied tints, from the fiery red of the beech and the amber of the maple to the lemon of the poplar, and the contrast of these with the darker hues of the Scots pines and spruce firs accentuates their beauty.

Storms on the heathland are ever awe-inspiring, but a night-storm is an experience not soon forgotten. The wind blows with terrific force; it is almost impossible to stand upright. Trees in the plantations twist and groan in torment; the woodland roars to the passing blast. Raindrops patter on the leaves like a continuous discharge of small shot, their fellows fall on the grass with tiny thuds, all merged in the great storm roar. In the occasional lulls some of the undercurrents are audible – the grating of the beeches, the swish of the firs, and the murmurous music of the aspens. One particular day there had been a heaviness in the air, a warning of trouble to come. Around the horizon the grey mist was banking up into semblance of clouds which covered the setting sun as with a pall. Gloom filled the air, and gloom settled on the souls of men. Who could be mirthful in such an atmosphere, under a lowering sky? Now and again there came a flash of light from the cloud-bank on the southern horizon, but the rumble of the thunder was lost in space. Dusk deepened into darkness, and the haunts of men were only evidenced by the light reflected over the brow of the hill, and the distant murmur as of a sullen swarm of bees, or the gurgling of a streamlet in an underground pool. Our footsteps on the hard road reverberated from the pine plantation, and we stopped by the lichen-covered palings. We knew where lay beneath the veil of mist the distant heather-covered Suffolk warren; the flowing river in the valley, and nearer still, in Norfolk, the dark straggling pine belts. A dim glimmer from the top of the opposite slope came from the warrener's lodge – a signal in the night. A night all too still; a calm that was weird. Small sounds were worrying; one would have welcomed a loud noise. The dropping of an acorn with muffled thud; the patter, patter, of a dead leaf as it was bandied from bough to bough on its descent to Mother Earth; the squeaking of a rat, the rustle of a hare or rabbit through the long grass, the flutter of a roosting bird – these maintained the tension. The silence penetrated every fibre; it would

97

have seemed presumption to talk louder than a whisper. One minute there would be an impenetrable darkness on the earth; the next, the lightning would illuminate the whole horizon. The rolling thunder was within hearing, rumbling over the southern ridge. Almost incessant was the lightning. During the flashes there appeared mysterious forms and shadows in the woodland glades. Vision said they were hobgoblins, elves, sprites of the forest; reason said they were trees and bushes. And ere vision could decide, the wood lay again in the deep of night.

But hark! there is a sound in the far distance – a dull roar. One could feel that a spirit was moving on the earth. Nearer and nearer it came; every living thing seemed to have been forewarned. Clear on the night air came the 'Chalk-up, chalk-up' of a pheasant from the pine belt on the borderland of heath and breck. And then – Babel – a confusion of tongues. It was as though Roderick Dhu had blown the fateful whistle, and

> *Instant, through copse and heath arose*
> *Bonnets, and spears, and bended bows.*

From every plantation came the scream of the pheasant; overhead and all around was the lapwing's plaint; and shrill and piercing in its intensity came the whistle of the stone-curlews from every heath, warren, and breck within audible radius. Skirting the wood came a vague shadow, with eyes scintillating in the gloom, and one could not repress a momentary start at the mournful 'Hoo-oo-oo-too-wit' of a tawny owl. A brighter flash than usual silhouetted its form against the dark background of pines; then it was lost in the darkness. With eyes and ears on the alert we awaited a repetition of that uncanny 'Hoo-oo,' but in vain. A moment later we had lapsed into somewhat of impassiveness, when not a yard behind us came that eerie note again, like the wail of a lost spirit in the avian Gehenna. Need one confess to a start, a quickening of the heart-beats? The croak of a moorhen far down in the valley came up on the storm vanguard of wind. From a calm, in which every voice of the night was distinct, to a raging gust which seemed to shake the solid earth – all in a minute. It was of short duration. The roar that presaged the storm, and the wind that whipped the oak leaves round and round and buffeted them hither and thither was soon far away beneath the night-pall. There was but a gentle murmuring in the tree-tops, a peaceful caressing, in partial atonement for the past. One could again hear the scurrying footsteps of the field-voles, or the sharp squeal of a pugnacious rat. Darker grew the night, sharper the lightning, louder the thunder, until even the birds of the air knew not whither they went, and lapwings were wandering round and round over the lights of the town in the valley until far on into the night, when the rearguard of the storm had passed away to the northward. Yet all this is quickly thrust into the recesses of memory when the sun rises over the swelling eastward heights. That is when the heathland is at its best. Mystery has receded, the face of the landscape is open and smiling. ...

The heathland in winter is mainly a dingy russet – bracken and heather giving the prevailing tone. There is little protection from wind or weather, and before the days when trees were planted, there are records of persons losing their lives in time of snow through wandering from the track. After a slight fall of snow cultivated land or unenclosed brecks on the heaths are easily distinguishable as white patches, the snow on the rougher parts being almost hidden by the vegetation. Snow on the heathland provides evidence of much almost unsuspected animal life. Here are the footprints of the hare, the forelegs close together and from 12 to 20 inches between the leaps; rabbit tracks doubling and crossing each other in all directions, and indicating which burrows are inhabited; a furrow with faint claw-marks alternating on either side as evidence of the passage of a mole; faint claw-marks in a long paw-print, and tail-tracks of the brown rat, while the forelegs of the water-vole are placed closer together and their hind legs further apart. Among bird-tracks those of the pheasants are unmistakeable – a three-pronged indentation with a continuous line between the footprints caused by the drooping hind-claw. When the meres have been frozen and snow-covered, herons, rabbits, hares, waterhens, pheasants and water-voles have crossed and indented the snow, so that when the snow is melting the hardened footprints remain in relief.

BLO' NORTON HALL
Virginia Woolf
(from *A Passionate Apprentice: The Early Journals*, 1990)

4th August 1906

It is a theory that the newer you are the better you like old things. No one but an American young woman, conscious of crudity as of some scourge of the flesh, would have plunged into such depths of age as we find here. The house is Elizabethan; & it has been too inconsiderable to restore – beyond what is needed to make it a living house; it is too remote & solitary & ancestral for anyone to wish to live here, except Americans who find all these qualities, I suppose, medicinal. Still, it is rather comfortable even for English people, to find that such houses go on unheeded & untended, accumulating quaintness & beauties with every year, all over England; despite the great towns & villas.

And age has a great charm.

Nothing of our own day could reproduce the harmony & exquisite peace of this little old house, as it struck our eyes, yesterday evening. It is so modest, & sound, & solid all through; as tho' the centuries had only confirmed its original virtues. As you were made honestly, they seem to say, so all time to come shall but prove & establish your virtue.

And such domestic beauty, all small & quaint & even humble as it is, appeals to ones sympathies. It is so good to find that humdrum people should live so respectably; beauty & splendour were then not for the surface alone, but they sank down & down, till all layers of the state were well steeped in them. A self respecting decorous place England must have been then! The American, I began to say, needs a deep bath of antiquity; & few English people, I think, could endure such a dose as Blo' Norton Hall is prepared to give them, without being drowned in it. We are to begin with 7 miles from a railway; & every mile seems to draw a thicker curtain than the last between you & the world. So that finally, when you are set down at the Hall, no sound what ever reaches your ear; the very light seems to filter through deep layers; & the air circulates slowly, as though it had but to make the circuit of the Hall, & its duties were complete.

Nor have such investigations as we could make today pierced behind the curtain. We seem to be in the middle of what in geography is called an 'undulating plain' well cultivated, but, apparently, almost deserted. The corn brims the fields; but no one is there to cut it; the churches hold up broad gray fingers all over the landscape, but no one, save perhaps the dead at their feet, attend to their commands; the windmills sail round & round, but no one trims their sails; it is very characteristic that the only sign of life in the land should be that produced by the wind of Heaven. How sleepy & ancient a people must be, who rely on the free gifts of Heaven still. But the wind seems fairly competent; the sails turn slowly, all day long. This, need I say it, is the kind of rash note an impetuous traveller makes; & it is only made because after all, such notes are the things one thinks before one begins to reason or to know. And like the images of childhood, they stay bright.

5th August

A second day reveals the fact, as facts go, that the country has possibilities. This morning for instance, we wandered into a lush fen, humming with dragonflies, & scented with meadow sweet. A pale windmill guarded it, stationary today I observe; for though the wind is God's wind, & will blow in spite of the Sabbath, one must not require it to work for human profit on a Sunday. Or how do the orthodox interpret these symbols? Again in the afternoon, we stepped some four miles out his way with Thoby. We had prudently to keep to the high road, which was flat, but umbrageous & lined with broad strips of green on either side. We passed the temples of three different sects, so that, reckoning by the number we met on the road there must be 10 orthodox Christians, 6 Methodists & 2^1/$_2$ Anabaptists in Hopton. Children count only as halves, because when they grow up they may think for themselves, & swell the number of the hostile sect, or, presumably build a fresh chapel for themselves. The Churches, I tell myself, & this is only a whisper after all – date from that era before the Black death, when sheep farming prospered, & piety throve: but now that the sheep are gone, & Americans live in the Halls of the landowners, how does piety thrive at all? And yet look at the great solid chapels! So thinking, arguing, & expounding we tramped along till we reached a crossroads, where the sign post waved in three different directions. Here was the appropriate place to part; one road led straight to Dalmatia & the wilds of Thessaly; the other back here to this profound seat of solitude, dug, I think, somewhere very near the heart of England. Dont I feel the steady beat of the great Creator as I write; & doesn't the Church there record its pulse this evening, & for six hundred years of evenings such as these?

The fens almost surround this house. And all the land is very flat, so that the landmarks resolve themselves into churches & windmills. The river, the Little Ouse deserves its diminutive; you may leap it – fall in as I did this afternoon – but all the same it is not a hazardous jump. You are sure of the mud at any rate. And there radiate various minor tributaries, ditches I should call them, did not I know of their relationship with the river, & these are sometimes fenced with barbed wire. Altogether, though a walk in the fen has a singular charm, it is not to be undertaken as a way of getting to places. Windmills have a way of staying absolutely still, or receding, to one who approaches them thus.

However, after leaping & circumnavigating, & brushing through reeds, & scrambling beneath barbed wire, it is pleasant to lie on the turf & try steering by windmills & towers to indicate on the map where you are precisely. Today I found the twin sources of the Waveney & the Little Ouse.

In a very short time unfortunately, it becomes clear how shortsighted was that opinion of mine that Norfolk had no inhabitants. It is not necessary here to go into details, which would be impolite; so I will only make the innocent remark that directly you begin to study the habits of creatures they become astonishingly frequent & well ordered. Here, it seems, one needs only but very little trouble in order to discover a whole network of society – Squires & Parsons & detached ladies living in cottages, who are all entertaining & paying calls, far more punctually & assiduously than in London.

But it is more to the point to remark that I found the real heath, not a mile from our door. It is a wild place, all sand & bracken, with innumerable rabbits, & great woods running alongside, in to which I plunge; down green drives as shady as any in the New Forest. It is a strange lonely kind of country; a carriage comes bowling over the hill, & you watch it pass & disappear & wonder where it comes from & whither it goes, & who is the lady inside.

Shall I confess, without meaning any kind of confession, that it is possible for one day to be much like another here, & not in the least dull?

I go for my usual walk; which has for me the interest of a discovery, because I go, armed with maps into a strange land. Windmills are my landmarks; & one must not mistake the river for a ditch. The heath attracts me most; because there are no fields. The fen plays you false at every step – I walked through a jungle of reeds & fell up to my nose in mud. And if one foundered here, the weeds would wave & the plover call, & no robin redbreast would bury one!

If this were the time or the place to uphold a paradox, I am half inclined to state that Norfolk is one of the most beautiful of counties. Indeed, let the artifice stand; for so there will be no need to expound it.

And truly, it would need a careful & skilful brush to give a picture of this strange, grey green, undulating, dreaming, philosophising & remembering land; where one may walk 10 miles & meet no one; where soft grass paths strike gently over the land; where the roads are many & lonely, & the churches are innumerable, & deserted. There is no use in a closer gaze at present. But it is worth saying that the more you walk here, & become initiated into the domesticities of the place – it is full of them – the more you love it, & know it. And that says as much for a place as for a person. It is so soft, so melancholy, so wild, & yet so willing to be gentle: like some noble untamed woman conscious that she has no beauty to vaunt, that nobody very much wants her.

It is one of the wilful habits of the brain, let me generalise for the sake of comfort, that it will only work at its own terms.

You bring it directly opposite an object, & bid it discourse; it merely shuts its eye, & turns away. But in one month, or three or seven, suddenly without any bidding, it pours out the whole picture, gratuitously. Some such surprise may be in store for me still; on the heights of the Acropolis the Norfolk fens may swim before me; & I know I shall have to wait many months before I can see Athens. Like the light that reaches you from the stars, it will only shine when some time after it has been shed.

So then, to come to the heart of the discourse, there is no use in presenting here a picture of Norfolk; when the place is directly beneath my eyes. I see at this moment a wall, coloured like an apricot in the sun; with touches of red upon it. The outline & angles of the roof & the tall chimney are completely filled with pure blue sky, as though some gigantic brush had laid a smooth wash of paint across the background. It is the kind of blue for a reason which I can hardly explain, that makes me understand why it should be said to 'drip' from the wings of a flying bird.

A certain look of dishevelment in the creepers & shrubs that climb the wall is token that there was a great gale the other morning;

which is further borne out by the recumbent posture of an apple tree in the middle of the lawn. It has spilt all its apples in the downfall. And a very keen eye or nose, or both, may detect a look & scent in the trees & the air which, in spite of the sun, hints at September. Without refining & matching words, no one could mistake the day for a summer's day. Yesterday, I took a bicycle ride to a place called Kenninghall. We will not talk about the bicycle; or there would be no time to deal with the church & the village, & some aesthetic outrage also would be committed upon our senses. Now Kenninghall is famous in the Ordnance map for a Saxon burial ground: & readers of Jefferies will take their chance of a bask upon such smooth turf. But at Kenninghall the Christian church alone was obvious; the curiously moulded tower, with its gilt clock, showed itself most decorously gray against the soft plumage of the trees. Moreover there were gravestones with home made elegies. As for instance the inscription upon Mrs Susan Batt (shall we say) of whom it is written.

She nothing took that plainness could not get
And most abhored [sic] *the running into debt*

which, I think, has the virtue of drawing a picture of the righteous old lady, albeit the lines are angular. Parenthetically, we may write down another fragment, retrieved from Market Weston:

His superior intellectual attainments
Could only be appreciated by
the Superior Few.
This they did:
But his moral worth
&c &c

This is broken up duly into long lines & short, set with capital letters, & cut deep black into a square sheet of marble. It is an eddy of the

105

eighteenth century formalism; when the superior few were not ashamed to call themselves so.

A very curious & interesting & entertaining article, I observe here (I blush I swear it) might be written upon Epitaphs; because when you have exhausted the surface oddity, there is really a solid lump of truth to be dug out beneath. I mean the attitude is perfectly honest; & so, very characteristic of the age & the people.

However, Mrs Susan Batt was no Saxon; & we must contrast the graves.

So on the authority of the map, we asked a small native for his Saxon burial ground, & were directed by him to the Christian Churchyard; Saxons they may have been to him; &, to the shame of Kenninghall be it spoken, no one there not even the photographer, knew where the Saxons were buried; or indeed had ever heard that there were Saxons. So taking the map's word for it, we decided to consecrate a mound in some gentleman's Park; certainly I could see no reason why Saxons should not have been buried there.

But as one had to climb a gate, & walk half a mile, we decided to do our conjectural meditations from a distance; the charm, I own, was not very potent, whether one must blame the distance or the doubt.

The advantages of a bicycle, almost I would say the advantage, is that it gets you to places. Our grandparents never saw Thetford or Diss, unless it was upon the wedding tour, in a high gig; or upon the Christening of the first born, or some other solemn feast, demanding the sanction of the market town.

But I can ride there in an afternoon; to buy postcards or grapes, or merely to look at certain curious old houses.

A very hot August day, a bare road across a moor, fields of corn & stubble – a haze as of wood fire smoke – innumerable pheasants & partridges – white stones – thatched cottages – sign posts – tiny villages – great waggons heaped with corn – sagacious dogs, farmers carts. Compose these all somehow into a picture; I am too lazy to do it.

106

At any rate after an hour's riding I dropped down into Thetford, which seemed to me with its girdle of wall & river, & the smooth turf slope outside something like an Italian town. Perhaps the knowledge extracted from the guide book that there was a nunnery here in the Middle Ages helped my imagination. Certainly I saw with my own eyes a Roman Catholic Padre step out of his monastery door, with a biretta on his head, & examine with long ecclesiastical nose the Dahlias in his neighbours garden. The rivers Thet & Ouse (I think) circle Thetford; & which ever way I went, seemed to take me across low stone bridges where anglers lounged, with their rods across the broad stream. Nurse maids were sitting on the rivers banks, leaning on the elbow over a paper novel, while their charges dabbled in the water. No one was ever able to say exactly what does go on in these medieval towns set in the heart of England at about this hour on a Summers afternoon. It is all so picturesque & accidental that to the traveller it seems a pleasant show got up for some benevolent purpose. For when you come upon stalwart men leaning their elbows on a parapet & dreaming of the stream beneath, while the sun is still high in the air, you reconsider what you mean by life. Often in London shall I think of Thetford, & wonder if it is still alive; or whether it has really ceased, peaceably, to exist any longer. No one would notice if the whole town forgot to wake up one morning.

But coming home in the evening through great open spaces of field it was born [*sic*] in upon the mind that something was alive enough. Call it what you will. For the whole air was rich with energy, & brilliant with colour.

'THE FIELDS OF DULDITCH'

Ronald Blythe

(Introduction to *The Fields of Dulditch*, 1976)

These bitter and remarkable stories [by Mary Mann] about half-starved East Anglian villagers at the turn of the century were published in 1902, the same year in which the Norfolk novelist Sir Henry Rider Haggard had paused in his creation of exotic tales to issue a devastating indictment of the nation's virtual abandonment of its agricultural industry. Called *Rural England*, Rider Haggard's inventory of the state of the countryside a third of the way through the great farming depression which was to last, except for the First World War years, until the 1940s, gives the economic facts of this disaster. In Suffolk and Norfolk this period was sometimes called 'the coming down time' as many old farming families and rural craftsmen lost their footing and were ruined. The field-workers suffered most of all. During the eighteen-eighties, Joseph Arch, champion hedge-cutter and union organiser, had made Norfolk a hearteningly successful centre for policies which promised to lift farm-labourers out of their serfdom but now, twenty years later, bad harvests, wage cuts and mass emigrations from the land to the towns, the railways, the colonies or the army, had demoralised many of those who remained at home.

Rider Haggard, in *Rural England*, describes village after village with forsaken cottages; Mary Mann reveals the interiors of those that are still inhabited. Although an exciting fantasist where his fiction was concerned, Rider Haggard is down to earth about British agriculture in decline, supporting the 'back to the land' call of the time whilst insisting that farmworkers should have decent prospects to return to. Mary Mann, on the contrary, allows her characters no prospects at all. To do so would be to undermine the tragic situation of what she calls their 'condition'. The almighty, in the role of the great 'Disposer' – the pitiless deity and the general fatalism alike suggest that the author knows her Hardy – has placed these wretched people in Dulditch and they have to accept their place. That, to Mary Mann, is the pathos of their lives.

108

She was a prolific popular novelist who published numerous country stories, most of them with Norfolk settings. Born Mary Rackham, the daughter of a Norwich businessman, Simon Rackham, she died at Sheringham in 1929. *The Fields of Dulditch* came towards the middle of an output which included such titles as *The Parish of Hilby, A Lost Estate, Susannah, The Parish Nurse, Astray in Arcady, Rose at Honeypot*, etc. It deserves re-issue because it contains brilliant eye-witness accounts of the intimate life of labouring families at a time when such poverty was not only normal, but was seemingly incurable. Mary Mann's compassion stems from seeing men and women as immutably planted in a location as a tree or a swede. As creatures thus imprisoned, her heart goes out to them. Although she reproduces the picturesque speech patterns of this lowly, grimly-rooted and – for her – blighted society with sufficient colour to entertain the reader, her central purpose is not to show rustic charm but rural plight. Howsomedever (as one of these late nineteenth century labourers would have said), she offers no solution other than the exhortations to endure which provided one of the high-minded supports to the status quo of the time. By enduring the misfortune of their birth, their ignorance, their incessant toil and their malnutrition, her characters receive their own special nobility, and it is this which ultimately concerns her. She describes first the barren soil of a particular life and then the little miracle of its flowering. Her understanding is greatest when it comes to the kind of nervelessness, apathy and inertia which results not so much from being stuck in a rut as from being helplessly tethered to a stunted growth. Although she occasionally comes dangerously near to sentimentalising these field-workers and their families, and sometimes patronises them in the conventional 'lady' manner, all in all she succeeds in being an uncomfortably truthful witness of their difficult existence and her sharp profile of what it was really like to be an ordinary villager eighty years ago challenges any nostalgic vision we may still hold of those days.

Of course, the chief interest to ourselves in such a book as this is not literary in the usual sense – although the actual writing is often very accomplished and vivid – but in its reportage of what were then the humdrum affairs of the farming world but which now can only be pieced together by the social historian. Its stories read less like plotted, imaginatively-shaped fictions of the traditional type than like brief biographies. They are sketched against 'an insignificant landscape, bleak fen-land, gorse-choked heath, familiar ponds and pits and puddles, rank turnip-fields, flat distances ...'. For Mary Mann, those who work this landscape are destined to find that 'the Book of Life is practically closed'. Yet, in spite of this, it is a far from negative conclusion that she ultimately draws. Her own veracity uncovers the solid worth of others and the reader is not left with a feeling that the Dulditchians are damned. The exposure of their actual lives, however, does contrast unmercifully, for example, with the kind of gentle village fiction known as the 'kailyard school', so popular at this time, in which cottagers displayed rustic adventures in prettily philosophical terms. A Mary Mann tale about what was happening in the average double-dweller in circa 1900 Norfolk bears no comparison at all with such bromides. What occurs in her writing is that, after setting off at a deceptively polite pace into the calm realm of the dialect story, the narrative suddenly ignites into something of more burning importance.

Against the stark facts of their education, religion, diet, illness, marriages, toil and death she constructs the individual shapes of her 'poor units of the brutish, measureless human undergrowth'. Even while allowing for the suppressed horror with which the better-off regarded the fate of the workaday poor and her almost total disregard of what is now called 'job satisfaction' – she dwells on the inscrutable deity 'which toss'd thee down into the field' but says little or nothing about the wonderful ploughing and harvesting that went on in them even at the miserable wage of eleven shillings a week – the cumulative effect of this book is both intriguing and moving. Intriguing because it has all the verisimilitude of an old photograph turned into language; moving because what happened then can be seen to affect so much that happens now.

Dulditch [Shropham on the edge of the Brecks and the author's home] has an impoverished bachelor squire, Sir Thomas, and a kindly but withdrawn Rector. The squire forgoes his annual holiday so that he can use the money to patch-up his cottages. The Rector is no saint to his maid, who prefers the hideously illustrated bible for which she has exchanged her life-savings to his services. 'I don't want him a-setting up ter tache me; efso be as ivver I want ter pray, I take it I kin pray without such as him.' She can't read her bible but she adores its 'gays' – its coloured pictures. In the 1860s Edward FitzGerald, the poet, asked a friend to find him a colourfully-plumed cockerel for his hens, stipulating 'only so as he be "gay" according to old Suffolk speech'. The Rector's maid epitomises the wilful East Anglian spirit which stubbornly ignores the rules. The ancient widower, Angel, who unsuccessfully courts her, on the contrary, knows his place. He goes to church in order to 'set under a gentleman' because 'him as prache at chapel bain't no better nor me ... 'Tis for th' quality to ha' th' haughtiness, and for we to ha' th' manners'. The quality, in the shape of the author, find it witty to call an epileptic Fitz-Brown. The farmyard poultry are ritually stoned – 'everybody stoned them'. To 'hull a ston' and lame th' old gander', or to break the wing 'o' th' old yiller hin', being considered ordinary sport. Big families sleep half a dozen to a room, their bed-clothes old coats. For the most part they eat 'light' dumplings consisting of flour, water and baking powder, potatoes, skim milk, peppered and salted bread soaked in hot water, cheese and various fruit and vegetable mashes.

Women, by working all hours, can earn up to six shillings a week stone-picking or singling-out. Men are frequently beer-drunkards. The old live in terror of the 'order for the house' – the workhouse. The sick have the club doctor and all manner of unofficial cures, from comfrey to touching a sore place with a dead hand. Elijah (a woman) has 'a sore', or cancer. The rheumatic are rubbed with horse-oils. There is the pauper lunatic asylum and there is suicide. To the inhabitants of Dulditch and to Mary Mann all this and more, the squalor of the houses and the brutality, is as to be expected as sun in summer. Her lovers and stalwarts, her brave and cunning girls and handsome 'first-team men' like Robbud, her cards like Jarge, her intrepids like the gal La'rences, her tragedies like Wolf-Charlie and Ben Pitcher's Elly, and her entire population of the village contend with these tough odds and sometimes overcome them. Like Biller and Becker, 'the unlovely, the loutish, the ungracious, and uncouth, whose births were shameful' as well as the beautiful and intelligent, they are all fixed in these penurious acres and 'are in their own obscure way holding their own there. ...' It required a special kind of honesty to counter-balance so many black facts with equally relevant actualities such as love, humour and the ability by some to stay undefeated.

A word must be said about Mary Mann's treatment of the old words. She heard them much as they would have sounded centuries before her own day and still untouched by modern influences. As old Angel says, 'These hare be th' wuds' and Mary Mann records them as easily as one for whom they are a second language is able. They tell of some of the side effects of a great industrial calamity when farming failed and an average village went broke.

Dialect and domestic detail aside, what are the issues which motivated these realistic stories and which make them so exceptional for their time? They are the issues which reduced the population of their author's village, Shropham, by nearly a third in her lifetime and left many of its cottages deserted. As wife of Shropham's principal farmer and living at the manor, Mary Mann knew all there was to know about the predicament of the labouring class. In her earlier novels she had kept it in some kind of middle-class check, although dealing with it compassionately, but in the 'Dulditch' tales, begun during the 1890s, she drops the role of the charming recorder of countryside romance and becomes, as a critic of another of her books wrote, 'unsparingly truthful'. Apart from a noticeably crusading attitude towards the evils of drink, she is strikingly non-Victorian about the facts of life in the average rural hovel, seeing in them the seeds of spiritual as well as physical death. She points at the vulnerability of Dulditch to disaster, and reveals its individual root causes in pain, ignorance, endless toil and simply by the fact that there was a group of human beings in her world with the dice loaded against their fulfilment and happiness. Dulditch exercises her radicalism. She sees both the admirable and the feckless brought down by circumstances that are entirely out of their control. She also observes the evil, commonplace by-products of an inbred and isolated community. She writes about fortitude, eccentricity, illegitimacy, animal-like or saintly extremes of conduct, class, alcoholism and, most movingly, about the fate of children. Building-up an inter-related series of village anecdotes in a light, practised but not very distinguished style, she soon becomes fascinating as, unlike the majority of people dealing with the lives of the poor at that date, she balances their entertaining quaintness of custom and talk with accounts of their terrors and triumphs which are disturbingly real. There are many things here which must have shocked the readers of Mary Mann's day – and which provide a valuable record for our own.

It must be added that Fairman Mann, the author's farmer husband whom she married when she was twenty-three, worked hard for the welfare of his parish, particularly where its education was concerned. Living at Shropham Manor and farming some 800 acres around the village, he assumed the responsibilities of a caring squire. Much of what he witnessed among his employees, on the Board of Guardians, as a churchwarden and school governor, etc., must have provided material for his wife's socially accurate reportage. The Dulditch stories stem from the closest involvement with the triumphs and difficulties they describe.

DRIFTING DOWN THE WISSEY

John Cowper Powys

(from *A Glastonbury Romance*, 1955)

When Mary arrived at the New Inn [in Northwold], punctually at ten o'clock, with their lunch tied up in white paper in a basket, she found John Crow seated on a bench outside the entrance, with two oars and a long boat-hook lying across his knees.

The wind had sheered round to due south and what there was of it was faint-blowing. The sky was covered with an opalescent vapour; the sun was warm; and the wandering odours that were wafted towards the girl from the neighbouring cottages had a sweetness in them beyond the pungency of burning peat: a sweetness that may have come from the new buds in the privet hedges, or from the dug-up earth clods in the little gardens at the back, where the spades and forks of the men still stood fixed in the ground awaiting their return when the day's work was over.

He rose with alacrity to welcome her, the two oars in one hand, the boat-hook in the other. 'I've got the key,' he announced triumphantly. 'It's at the end of Alder Dyke on the big river. They say we'd better go there by Foulden Bridge.' He lowered his voice and bent down his head. 'Did any of them try to stop you coming? Did Philip say anything?'

She shook her head and stood for a moment without moving, her face averted, looking dreamily down the street. 'This will never happen to me again,' she thought. 'I am in love with him. He is in love with me. I shall never forget this day and I shall never feel just like this ever again, whatever happens.' She turned towards John. 'I don't care where you take me,' her look said, 'or what you do with me, as long as we are together!' But her lips said, 'Do you mind going in and getting some more of that wine, John? I didn't want to make my basket too heavy, so I left on the table the bottle of milk that Aunt Elizabeth made me take.'

He propped up the oars and the boat-hook against the house and went in. Mary moved away, crossed to the other side of the road and bending over a low brick wall stared at a manure-heap in which three black hens were scratching. The manure-heap with the three black fowls became at that second a sort of extension of her own personality. She felt at that moment, as she rested her basket on the top of the wall and heedless of her sleeves stretched her arms along its surface and ran her bare fingers through the cool stone-crop stalks, as if her soul was scarcely attached to her body. Almost without allowing her happy trance to be broken she took down her basket from the wall, recrossed the road and met John at the instant he emerged. 'Sorry to have kept you,' he chuckled, 'but I've made them give me a flask of brandy as well as a flask of port. That's the best of having a great coat on, even on a hot day. Its pockets are so useful.'

They walked rapidly now side by side past the churchyard and past the gardener's cottage at the drive-gate where Ben Pod had counted the cars. They came to a narrow foot-way that led them across the little river by a bridge that was scarcely more than a plank, and after that across the fields to the big river. Here at Foulden Bridge, which they did not cross, they debouched from the path; and turning to the left, followed the river bank downstream.

They had not spoken a word since leaving the Inn. Mary grew conscious, just before they got to Foulden Bridge, that she had been repeating to herself as she walked along, 'That's the best of a greatcoat on a hot day. Its pockets are so useful.' What she had been thinking was, how bony and thin was John's hand as it clutched the boat-hook which swung horizontally between them like an antique spear.

John was delving in his memory for something; something important. There had been several patches of yellow marigolds along the path they had followed and these had excited a tantalising feeling in his mind that he could not fathom. Those gleaming yellow flowers kept leading his memory to the verge of something and then deserting him and turning into a blur of blackness! Tom Barter had to do with it; but it was not Barter. This preoccupation with an obscure past, although it made him grave and silent, did not lessen his delight in his companion's presence. They were indeed, both of them, thrillingly happy, these two flesh-covered skeletons, drifting so lingeringly along

115

the banks of the Wissey, but John's happiness was much more complicated than Mary's. His return to his native land played a part in it; the revival of local memories played a still larger part; and this latter feeling was so intimately associated with Tom Barter that to oust that sturdy figure from its place was impossible. He kept reverting to the marigolds, especially to their stalks in muddy water, and he kept thinking too of the stickiness of certain lumps of flour-dough mixed with cotton-wool and treacle that Tom and he had used for bait for roach and dace. Perch, that more rapacious fish, despised these harmless pellets; and he wondered whether it could be the black stripes ot these deep-water fish and their enormous mouths, or the stickiness of this bait for the others, or a certain kind of home-made gingerbeer that their grandfather's cook used to make, and not the marigolds at all, that had been the tap-root to his rapturous sensation. It was not that this tantalising sense of being on the edge of some incredible life-secret interfered with his feeling for Mary. It was that his possession of Mary had become a calm-flowing tidal-stream which released and expanded all the antennae of his nature. These responses leapt up towards the unknown, like those great, slippery fish at Harrod's Mill. Tom Barter, marigold-stalks, fish-scales, dough-pellets – all these, and the secret they held, depended, like the long shining river-weeds upon which his eye now rested, upon the flow of that stream of contentment which was his possession of Mary.

They were walking now very close to the river bank and it was not long before they reached Dye's Hole. This spot was really a series of deep holes in the bed of the Wissey where the stream made a sweeping curve. Over these dark places in the swirling water bent the trunks of several massive willow trees and between these trees and the edge of the stream there was a winding path, too narrow to be trodden by horses and cattle, but interspersed with muddy footholds and beaten-down clearings amid the last year's growths, where it was just possible for two people to stand close together having the willow trunks behind them and the dark water in front.

John stopped when he reached the largest of these little clearings, and standing on the trodden mud balanced the two oars and the boat-hook against the branches of an elder bush which hung over a narrow ditch on the side of their path opposite to the river. Then he turned round and facing Dye's Hole waited for the girl to come up. The back of his head touched the vivid green shoots of a gigantic willow tree whose roots, like great thirsty serpents, plunged below the flowing water. As soon as the girl reached him he took her basket from her and laid it down on the ground, taking care to place it where a fragment of an old post, of dark, rotting wood pierced by three rusty nails, would prevent it from toppling over into the ditch. As he placed it there he chanced to touch, between it and the post, a newly grown shoot of water mint; and at once a wafture of incredible aromatic sweetness reached his brain. ...

Alder Dyke! Alder Dyke! It was not marigold stalks nor the smell of dough. It was alder boughs that brought Tom Barter and that unknown ecstasy into the arteries of his soul! He made a fumbling forward movement with his arms as he touched these alders, as if welcoming a living person, and Mary divined, merely from the look of his lean vagabond's back, that some new emotion, entirely unconnected with her, had taken possession of him. When he dived into the mass of entangled boughs he plunged his hands into it and only after pressing an armful of rough twigs against his mouth and cheeks did he turn his head towards her. Any ordinary girl would have been disturbed by the nature of the crazy sound he now made to express his feelings and to summon his mate to enjoy Alder Dyke with him! It was more like the whinnying of a wild horse than anything else and yet it was not as loud as that; nor was it really an animal sound any more than it was a human sound. It was the sort of sound that this thick bed of alders itself might have emitted when tossed and rocked and torn by some fierce buffeting of the March winds. Instead of getting angry with him or thinking to herself 'Who is this man I have given myself to?', instead in fact of *thinking* anything at all, Mary simply put down her basket and ran hastily to his side. Without a word she threw her arms round his neck and pressed her lips against his cold leaf-smelling cheek. An alder twig had chanced to scratch his skin and the girl tasted now the saltish taste of spilt blood. John's cap had been already switched from his head by his dive into the mass of boughs, and Mary instinctively snatched off her own hat. Thus they swayed together for a minute like two wild ponies who in joy bite furiously at each other's necks. Then, using all his strength, though she was nearly as tall as he, he lifted her up and trampling forward like a centaur with a human burden plunged headlong deeper and deeper among those twisted branches.

When he reached the banks of the deep ditch itself he turned towards its mouth, and after an angry and tender struggle to keep the twigs from striking the girl's face, emerged triumphantly at a grassy open space where the Dyke ran into the river. There lay the boat he was looking for, moored by a padlocked chain to a stake in the ground, its rudder embedded in mud, its bottom full of dark rain-water. He put the girl down and the two stood side by side staring into the boat. ...

The river weeds, below the tide that bore them on, gleamed emerald green in the warm sunshine. Across and between the weeds darted shoals of glittering dace, their swaying bodies sometimes silver white and sometimes slippery black as they turned and twisted, rose and sank, hovered and flashed by. Beds of golden marigolds reflected their bright cups in the swift water; and here and there, against the brownish clumps of last year's reeds, they caught passing glimpses of pale, delicate-tinged cuckoo flowers. Every now and then they would come upon a group of hornless Norfolk cattle, their brown and white backs, bent heads, and noble udders giving to the whole scene an air of enchanted passivity through which the boat passed forward on its way, as if the quiet pastures and solemn cattle were the dream of some very old god into which the gleaming river and the darting fish entered by a sort of violence, as the dream of a younger and more restless immortal. ...

'I'll make him stop in a minute!' she kept saying to herself; and then something in the very effort they both were making, he to row and she to steer, something almost religious in their united tension, compelled her to concentrate upon what she was doing and to hold her peace. Past deep, muddy estuaries the boat shot forward, where the marigolds grew so thick as to resemble heaps of scattered gold, flung out for largesse from some royal barge, past groups of tall lombardy poplars, their proud tops bowing gently away from the wind, past long-maned and long-tailed horses who rushed to look at them as they shot by, their liquid eyes filled with entranced curiosity, past little farm-houses with great, sloping red roofs, past massive cattle-sheds tiled with those large, curved, brick tiles so characteristic of East Anglia, past sunlit gaps in majestic woods through whose clearings tall, flint church towers could be seen in the far distance past huge black windmills, their great arms glittering in the sun as they turned, grinding white flour for the people of Norfolk, past all these the boat darted forward, rowed, it seemed, by one relentless will-power and steered by another. And as he swung his arms forth and back, repeating his monotonous strokes with grim pantings and with a glazed, unseeing look in his eyes, it seemed to John as if merely by making this blind quixotic effort he was on the way to insure a happy issue for their love. ...

The silver-scaled dace and red-finned roach that their swift movement disturbed seemed actually to pursue this furiously speeding boat. The quivering poplars seemed to bow down their proud tops to watch these two; the cattle lifted their heads to gaze at them as they swept by; beneath air-region after air-region of tremulous lark-music they flashed and glittered forward; water-rats fled into their mud-burrows or plopped with a gurgling, sucking sound under the swirling eddies that their boat made; moor-hens flapped across their way with weak, harsh cries; small, greenish-coloured, immature pike, motionless like drowned sticks in the sunny shallows, shot blindly into the middle of the river and were lost in the weeds. The prolonged struggle of these two with the boat and with the water became in a very intimate sense their marriage day upon earth. ...

119

'You run off and explore, my pretty one!' he said. 'I'll deal with the boat.' When she was gone he thought to himself; 'It's the way she parts her hair and pulls it back and twists it, that I like so well. Who would have guessed that I'd find her like this the first minute I got to my native land?' He frowned a little and then closed his eyes. Though it was warm enough to be May rather than March, it was too early for that confusing murmur of insects which is the usual background for a hot afternoon. When the rustling of her steps died away an incredible silence descended on the place. The newborn reeds were too young to play with the flowing river. The noon had become afternoon. The larks were silent. The fish had ceased to rise. There were no swallows yet and the few spring flies that hovered over that weedy ditch were safe from attack whether from the firmament above or the firmament below. The only sound that reached his ears was the sound of a faint trickle of water which came from some infinitesimal ledge in the bank above his head and fell down drop by drop into the ditch. Not a breath of wind stirred, Not a leaf-bud quivered. Not a grass-blade swayed. There was only that elfin waterfall and, except for that, the very earth herself seemed to have fallen asleep. 'This is Norfolk,' he said to himself; and in that intense, indrawn silence some old atavistic affiliation with fen-ditches and fen-water and fen-peat tugged at his soul and pulled it earthward. And there came to his nostrils, as he lay with his eyes shut, a far-flung, acrid, aromatic smell. It was not the smell of mud, or leaf-buds, or grass-roots, or cattle-droppings, or ditch-water. It was not the smell of last night's rain, or of the sleeping south wind. It reached him independent of the eel slime that still clung about the bottom of the boat. It was the smell of East Anglia itself. It was the smell to greet which, on uncounted spring mornings, his Isle-of-Ely ancestors had left their beds and opened their back doors! It was the smell that had come wandering over the water-meadows on afternoons like this, to the drowsy heads of innumerable John Crows, resting from their ploughing with their ale mugs in their blistered hands, and their minds running on ewes and lambs and on bawdy Cambridge taverns!

THE EAST ANGLIAN BADLANDS (1991)
Richard Mabey
(from *Country Matters: Selected Writings 1974-99*, 2000)

In 1668 the Norfolk village of Santon Downham was buried under a sandstorm, a blow-out from an inland dune system at Lakenheath Warren, a few miles to the south. It was, by any reasonable English standards, an outlandish occurrence. But this was the Breckland, 'a vast Arabian desert' straddling the Norfolk-Suffolk borders which had long been notorious with travellers. Many used to cross 'the horrible Brandon sands' in the dawn to avoid upsetting the horses, and there was a kind of wooden lighthouse to guide anyone unfortunate enough to be benighted. Seven years after the Santon storm the diarist John Evelyn noted that 'the Travelling Sands have so damaged the country, rolling from place to place, and quite overwhelmed some gentlemen's estates', and he urged them to plant 'tufts of firr' to stabilise the sand.

They didn't need much encouragement. As the fashion for improvement gathered pace during the late eighteenth and nineteenth centuries Breckland landowners went in for all manner of schemes to make their local wilderness bear fruit. They planted thickets for pheasants, turnips to enrich the soil and pine hedges to check the winds. Eventually – with more than a suggestion that poetic justice had been done – Santon Downham rose again as the local headquarters of the Forestry Commission, whose vast pine plantations had become the biggest single enterprise to keep the sand in its place. In the 1940s Lakenheath Warren vanished under the runways of an airfield (now the US base that despatched the Libyan strike force). During the last

121

twenty years all the remaining open dunes have been tidily fenced off and labelled as nature reserves. Breckland has been very nearly brought to heel, and for the first time not everyone feels comfortable about this particular triumph of man over the waste.

For much of its recent history Breckland has been regarded as a classic piece of wasteland, somewhere to lose unpopular and land-hungry activities like battle-training and commercial forestry. There weren't many other obvious uses for an infertile plain which had the lowest rainfall in Britain, and which was almost devoid of the features usually regarded as making a picturesque landscape. I doubt if there is another comparable tract of rural England (it covers some 400 square miles, from Bury St Edmunds in the south to Swaffham in the north) that is so little known and so impatiently rushed through by travellers. When I first began exploring East Anglia thirty years ago it felt like an occupied zone, an intimidating gauntlet of barricaded shooting estates and military bases.

Yet everywhere there were reminders of the old waste clinging on in the margins. You could pick up neolithic arrowheads in the fields. Species of wild flower grew on the road verges that didn't crop up again until you reached the East European steppes. Nightjars seemed to find echoes of their ancestral habitats in the new forestry clearings, and churred in ever increasing numbers through the summer dusks. I began to find modern Breckland a haunting and evocative place, a ghost of the old landscape of immense sandy heaths and stony scrubland, and when dust-devils were whirling across the carrot fields and through the stunted pine wind-breaks it didn't seem implausible that flocks of great bustard stalked the plains only a hundred and fifty years ago.

Given the seemingly run-down state of the place, it was a rather perverse fascination. But attitudes towards landscape change, and just as it seemed to be on its last legs, the Breckland has come into its own. It has even received the ultimate tribute of having a District Council named after it (though rather confusingly much of this lies outside the Breckland proper).

A better guide to its status may be the changing patterns of land-use, in which both the leisure industry and low-intensity farming are making strong showings. The annual tally of visitors to the Forestry Commission's Thetford Forest Park has passed the million mark. The Dutch firm Center Parcs have created one of their holiday villages in a pine plantation on the Iveaghs' estate at Elveden. And last year, in a move which challenged the assumptions underlying centuries of agricultural development, the government designated the region as one of the first Environmentally Sensitive Areas (ESAs) in which farmers are encouraged to return to methods which will conserve historic or locally distinctive landscapes. The scheme is beginning to work quite well. But if some farmers are doubtful about taking part it isn't simply that they are unimpressed by the scale of grants and compensation. To *not* improve the land, to deliberately court infertility, goes against a whole tradition of husbanding instincts, and at a time when we are becoming sensitive to the consequences of deforestation and land degradation in the Third World, smacks of a peculiarly western brand of hypocrisy and indulgence. But the argument is nothing like as black and white as plenty versus barrenness, and the example of the Breckland may have something to teach us about a discriminating attitude towards fertility.

But there is no avoiding the fact that the Breckland is a prime home-grown example of what deforestation can lead to. Up to a couple of hundred years ago it was the nearest thing Britain had to a dust-bowl. In parts this may have been its natural state. The area is defined by deposits of sands and gravel that were washed here by glacial meltwaters, and there may have been areas of especially loose sand on exposed ridges that never sustained a permanent woodland cover. But most of the open areas were created or encouraged by human activity. The light soils made forest clearance relatively easy, and in prehistoric times it was one of the most densely populated areas of Britain. Grazing by semi-domesticated cattle would soon have converted what remained of the woodland to a mixture of wiry grass and heather. A large and sprawling network of trackways and drove roads connected the region with the Icknield Way and trading settlements on the East Anglian coast.

Amongst the most important items of trade ferried along these tracks were worked flints, for use in knives, weapons and farm implements. Flint is abundant throughout East Anglia, but Breckland had some of the best quality, and became a centre for flint-knapping skills. At Grimes Graves, just north of Brandon, there is a prehistoric flint-mine in which, to date, some 540 shafts have been uncovered. The strictures of Health and Safety regulations have rather dulled the experience of clambering down into these austere chambers in the chalk. But behind the grilles you can still see the scratch-marks made in the faces by deer-antler picks four thousand years ago.

Early farming itself was a less rewarding business. The thin soils soon began to lose their fertility, and at some unspecified date the system that eventually gave the region its name evolved. A field would be cultivated for a few years and then abandoned for as many as twenty to give it time to recover. These long-term fallow plots were named after an Old English term *brek*, meaning a tract of land broken up for cultivation and then allowed to revert. You can glimpse what these archaic stony plots were like in parts of Weeting and Thetford Heath National Nature Reserves.

Sheep-grazing was the most sensible use for both the grasslands and the brecks, and large flocks were roaming the region by Roman times. In the Middle Ages they were joined by rabbits, which were kept in enormous high-banked warrens. By the middle of the eighteenth century there were reckoned to be more than 15,000 acres of organised warren in the Brecks, and the traveller and agricultural reporter Arthur Young (1741-1820) quoted the figure of forty thousand rabbits as the production of just one warren.

At this time Breckland was probably as wild and inhospitable as it has ever been, with the areas of eroded sand growing as grazing pressure increased. This was the heyday of the exploration of Britain, and inquisitive travellers like Young, William Gilpin, the antiquarian Dr Stukeley and Charles Kidman all visited the region. Almost without exception they regarded it loathsome and treacherous. Only the duc de La Rochefoucauld, a waspish eighteen-year-old French nobleman who

toured East Anglia in 1784, saw some merit in the place – in the rabbits
if nothing else. Commenting on the landscape between Bury and
Thetford, he wrote:

The whole of the country through which the road runs for a distance of eight
miles is covered with heather in every direction as far as the eye can see ... no
trees, no cultivation, everywhere sand, everywhere little clumps of reeds and
bracken. A large portion of this arid country is full of rabbits, of which the
numbers astonished me. We saw whole troops of them in broad daylight and we
could almost touch some of them with our whips. I enquired the reason for this
prodigious number and was told that there was an immense warren which brought
in 200 guineas a year to the owner, being let to a farmer ... In the eyes of the law,
rabbits in a warren are as sacred a piece of property as the land itself, and to
transgress the laws of property is a capital offence ... The dry sand which
pervades the district militates against improvements and I do not believe that it
will ever be possible, in such an unfavourable soil, to put the twenty miles of
country which we covered in the course of a day under cultivation.

In this he underestimated the ingenuity and ambition of the local
squires. During the early years of the nineteenth century the farming
systems of the Breckland were totally transformed. Between 1800 and
1820 forty-nine Parliamentary Enclosure Acts took in nearly 120,000
acres of grass and heathland. Common rights were extinguished and
the rabbit warrens abolished. Pine wind-breaks – cut back like hedges
to encourage lateral growth – made their appearance (and produced
such distinctive rows of contorted trees that now, ironically, they are
regarded as crucial elements in the 'landscape heritage'). Increasingly,
the small farms were bought out by the large landowners, a process
which accelerated once the great agricultural depression had set in in
the 1870s. Breckland became a region of vast private estates –
Elveden, Euston, Culford, West Stow, Stanford – many of them more
than 10,000 acres in extent and able to turn the slump to their
advantage by using their rough land for raising pheasants. Breckland
became for a while the pheasant-shooting centre of England, and was

the site of some terrible *battues*. The Maharajah Duleep Singh, who rebuilt Elveden into a passable imitation of a north Indian palace in 1870, once slaughtered 789 partridges in a single day. Tom de Grey, the sixth Lord Walsingham, used to go shooting dressed in a snakeskin waistcoat and a hat made from a whole hedgehog. On a winter's day in 1889, in the marshy heathland round Stanford, he bagged sixty-five coots, thirty-nine pheasants, twenty-three mallard, seven teal, six gadwall, four pochard, one goldeneye, three swans, three snipe, one woodcock, one pigeon, two herons, two moorhens, sixteen rabbits, nine hares, one otter, one pike (shot underwater) and a rat. Game shooting continues in the Brecks, and has left some unhappy local legacies, not least a rather cavalier attitude towards bird protection laws and an entrenched hostility towards public access.

But once farming became prosperous again after the war, landowners returned to the business of improving their cultivated areas. Now the sandy soils grow high quality carrots and asparagus, and much of the cultivation is sub-contracted out to specialist growers, who undertake the whole business from sowing to harvesting.

Bill Nickson, the Ministry of Agriculture Project Officer for the Breckland ESA, keeps a personal copy of the Ministry's journal for May 1952 (his birth month) as a benchmark against which to measure changing attitudes. It contains an exhortation from the then Minister, Thomas Dugdale, to produce more food from our own soil, and a book review of *The Elveden Enterprise* which described enthusiastically how a large part of this Breckland estate had been converted from the heath. 'They were responding to the needs of their time, just as they are now,' he reflects. The needs of the time now are seen in terms of the preservation of the heathland and the fallow 'brecks', and Bill is empowered to offer grants to farmers for various initiatives aimed at meeting these objectives. By the end of 1989 there were agreements for the conservation of 1300 hectares of heath and dry grassland, in which farmers agree to restrict their use of pesticides and fertiliser and manage the grass by grazing. There have also been agreements over some 300 hectares for the encouragement of rough flower-rich strips at the edges of arable fields. This is a small step towards an option which has sadly not yet been taken up at all, that is, allowing arable fields to revert to fully fledged brecks. Agreements have been entered into by both large and small landowners, but there are still vast tracts of the Breckland which are impervious to current ideas about conservation and access. Much of the land around Rushford, for instance, is in foreign ownership, and in the wake of the rabbit and pheasant there is now a third generation of Breckland sporting beast: the thorough-bred horse. The new stud farms, done up with neo-classical porticos and smart post-and-rail fences, stand out like South Forks in the tousled Breck prairieland.

But you get used to incongruous sights. I am up here in early summer, and the new unsprayed field-edges, full of mignonette and poppies, are also bristling with soldiers in camouflage. It is the middle of a big NATO exercise to simulate an aerial invasion of Britain, and I am rather lucky to get a guided trip round the Stanford Battle Area. Bob Berry from the Property Services Agency (PSA) which undertakes estate management for the army, is an expert and enthusiastic advocate of the MoD's new attitude towards conservation. He shows me hardwood plantings deliberately edged with scrub (equally good, eventually, for nesting birds and lurking tanks) and cleared pine plantations that they are attempting to return to a heather cover. The sheep that graze much of the 17,000 acres of land are worked according to the upland hefting system, in which small, clannish flocks graze their own patch of territory and need the minimum of shepherding.

The local birds seem ineffably unconcerned about the furious activity involved in the exercise. Swallows are commuting to nests in old pillboxes. Two curlews do a display flight around a low-flying helicopter. They have an ally in the camp commandant, who is also chairman of the Stanford conservation group. During the lambing and nesting season, he puts out radar traps to catch speeding tanks. War-games are not always played by such sentimental rules.

We drive up to the highest point in the Battle Area, Frog Hill. The view over miles of pale, stony grassland, studded with pine and scrub, is extraordinary, like nothing else in this country except perhaps the New Forest. You can just catch glimpses of Langford, Stanford and Tottington churches, all that remains of the villages that were appropriated to create the Battle Training Area during the war. As in many similar areas, the army promised that the villagers could return after the cease-fire. It never happened, and the only way the dwindling number of surviving inhabitants can return to their birthplace is to be buried there.

I ask Bob Berry whether there are any better prospects now of the general public being able to visit one of the outstanding wild open spaces in lowland England. But he is sceptical. Detente means that more troops are scheduled to return from Germany, and the MoD feels it needs more training areas, not less. Hopeful visitors must be satisfied with occasional marshalled coach trips in the summer.

Only on the Forestry Commission's land is one free to walk about at will in the Brecks. This was one of the first areas to be planted up by the Commission in its post-Great-War mission to increase the nation's strategic timber reserve. Now it is the largest single landowner in Breckland, with 21,000 hectares. Most of this is planted up with Corsican pines, which for decades put the countryside here under a forbidding and monotonous drape. But many of the early plantings are coming round for felling, and landscape is perceptibly more open. The FC is also now committed to promoting nature conservation and public enjoyment of its estates, and nowhere is this policy more evident than the Brecks. Les Simpson, their local officer, tells me that they are now paying almost a full tithe – dedicating eight per cent of their land purely for conservation purposes. There are nature trails and a red squirrel project, and the Forest Park, which includes a fair amount of the commercially worked area. On some sites the Commission is creating unusually large clear-fells of up to 30 hectares for reasons that have little to do with timber management. Beyond Emily's Wood, north of Brandon, the aim is to give travellers along the A1065 an idea of what the open prospects of Breckland might once have looked like, stretches of rough land clear to the tree belts on the horizon. Down in

Wangford Warren there is an immense clearing specifically for the benefit of nightjars, woodlarks and hunting goshawks. (A while ago, with typical local opportunism, there was a sign outside the nearby farm which anounced 'Goshawks!' as lesser holdings do their honey and free-range eggs.)

Meandering between these forest clearings, watching the tree pipits doing their melodramatic free-fall song-flights, was the pleasantest part of my visit. And at night, with the vegetation underfoot smelling of fern and foxes, and the nightjars gliding out like ghostly kites against the silhouetted trees, there was a palpable sense of the old wilderness.

But much of the rest of Breckland seems to have become a curmudgeonly and inhospitable place. There is almost nowhere to walk. The network of ancient tracks that pass across the estates south of Elveden are all blocked off by curt Private signs. Even England's oldest road, the Icknield Way, summarily peters out once it leaves the FC's Kings Forest. Only the Roman Peddars Way, opened up after long and patient negotiation by Breckland local authorities, is an uninterrupted right of way, and on this I was turned back by a noxious cloud of smoke from a vast field-fire of rotting bean haulm. Feeling decidedly tetchy, I began to wonder if the time might not be approaching when, in the public interest, the whole of Breckland should be looked on – and administered – as a national asset. My private dream of the army leaving Stanford to become England's first American-style 'roadless area' will probably remain a fantasy. But public opinion is changing. More than a century ago, in his extraordinary description of the Dorset heathland in *The Return of the Native*, Thomas Hardy predicted that, 'The New Vale of Tempe may be a gaunt waste in Thule: human souls may find themselves in closer and closer harmony with external things wearing a sombreness distasteful to our race when it was young.' It would no longer seem out of place for the Breckland to become an Area of Outstanding Natural Beauty, or even a lowland National Park. Such possibilities are being whispered behind closed doors amongst those many conservation groups that currently keep an eye on the region's ecological health. They have noticed a worrying and widespread deterioration lately. Local specialities are declining. The heather is dying back. There is a growing belief that the place is probably over-grazed and over-manured, and that perhaps what is needed is a return to the old breck system itself – cultivation followed by a long fallow period. It is, ironically, a system that the much-abused Forestry Commission are already almost following. Their policy of short term rotations followed by large clearances is like a condensation of the prehistoric farming systems here. If they could be persuaded to allow longer periods before replanting they might produce a model for the Brecks, a landscape that, as Hardy put it, was 'impressive without showiness, emphatic in its admonitions, grand in its simplicity'. And, alternating forest with fallow, it would also be a salutary place for meditating upon the fact that fertility is not something which can be endlessly exploited without, so to speak, a break.

A LAMENTABLE TRAGEDY
Caroline Davison

A walk through the windswept open fields and pine belts of the modern-day Brecklands can be a lonely experience. Long straight tracks, clogged with sand, pass rusting farm machinery, derelict houses and ruined churches. The solitary hiker might conclude that every one else has fled. Blackish-green blocks of fir trees cast long shadows, muffle sounds into soft thuds. It is the kind of unvisited place where bad things might happen, and no-one would ever know.

The landscape here has been transformed by human activity, and seems to resent it. Much of the primeval wood had already been cleared before the Romans left, exposing a thin soil, prone to erosion, and easily exhausted. The Anglo-Saxons, who followed, settled in the fertile river valleys but as the population expanded it became necessary to colonise the poorer soils. Burgeoning villages built churches, sometimes two or three in a parish. Farmers developed a system where sheep grazed the heaths during the day, and spent their nights on the fallow arable land, their manure enriching the desiccated earth.

Even so, the consequences of clearing the trees could not be escaped. Over-cultivated soil turned into sand, taken up by the wind into corrosive dust clouds and drifts. The unforgiving flint and chalk sub-soil provided no sustenance for famished crops – only coarse grass and heather thrived. Sheep and rabbit farming continued to be profitable, so greedy landowners over-stocked commons, and demolished houses for more grazing. Rural populations dwindled and, one by one, the churches crumbled. In 1401 a mournful resident of Blo Norton wrote:

...by reason of pestilences and mortalities, barrenness of lands, ruin of buildings, the malice of the times and especially the fewness and the poverty of the parishioners...the church is so ruined in roof and wall that it almost daily threatens to fall.

Evicted villagers swelled the towns, scraping a living, no doubt full of resentment over their loss. Bracelets of ruined and lost churches loosely encircle Swaffham and Watton, marking this pattern of migration. The Brecks became an inhospitable desert, the home of outlaws, a shunned landscape through which respectable travellers hurried. And so the scene was set for a lamentable tragedy.

The small market town of Watton lies on the north-east edge of the Brecks. The village sign today shows two children reclining beneath a spreading tree. Unsuspecting visitors might assume that this is an evocation of a summer idyll. But these children are the *Babes in the Wood*, the doomed brother and sister, cruelly betrayed by their evil uncle, and left to die, their plight first recorded in Thomas Millington's ballad, of 1595:

131

Knowing Your Place

The Norfolk Gentleman, his Will and Testament, and how he committed the keeping of his children to his own brother, who dealt most wickedly with them, and how God plagued him for it.

It was later adapted as a play, *Two Lamentable Tragedies*, and included the story 'of a young child murthered in a wood by two ruffins with the consent of his unkle.'

The well-meaning but disastrously naïve father had willed that if his offspring should die before adulthood their inheritance was to go to his brother. Before a year and a day had passed, the wicked uncle employs two men to take the children to the wood, in order to do away with them. Despite the 'furious mood' of the two ruffians, one of them finds his heart melted by the sweet infants. Knowing no other way but violence, he kills his accomplice to save them. Afterwards he disappears into the green twilight, in search of bread, never to return. Perhaps he, too, lost his way.

The children have been torn from their home, roughly treated, and forced to witness a brutal, bloody murder, before finally being abandoned. They stumble about aimlessly, scared and hungry, before sliding into exhaustion and death.

> *These pretty babes, with hand in hand*
> *Went wandering up and down,*
> *But never more could see the man*
> *Approaching from the town.*
> *Their pretty lips with blackberries*
> *Were all besmear'd and dyed*
> *And when they saw the darksome night*
> *They sat them down and cried.*
>
> *Thus wandered these poor innocents*
> *Till death did end their grief*
> *In one another's arms they died*
> *As wanting due relief*

No burial this pretty pair
Of any man receives
Till Robin Redbreast piously
Did cover them with leaves.

It is hard to imagine a more hopeless tale.

This story has always been associated in Norfolk with Wayland Wood, a pocket of wild wood, just outside Watton, which has somehow miraculously avoided destruction. The old name *Waneland* is, in part, derived from the Viking *lundr* or 'sacred grove', suggesting past cabalistic practices. Perhaps those pagan customs survived as folk memories, reflected in this story of sacrificed innocents. The alternative name, Wailing Wood, provides a setting fit for such a sorrowful drama. Legend has it that the crying of the forsaken children can still be heard on moonless nights.

The ballad may have been concocted by Protestants to besmirch the character of the popish de Greys who lived at Griston Hall in the neighbouring parish. Thomas de Grey was seven years old when his father died and he became the ward of his uncle, Robert. When the boy was eleven he went to visit his step-mother, and never returned, either dying at her house, or on the way home.

A rumour sprang up that the boy's uncle had killed him for his inheritance. There was, after all, a pattern in the lives of the population of violence and injustice. Defenceless Tom's inheritance was stolen from him by a grasping aristocrat just as the land had been stolen from them. But why was his body never seen again? The old boy retelling the yarn might have leaned across the fire to whisper into the eager ears of the ballad writer, with a jerk of his head in the direction of the dark shadows, looming outside. 'The Wailin' Wood, tha's where he's hid.'

At the end of the 16th century the wood – much bigger then – was still the 'desert place' of Shakespeare, where malevolent fairies, wild beasts and outcasts lurked; a place both magical and forbidding for the medieval peasant living on the edge of the sand lands. The forest represents a threat to reason, and this Jungian symbol of the dark collective unconscious appears in many fairy tales, one of the best known being *Hansel and Gretel*. Its narrative of siblings abandoned in a wild wood bears a striking resemblance to the *Babes in the Wood* tragedy. Similar tales have been found around the world, 'the children and the ogre' in the international system of classification (number 327A). This archetypal story has a complex plot rich with metaphor. The birth mother dies. The father is persuaded by his new wife that they will be better off without his off-spring. Forsaken, the lost little ones wander hand in hand, just like their Norfolk counterparts.

In the classic tale the brother and sister eventually stumble upon a cottage made from sweets and cake – a realisation of their fevered dreams. But it is home to a witch who locks up the boy, forcing the girl to fatten him for eating. The Gretel character manages to push the witch into the oven, and the siblings finally make there way back home, where they find the wicked stepmother dead, and their father overjoyed to see them.

This tale of extreme behaviour was designed to enthral, terrify and then reassure its audience. The story teller took the defenceless infants into the most dangerous places imaginable, before providing the satisfactory conclusion – the ultimate escape from the wood, laden with treasure, reconciliation with the father, death of all the mean-hearted characters, and a life happy ever after. In the Norfolk version there is no such flight of fancy. The children are lost, they starve, they die. The wood takes its revenge.

Is it a coincidence that the tale of these innocent babes ends tragically on the edge of the Brecks, caught here between the bad lands and the sacred grove? Families listening to the ballad would have known all about the thankless toil against irreducible nature. They, too, had been abandoned to their fate by ruthless patriarchs, and had descended into the deep, dark places of the soul. The scouring sands had scraped away at hope, and flint had entered their hearts. They would not have believed the story with a happy ending.

A DISTANT CRY

The Norfolk Coast

'THE SHRIMP AND THE ANEMONE'
L.P.Hartley and Hunstanton
Peter Tolhurst
(from *East Anglia: A Literary Pilgrimage*, 1996)

L.P. Hartley never lived in Norfolk, but it is no coincidence that his two best known works, the *Eustace and Hilda* trilogy and *The Go Between* are both set in the county during the years of his Edwardian childhood. Brought up in the Fens, it becomes clear from his accurate depiction of Hunstanton and the surrounding countryside in *The Shrimp and the Anemone*, the first volume of his trilogy, that Hartley knew this corner of Norfolk intimately from family holidays and his love of church architecture. In this first volume the world is seen through the eyes of the young Eustace, a delicate self-portrait of the novelist, and traces the complex relationship with his dominant elder sister Hilda that unfolds with disastrous consequences. The destructive nature of this relationship is beautifully captured in the opening sequence when Eustace, playing in the rock pools at the foot of the cliffs, tries ineffectually to save a shrimp from the devouring clutches of an anemone.

The Cherrington family's move to Anchorstone (Hunstanton) is prompted by the boy's fragile health – like Hartley he suffers from a weak heart. His father decides that the town's elevated position, both physically and socially, is preferable to the cramped accommodation above his accountant's office in Ousemouth (King's Lynn). Eustace, who loves statistics, is comforted by the knowledge that Anchorstone has the 9th lowest death rate in England. There are clear parallels here with Hartley's own upbringing. He was born into just such an upper

137

middle class family, his father having abandoned his solicitor's office to become director of a local brickworks near Peterborough. The family fortune secured Hartley a place at Harrow and a scholarship to Oxford, but in *The Shrimp and the Anemone* Eustace's education is paid for out of a legacy from Miss Fothergill in recognition of the boy's friendship.

The Victorian seaside resort of Hunstanton, bleak and exposed on the edge of the cliffs, peers out across the Wash to the distant outline of the Lincolnshire coast. Shortly after the Great Eastern Railway reached the town in 1862, the Le Strange family at Hunstanton Hall developed part of the estate as a health resort. Hotels sprang up around the green, then the pier, the theatre and convalescent home followed in quick succession. Streets of late Victorian villas with turrets in the French chateau style and Edwardian Tudor semis built in local brown carrstone still give the residential areas a respectable uniformity which, as the architectural historian Nicholas Pevsner observed, are 'not a bit cheerful'.

In Anchorstone, houses arranged in neat formation read like a roll of honour from the Boer War; Ladysmith, Omdurman, Bulawayo and Rorke's Drift. Hartley, like his great admirer John Betjeman, manages to define social distinctions in architectural terms with great subtlety. In Pretoria Street stands Mafeking Villa 'as dingy as ever, the "Apartments" notice still askew in the window, the front garden – a circular flower-bed planted with sea shells set in a square of granite chips – discreetly depressing'. Further along the 'beetling heights and stately pinnacles' of the lodgings in Palmerston Parade 'always moved Eustace to awe'. To the impressionable child they suggested the west front of Peterborough Cathedral, but above all he was struck by the magnificence of the Wolferton Hotel where, to sit among the palms in its glass wintergarden looking out to sea, seemed to Eustace one of the 'supreme rewards of human endeavour, and its noble zigzag fire-escape had kindled in his imagination conflagrations of unparalleled splendour.'

Hartley evokes the seaside atmosphere of Edwardian Anchorstone with great charm. Eustace and Hilda play out their childhood dramas on the sands against a backdrop of the town's famous striped cliffs; a layered cake of white chalk and gingerbread carrstone filled with that thin band of red chalk peculiar to the locality. The zigzag path to the top, the 'Try your Grip' machine and the three shelters between the pier and the lighthouse mark their territory. Later Eustace gazes out over the accumulating clutter of cheap entertainment which threatens the safety of a world he is about to leave behind:

Eustace turned round to look at the two promenades, stretching away with their burden of shops, swingboats and shabby buildings dedicated vaguely to amusement; next came the pier striding out into the sea, and beyond it the smoke-stained sky above the railway station.

Throughout, the narrative is punctuated with references to the town's landmarks, those 'anchorstones' which both excite and comfort the sensitive child. As the family leaves for a trip to the downs, Eustace surveys the town from the top of the carriage, noticing with pleasure; 'Certain interesting and venerated landmarks such as the soaring water tower, a magnificent structure of redbrick which he never passed under without a thrill, thinking it might burst with the weight of the water imprisoned in it'. Receiving the news that he is to leave Anchorstone for boarding school, Eustace clings to those features which, until then, have structured his world.

[He] felt as if the landscape of his life was streaming by him while he, perilously balanced on a small white stone in the midst of the flux, searched in vain for some landmark which would confirm his sense of the stability in existence.

A few miles south of the town the village of Frontisham (Snettisham) is memorable as the scene of Eustace's mystical experience. It was often the destination for excursions by the Cherringtons in the landau, and on arrival they would take tea in the garden of the Swan Hotel from where the west window of the church

139

was clearly visible. For Hartley, a knowledgeable ecclesiologist, the magnificent west window was simply unsurpassed and by way of confirmation he quotes from the church guidebook:

> Inferior in mere size to the west window of York Minster and to the east window of Carlisle Cathedral, the window at Frontisham easily surpasses them in beauty, vigour and originality. It is unquestionably the finest example of flamboyant tracery in the kingdom; confronted with this masterpiece, criticism is silent.

Eustace knows this passage by heart and gazing transfixed at the tracery he becomes overwhelmed in the presence of perfection; a realisation evoked as much by the language of the guidebook as by the window itself. In a descriptive passage of sustained power, Eustace's reverie intensifies into something akin to a religious experience as his tortured body is born aloft and we witness the martyrdom of the boy saint.

> Disengaging himself from the tea table he floated upwards. Out shot his left arm, caught by some force and twisted this way and that; he could feel his fingers, treble-jointed and unnaturally long, scraping against the masonry of the arch as they groped for the positions that had been assigned to them ... Splayed, spread-eagled, crucified (but for fear of blasphemy he must only think the shadow of that word) into a semblance of the writhing stonework.
>
> Meanwhile the interstices, the spaces where he was not, began to fill with stained glass. Pictures of saints and angels, red, blue and yellow, pressed against and into him, bruising him, cutting him, spilling their colours over him. The pain was exquisite, but there was rapture in it too. Another twitch, a final wriggle and Eustace felt no more; he was immobilised, turned to stone. High and lifted up, he looked down from the church wall, perfect, pre-eminent, beyond criticism ... to be admired and worshipped by hundreds of visitors ... Eustace, Eustace of Frontisham, Saint Eustace.

Even the exciting ascent of Frontisham Hill on the way home fails to compensate the boy for an experience so abruptly terminated by the sound of his father's voice ordering more tea.

As a child Anchorstone Hall, enclosed in its landscaped grounds, had always seemed beyond the reach of Eustace, but returning from another excursion, the Cherringtons take a detour round the edge of the park. Eustace catches his first glimpse of the building and in that instance recognises his ambition:

> Suddenly a great sheet of water opened out before them, and beyond it rose the chimneys and turrets and battlements of Anchorstone Hall. The moon made a faint pathway on the water, but the house was still gilded by the setting sun, Eustace was enchanted 'Oh isn't it lovely? If I ever made enough money to buy it, will you come and live with me there Hilda?'

Sooner than expected, Eustace finds himself briefly within the ancient walls of the Hall having been rescued in the park by Dick Staveley after he had become lost in a storm. Contact is renewed shortly afterwards when Dick is out riding on the sands. Eustace is greatly impressed by the announcement that his family are Lords of the Foreshore, a direct reference to the head of the Le Strange family who held the hereditary title, Lord High Admiral of the Wash, a position which allowed him to claim anything on the beach or in the sea as far as a man could ride a horse or shoot an arrow. In the novel this archaic rite becomes a metaphor for the way that the lives of Eustace and Hilda fall claim to the Staveleys.

In the second volume, *The Sixth Heaven*, Hartley draws heavily on his experiences as an undergraduate to recreate the dazzling social life of Oxford in the 1920s. Here Eustace finds doors open into a world of privilege to which he has always aspired. Hartley, too moved easily in some of the most glamourous literary and social circles. A frequent guest at Garsington Manor, the home of Lady Ottoline Morrell, he transposed her weekend house parties to Anchorstone Hall in his trilogy where Eustace is befriended by Lady Nelly Staveley, a character based partly on the author's life-long friend Lady Cynthia

Asquith. He eventually persuades Hilda to join him, determined that she should marry Dick Staveley, heir to the family seat, thereby fulfiling his desire to enter that grand monde of elegance and tradition at the pinnacle of English society.

Later, in the company of Lady Nelly, he explores the grounds, taking in the architectural splendours of the hall's main front which comes as a relief from the 'self conscious Elizabethanism' of the Victorian wing. 'The image of the house was spread out before them, the pink of the Banqueting Hall, the glinting, lively grey of the flint-flecked front; elongated and wavey, inflexions of the chimneys trembled into the rushes at their feet. The house had the mirror to itself'. On another occasion Eustace stumbles across a ruined chapel in the grounds. Here he is disturbed by Dick who casually breaks off a fragment of carved stone from the font, handing it to Eustace as a memento, but for Eustace it comes to assume a greater significance. Later in Venice with Lady Nelly, his thoughts return to this precious spot:

... of all the places in Anchorstone Hall this was his favourite, perhaps because, being a roofless ruin and belonging to the past, it did not repel his imagination with the pride of alien ownership. They had laughed at him, at home, for bringing away the carved fragment ... But Eustace had a strong feeling for relics and it should even earn its passage by acting as a paper-weight. The stability of paper-weights appealed to him. They tethered things down, they anchored the past. The Anchor Stone!

Throughout the weekend the pleasure Eustace experiences as a guest of the aristocracy is tainted by the feeling that they share a life within the carefully structured defences of Anchorstone Hall that he can never really penetrate. After church he stops in front of the duck pond: 'So strangely did he feel his childhood pressing round him, usurping his present self, that the Tudor gateway seemed a barrier against him, the public.'

Eustace only experiences a real sense of belonging at the end of the trilogy, while revisiting the scenes of his childhood for the last time.

Riding out through the park which 'welcomes him into the past' he is at last happy in the knowledge that he has Sir John's permission to go wherever he chooses. Passing the ruin which all those years ago heralded the approaching downs and their picnic, 'the roofless, gabled church which the sky poured into, made him feel as if a lid had been taken off his own mind. He passed by it slowly, his eyes dwelling with pleasure on all its broken but enduring surfaces.'

Hartley returned to the theme of desecration when Eustace finds the 'mysterious round white summit of the lighthouse', Anchorstone's most potent landmark, has been decapitated. Painted a hideous maroon, it has become the Old Lighthouse Tea Rooms. 'The god has deserted his shrine and commerce has taken over'. But before Eustace drifts into unconsciousness the reader is left with a single image of lasting beauty:

Over the Lincolnshire coast the sun was going down in calm magnificence. A few clouds, bars of indigo, bright at the edges, rested on the lower part of the great orb; below, the sea already shimmered with the opalescence of approaching twilight. The wind had dropped but the water was still ruffled by the energy of its breath. A procession of ripples, tipped with palest gold, rolled purposefully towards Eustace.

The commercial pressures, symbolised for Hartley by the tea rooms, have finally transformed Hunstanton from an attractive Edwardian town, into the kind of resort found anywhere along the coast. The railway station and the Sandringham Hotel have both gone, the pier swept away and the water tower, built with those same Fletton bricks that made the Hartley fortune, has been converted into flats. Only the striped cliffs, the rock pools and the view out to sea remain as Eustace would have remembered them. Death duties and another disastrous fire eventually forced the Le Strange family to vacate their ancestral home, but Ringstead Parva church survives, the most ancient and ruinous of the landmarks so dear to Eustace. Its 'enduring surfaces' a little more eroded by time, it stands abandoned and unapproachable in the middle of a wheat field guarding the entrance to Ringstead Down.

ADVENTURES AMONG BIRDS
W. H. Hudson
(from *Adventures Among Birds*, 1913)

There are few places in England where you can get so much wildness
and desolation of sea and sand-hills, wood, green marsh, and grey
saltings as at Wells, in Norfolk, the small old red-brick town, a mile and
a quarter from the beach, with a green embankment lying across the
intervening marsh connecting town and sea. Here you can have it all in
the space of a half-day's prowl or saunter – I cannot say 'walk,' seeing
that I am as often standing or sitting still as in motion. The little village-
like town in its quietude and sense of remoteness from the world is itself
a restful place to be in; going out you have on the land side the quiet
green Norfolk country of winding roads and lanes, old farm-houses and
small red villages which appear almost deserted. As I passed through
one the other day, the thought was in my mind that in this village not
one inhabitant remained, when all at once I caught sight of a very old
man, shrunk and lean and grey, standing in a cottage garden behind its
grey palings. His clothes, too, like his hair and face, were a dull grey, so
like the hue of the old weathered and lichen-stained wood of the palings
as to make him almost invisible. It was an instance of protective
resemblance in the human species. He was standing motionless, leaning
on his stick, peering at me out of his pale dim eyes as if astonished at
the sight of a stranger in that lonely place.

But I love the solitariness on the side towards the sea best, the green
marsh extending to Holkham on your left hand, once a salt flat
inundated by the sea, but long reclaimed by the making of that same

144

green bank I have mentioned – the causeway which connects Wells with the beach. On the right side of this bank is the estuary by which small ships may creep up to the town at high tide, and the immense grey saltings extending miles and miles away to Blakeney. Between the flats and the sea are the sand-hills, rough with grey marram grass; then the beach, and, if the tide is up, the sea; but when the water is out, you look across miles of smooth and ribbed sands, with no life visible on its desolate expanse except a troop of gulls resting in a long white line, and very far out a few men and boys digging for bait in the sand, looking no bigger than crows at that distance. Beyond the line of white gulls and the widely scattered and diminished human forms is the silvery-grey line of the sea, with perhaps a sail or two faintly visible on the horizon.

What more could anyone desire? – what could add to the fascinations of such a retreat? A wood! Well, we have that too, a dark pine wood growing on the slopes of the sand-hills on the land side and extending from the Wells embankment to Holkham a couple of miles away. Many an hour in the late afternoons and evenings have I spent in that perfect solitude listening to the sea-wind in the pines when the sound of wind and sea were one, and finding the deep shelter warm and grateful after a long ramble over the sands and dunes and marshes.

For I go not to Wells in 'the season,' when days are long and the sun is hot, the scattering time for all those who live 'too thick,' when even into this remote spot drift a few of the pale town-people with books in their pockets and cameras and green butterfly-nets in their hands. The wild geese are not there then, they are away breeding in the Siberian tundra or Spitzbergen; and for that wild exhilarating clangour which they make when passing overhead to and from the sea, and for the cra-cra of the hooded crow – his harsh war-cry and curse on everything – you hear lark and titlark, dunnock and wren, with the other members of the 'feathered choir' even as in all other green places.

Autumn and winter is my time, and at no other place in the kingdom can the grey geese be seen to better advantage, despite the fact that to this spot the wild-fowler comes annually in numbers, and that many of the natives, even the poorest, possess a gun and are always on the lookout for geese. The birds come in undiminished numbers, probably because they find here the one green spot on which they can repose in comparative safety. This spot is the reclaimed marsh or meadowland which I have mentioned as lying between the Wells embankment and Holkham. It is not a perfect sanctuary, since the geese are shot a few times during the winter by the lord of the manor and his guests; but the dangerous days are so few and far between at this place that the geese have come to regard it as a safe refuge, and are accustomed to congregate daily in large numbers, two or three thousand or more being often seen together ...

To find at this spot that I was able to look at a flock of a thousand or two of geese at a short distance has been one of my most delightful experiences in bird-watching in England. I had heard of their tameness from others, but could hardly credit it until witnessing it myself. The best time was in fine weather as we occasionally get it in October and November, when the wind is still and the sunshine bright and warm, for the birds are then in a drowsy state and less vigilant than at other times, especially after a moonlight night when they have been feeding on the stubble and pastures. You can then get quite near to them and see them at their best, and with a good binocular bring them as close to your eyes as you like. It is a very fine sight – this assemblage of large wild birds on the green turf sitting or standing in every attitude of repose. At a distance they look almost black; seen closely one admires the shading of their plumage, the dark upper barred greys and browns, and the buff colouring on neck and breast and pink beak and legs. The sight is peculiarly fine when, as frequently happens, great numbers of birds of other species gather at the same spot as if a parliament of the feathered nations were being held. Rooks and crows, both black and hooded, and daws are often there in hundreds; lapwings too in hundreds, and black-headed gulls and starlings and wintering larks, with other small birds. The geese repose, the others are mostly moving about in search of worms and grubs. The lapwings are quietest, inclined to repose too; but at intervals they all rise up and wheel about for a minute or so, then drop to earth again ...

My best evening was on October 29, for at the close of that day the sky cleared and the geese returned, not in detachments, but all together a little earlier than usual. I was out on the marsh towards Blakeney, a mile and a half or so from Wells, when, about half an hour before sunset, a solitary goose came flying by me towards the sea, keeping only a foot or two above the ground. It was a wounded bird shot somewhere on its feeding-ground, and, being unable to keep with the flock, was travelling slowly and painfully to the roosting-place on the sand. When it had got about a couple of hundred yards past me a few redshanks rose from the edge of the creek and, after wheeling round once or twice, dropped down again in the same place, and no sooner had they alighted than the goose turned aside from his course and, flying straight to them, pitched on the ground at their side. That is just how a bird of social disposition will always act when forsaken by his fellows and in distress: it will try to get with others, however unlike its own species they may be – even a goose with redshanks; and this, too, in a most dangerous place for a goose to delay in, where gunners are accustomed to hide in the creeks. It was evident that he was ill at ease and troubled at my presence as after alighting he continued standing erect with head towards me. There he remained with the redshanks for full fifteen minutes, but he had not been more than two minutes on the spot before a passing hooded crow dropped down close to and began walking round him. The crow will not attack a wounded goose, even when badly wounded, but he knows when a bird is in trouble and he must satisfy his inquisitive nature by looking closely at him to find out how bad he really is. The goose, too, knows exactly what the crow's life and mind is, and no doubt despises him. I watched them intently, and every time the crow came within a couple of feet of him the goose bent down and shot out his snake-like head and neck at him. If my binocular had been able to catch the sound as well as the sight, it would have conveyed to me, too, the angry snake-like hiss which accompanied the threatening gesture. And each time this gesture was made the crow hopped away a little space, only to begin walking and hopping round the goose again until

147

he had satisfied his impudent curiosity, where-upon he flew off towards his roosting-place.

Then, after a few minutes, from a great way off in the sky came the sounds of approaching geese, and the wounded bird turned his breast towards the land and stood with head held high to listen to and see his fellows returning uninjured with crops full of corn, boisterous in their happiness, to the roosting-place. The sound grew louder, and presently the birds appeared, not in a compact body, but in three single lines or skeins of immense length, while between these widely separated lines were many groups or gaggles of a dozen to forty or fifty birds arranged in phalanx form.

I had been witnessing this evening return of the geese for a fortnight, but never, as now, united in one vast flock, numbering at the least four thousand birds, the skeins extending over the sky for a length of about a third of a mile. Nor had the conditions ever been so favourable; the evenings had been clouded and it was often growing dark when they appeared. On this occasion the heavens were without a cloud or stain and the sun still above the horizon. I could see it from the flat marsh like a great crimson globe hanging just above the low, black roofs of Wells with the square church tower in the middle. The whole vast aerial army streamed by directly over me and over their wounded fellow below, still standing statuesque and conspicuous on the brown, level marsh. In two or three minutes more the leading birds were directly above the roosting-place on the flat sands, and at this point they paused and remained stationary in mid-air, or slowly circled round still keeping at the same height; and as others and still others joined them, the whole formation was gradually broken up, skeins and phalanxes becoming merged in one vast cloud of geese, circling round like a cloud of gulls. Then the descent began, a few at a time detaching themselves from the throng and sweeping obliquely downwards, while others, singly or in small parties, with half-closed wings appeared to hurl themselves towards earth with extraordinary violence. This marvellous wild-wing display continued for four or five minutes before the entire multitude had come to the ground. Altogether it had

148

been the most magnificent spectacle in wild-bird life I had ever witnessed in England.

It was not until all were down and invisible, and the tumult of the multitudinous cries had sunk to silence, that the wounded bird, after some moments of indecision, first taking a few steps onwards, then returning to the side of the redshanks, as if reluctant to part from those little unhelpful friends lest he should find no others, finally set off walking towards the sea.

There were no gunners out on the shore at this point just then and he would be able to reach the flock in a little while, although he would not perhaps be able to follow them to the farmlands on the morrow or ever again.

Rough and rainy days succeeded that rare evening of a wild-wing display on a magnificent scale; then followed yet another perfect November morning like that on which the martins had abandoned their stricken nest. A clear sky, a light that glorified that brown marshy world, and a clear sharp air which almost made one think that 'miracles are not ceased,' since in breathing it in the shackles that hold and weigh us down appear to drop off. On such a morning it is only necessary for a man to mimic the actions of a crane or stork by lifting his arms and taking a couple of strides and a hop forward, to find himself launched in space, rising to a vast height, on a voyage of exploration to 'heavens not his own and worlds unknown before.' It is the nearest we can get to the state of being a bird.

On that side where the large sun was coming up the sky was all a pale amber-coloured flame, and on it, seemingly at a great distance, appeared minute black floating spots, which rapidly increased in size and presently resolved themselves into a company of hooded crows just arrived from their journey over the North Sea. And no sooner were they gone journeying inland in their slow-flapping laborious manner, than other crows and yet more crows succeeded, in twos and threes and half-dozens, and in scores and more, an endless straggling procession of hoary Scandinavian or 'Danish' crows coming to winter in England. And from time to time fieldfares, too, appeared, travelling a little faster

149

with an undulatory flight, but keeping strictly to the crow-line; and these too appeared to be fatigued and journeyed silently, and there was no sound but the low swish of their wings.

A morning and a bird life to rejoice the heart of a field naturalist; yet this happiness was scarcely mine before a contrary feeling supervened – the same old ineffable sadness experienced on former occasions on quitting some spot which had all unknown been growing too dear to me. For no sooner am I conscious of such an attachment – of this queer trick of the vegetative nerves in throwing out countless invisible filaments to fasten themselves like tendrils to every object and 'every grass,' or to root themselves in the soil, than I am alarmed and make haste to sever these inconvenient threads before they get too strong for me, and take my final departure from that place. For why should these fields, these houses and trees, these cattle and sheep and birds, these men and women and children, be more to me than others anywhere in the land?

However, I made no desperate vow on this occasion: the recollection of the wild geese prevented me from saying a word which could never be unsaid. I had planned to go that morning and bade a simple good-bye: nevertheless my heart was heavy in me, and it was perhaps a prophetic heart.

The black straggling procession of crows, with occasional flocks of fieldfares, had not finished passing when the train carried me away towards Lynn, skirting the green marshes or meadows sacred to the wild geese. And here, before we came to the little Holkham station, I had my last sight of them. Looking out I spied a party of about a dozen Egyptian geese, on a visit to their wild relations, from Holkham Park close by, and as the train approached they became alarmed and finally rose up with much screaming and cackling and flew from us, showing their strongly contrasted colours, black and red and glistening white, to the best advantage. Now a very little further on a flock of about eight hundred wild geese were stationed. They were all standing with heads raised to see the train pass within easy pistol shot; yet in spite of all the noise and steam and rushing motion, and of the outcry the semi-domestic Egyptians had raised, and their flight, these wild geese, the most persecuted and wariest birds in the world, uttered no sound of alarm and made no movement!

A better example of this bird's intelligence could not have been witnessed; nor – from the point of view of those who dream of a more varied and nobler wild-bird life than we have now been reduced to in England – could there have been a more perfect object lesson.

A TIDE IN THE AFFAIRS
Richard Mabey
(from *Country Matters, Selected Writings 1974-99*, 2000)

I was nearly eighteen before I succeeded in getting as far north as the Norfolk coast. One summer a friend whose father had a converted lifeboat moored at Blakeney invited a group of us to spend a few days there. We went up in his Land Rover, eight of us, scrabbling about in the back like over-excited puppies. For all of us, East Anglia was something of an unknown quantity. It had a reputation as a bit of an outback, on the way to nowhere, and as its prospects began to unfold before us north of Newmarket, it looked like a very strange country indeed. American bomber bases glinted ominously in distant heaths. Asparagus grew in sandy fields. The roads were lined with stunted pine windbreaks, unlike any hedges I had ever seen. Then, further on, there were no margins at all, and the great washes of sugar beet and barley broke abruptly against the flint walls of medieval churches. When we swung into the long straight reach of the Icknield Way, north of Brandon, Justin, our driver and host, sensing our excitement but also aware of the responsibility of having such a gathering of greenhorns in his charge, hunched down towards the dashboard and showed us how he could change into four-wheel drive with his foot.

We saw more kicking out – and the same mixture of nonchalance and authority – that evening in a Blakeney pub. One of the regulars was Crow, a ruddy-faced village elder, yarner and Jack-of-all-trades, whom we came to adulate in a rather silly way as a local 'character'. He, of course, made merciless fun of us by acting out the role for all his worth. That night he showed us a natty trick he had with the bar skittles. He would aim the ball somewhere between the door-knob and the photograph of the pre-war lifeboat crew that hung on the wall, and on the backswing give it a flick with his foot that made it swoop round and knock every skittle flat. Crow was in his late fifties then, the same age as most of the lifeboatmen in the photo. The picture had been taken after a momentous rescue in which conditions had been so terrible that the men's hands had been frozen solid to the oars. Norfolk, that evening, looked like a place where one might have to flex all manner of undiscovered muscles.

Yet even on those first visits the place sounded old chords. It was the first time I had gone tribal since I was a child in the early fifties. I was with another gang then and we spent our school holidays in the grounds of a demolished eighteenth-century mansion behind our road. We went out there first thing, built camps up trees and in holes in the ground, churned milk on upturned bicycles, baked potatoes in wood fires, fought off invaders from the council estate on the far side of the park, and then went home for tea. We used it as our common, and always referred to it, rather imperiously, as 'The Field'. Everywhere else, just as airily, was 'Up the Top'. And up the top, in ecstatic daydreaming on the hills to the south of our road, was where I spent most of the remainder of my youth. It was a patch of country that I clung to like a secret code, full of touchstones and private vistas that had to be visited in a precise and rigid sequence. It was right enough for a brooding adolescent, but when Norfolk arrived I was glad to be back with some company again, and with a landscape that seemed to have some of the perennial new-mintedness of those childhood mornings in The Field.

We spent that first Norfolk night, as we were to spend many more in the years to come, crammed into the eccentric cavities of the old lifeboat (which was called, for reasons beyond any fathoming, *Dilemma X*). The lucky few had bunks, the rest of us found what spaces we could under tables and in the wheelhouse. In the morning I wriggled stiffly out of my own cranny near the bilges, found a porthole, and looked out on the sight that has kept me in thrall to this coastline ever since: a high tide swirling in over a mile of saltmarsh and lapping the concrete quay where we were moored. There was not a single point of stillness. Terns hovered above the water and spikes of sea-lavender bent and bounced under the tide-race. Even the mud was alive, and slid out of the receding water with the moist shine of a new-born animal.

Saltmarshes don't fit into our conventional views about landscape. They are neither sea nor dry land. Most of the time they have the comfortably timeless look of old pastureland, yet twice a day they are reshaped by the sea. The men who go out on them to dig for lugworm and mussels also live odd hybrid existences, hunter-gathering in season, odd-jobbing on farms and gardens in the summer. They use the language of land-workers to describe the mudflats, and talk of fields and valleys and ditches; yet they know that no tractor could drag them out if they were caught by tides that come in faster than a person can walk.

The local ferrymen showed their indifference to the shifting contours of Blakeney Channel by bringing in their boats at the lowest possible water holding the tiller with one hand and rolling a cigarette ('wibbling' they called it) with the other. We were altogether more timid when it came to the sea, and one trip up the spout on *Dilemma* per visit was quite enough. Even then we didn't venture out to the open sea, but to the Pit, a natural haven formed and sheltered by the long shingle spit known as Blakeney Point.

The Point was an enchanted oasis of lagoons and shifting sand-dunes, where seals basked and the air was full of the clamour of oyster-catchers and redshank. Even when rain hung over the mainland this 3-mile-long peninsula often lay under its own mysteriously clear strip of blue sky. It was our Coral Island, and on hot days I can still conjure up the coconut and honey scent of the sea-pinks and tree lupins. (Once or twice, walking over the marshes at nearby Stiffkey, I have seen a true mirage of the Point. It floated high above the horizon, stretched by the heat haze so that its dunes looked like the walls of a Moorish castle.) When the tide went out it left little pools, not more than two or three feet deep, and warm enough to doze in. Occasionally we would see a great flock of terns swirling like ticker-tape above one of these pools, and raining down after the shoal of whitebait that had been stranded there. We never bothered to try and catch fish ourselves, but we grubbed for cockles and cooked bundles of marsh samphire (wrapped in silver foil – we were no purists) over drift-wood fires.

But though we thought sometimes of spending whole days and nights out there, curled up under the dunes, the fantasy of being castaways was never strong enough to keep us from the sociable pleasures of the mainland in the evenings. So when the tide was right we would row back to *Dilemma*, on to the flats on the landward side of the Pit, and then walk to the pub at Morston across a mile of glassy mud and rickety plank bridges, with black mud squirting between our toes. It was a hilarious, slithery journey even in the daylight, and how we used to make it back after closing-time I do not know. Justin, never one to shirk his captain's responsibilities, wouldn't allow us to use torches in case we dropped them and fell away ourselves with night blindness (some of the creeks under those bridges were 10 feet deep). So if there was no moon the only light was the phosphorescence that rippled about our feet as we splashed into the shallow water. Sometimes we could see our last footprints glowing for a brief instant in the damp sand behind us, as long-lived a trace as anyone leaves here. I learned much later that it was partly these marsh-lights that Justin thought had given samphire, the plant which grew in these muds, its name. Never having had a reason to see the word written, he thought it was 'sand-fire'.

In wintertime the Point was too wild and wind-torn for our tastes, but we still haunted the marshes north of Morston, and took long, tacking walks along the sea-walls. At New Year the sky here is often the purest, sharpest blue, and is etched with vast flights of wintering birds – wild geese, wigeon, flocks of waders swirling like smoke over the distant slack water with their pale underwings flashing in the sun as they turn.

I've never understood those who find marshes desolate places. They can be remorselessly hard, especially in winter, but they are never oppressive. They are too open for that. If you look east or west along these flats you can sometimes see for a dozen miles, up to the edge of the Wash, if you are lucky. The view would swallow you if it were not for the rim of the sea itself. It is a shifting edge, but it puts a comforting limit to things. On the tideline, you know where you are. Stand by it and look due north and there is nothing between you and the Arctic Circle. The North Sea here is as dark as anywhere in Britain, and the locals still often refer to it by its stark ancient name, the German Ocean.

Yet turn round and look inland and you could be in the Chilterns. In the mile or so that lies between the sea and the coast road the marshes gradually assemble themselves. Nearest you are the bare sands and the plastic, shifting muds; then the pastel wash of the first plants, the silver wormwood and lilac sea-lavenders; then the claimed land locked up behind the sea-walls; and finally, backed up against the low swell of the coastal hills, the little villages with their mighty churches, as compact and bright as if they were tucked in a secure inland valley.

It's hard to feel lonely where there is a tide. Whatever else it may be, it is reliable. A tide will come in, always more or less on time, and always, eventually, recede. The signs the spent water leaves on the sand and mudflats are like vanishing footprints. They are soft-edged, fleeting, curiously tidy. Perhaps it is this husbanding by the sea that gives marshy landscapes what affinities they have with more slowly moulded sceneries inland. It is as if a whole round of seasons – or a whole generation of farming – were enacted twice a day.

Every few years the sea breaks in more savagely, but even then the changes are transient. Early in 1976 a great storm breached sea-walls right along the coast and all the shoreline habitats – beaches, sand, mudflats, saltings – were thrown together in a mad jumble. The sea sprayed tongues of shingle far into the marsh and hollowed out muddy pools in the middle of the beach. In many places the rows of sea-blite bushes that grow along the margin between beach and mud were completely buried by shingle. But by August that year their shoots had already started to reappear above the surface. I dug down below one of these new sprigs, down to the old and already decaying parent plants, and saw the new shoots, pallid but indomitable, pushing their way up through more than 2 feet of heavy pebbles.

These harsh conditions demand a measure of adaptability from everything that lives here. Once or twice a year, when high spring tides are boosted by north-easterly winds, the seaward edge of Blakeney floods. In the summer everyone gathers round the quay to see the tide in, and it becomes a kind of coastal village green. The car park attendant's booth bobs free and floats off, the bus stop is moved, and as the water starts lapping the steps of the knitwear store in the High Street, the more adventurous boat-people go shopping in their tenders. This narrow street is steep enough to give a view over the whole quay and out into the Pit, and you can see how the tide drives everything remorselessly before it – spectators, cars, boats and all – like flecks of spindrift on the shore. When Blakeney Channel was wider and the quay used commercially, the cargoes had to be edged down this slope in carts braked by backward-facing horses. Steep land, high water: the influence of the elements of a landscape can be ineluctable. I've watched a bulldozer, clearing up flotsam after one of these flood tides, run gently out of control down the hill and over the edge of the quay. And once, when we were trundling a piano down the street to the pub, it began to move so fast that the wheels glowed hot and hissed in the puddles.

The tribe has broken up now and its members gone their separate ways, and when I come back to this stretch of Norfolk I am usually by myself. But the marsh landscapes are as familiar company as they ever were. I still follow the old route up – past the airfields and squat pines, along the road from Fakenham that edges, maddeningly slowly, towards the coast. Then through the gorse and heather of Salthouse Heath, which lies on a ridge of sandy gravels dumped here by the last ice-sheet. You see the first glint of water, then as you tip sharply down through the narrow strip of arable fields, the marsh suddenly fills the whole horizon, criss-crossed with silver dykes. You feel age and time falling away. Where you stand was the coastline five hundred years ago. What you are looking at now is a sight that has never been seen exactly so before, nor ever will be again.

I drive as fast as I dare to Morston, kick off my shoes and run out over the mud towards that thin blue line that hangs over the tide's edge, and wonder why I have ever left.

GREAT EYE FOLLY
Sylvia Townsend Warner
(from 'Bathrooms Remembered', 1963; and *Letters*, 1982)

So many of the houses I have lived in have afterward come to violent ends that I wonder my friends still invite me under their roofs. For there is yet another: it died by the act of God, and a wave was its winding sheet.

It stood on the north coast of Norfolk – a coast always under menace from the sea. I remember a man pointing to a long-shore fishing boat and telling me that precisely beneath it there had been a bridge over a stream, and that his grandfather as a boy had seen wagons loaded with corn driven over it. Further out, there was a submerged market town, larger than the market town inland, and the bells in its church tower could be heard ringing in a ground swell. The usual Ys legend, in fact, only distinguished by an insistence that all this was pretty recent, was almost still something being talked about. The house was called the Folly, and it had a legend, too. It had been built by a lady in the market town (the visible one), who had loved a sea captain. Every night, she drove out to it along the causeway over the sea marsh to a light in a beaconing lamp in its window. After her day, it was used by coast guards, and it was they, so I was told, who put the battlements on its roof. When the coast guards moved to a new station further along the coast, the Folly was abandoned, and stood empty till a family from London bought it as a holiday house and put in two bathrooms.

The lady of the lamp, the battlements, the two bathrooms, the schoolteacher on the roof – they were known far and wide; they were part of the story, part of the legend. And we, by renting the Folly for the winter, excited local interest much as though we were the first page of another chapter. Even if we did not prove so notable as the schoolteacher – also a winter tenant, who, when the house was cut off by a series of high tides flooding the marsh, was seen walking on the roof and believed to be signalling, though as it was impossible to get to her no one could learn what she meant, till the flood withdrew and she explained to enquiring visitors that she had been admiring the spectacle – even if we did not prove so notable as she, we were at least notable in going there at all that time of year.

'You aren't afraid of the old waves, then?' shouted the man who was delivering coal. Waiting for a pause between one wave and another, I said we hadn't been afraid so far. He stared at me as if I were something a long way out to sea.

It was a two-storey house, stockily built and looking assertively bolt upright on its little hillock, a residue of rabbity turf and crouched gorse bushes on the eroded beach. On either side of the hillock the pebble ridge stretched featurelessly away. In front the beach sloped sharply downward; at low tide it was quite difficult to clamber up its subsiding lower terraces. Behind was a wide stretch of sea marsh, and a causeway connecting us with the real land, where people lived and vegetables grew and where we went for supplies of drinking water. On a calm day, we could hear the sounds of real land – a cock crowing, a car hooting; for the rest, we heard nothing but wind and sea and sometimes snatches of conversation from passing boats. I was several times terrified during that winter; never, I think, frightened. The boom and explosion of the waves breaking along the wide stretch of beach, the snarl of the pebbles dragged back and forth, was so compulsive, so hallucinating, that by dint of always being aware of it I scarcely noticed it. It was only when the sea broke its own spell, perhaps by some exceptionally ringing rattle of spray against the windowpanes, perhaps by one of those silences that presage a wave much larger than the others, that I was tossed into terror. It was a stormy winter. We grew accustomed to being shouted down by waves, we grew accustomed to being flayed by winds. It soon seemed natural to me that if I wanted to empty the trash basket into the rubbish pit I should cross the hillock on all fours. It was much harder to grow accustomed to the indoor inclemencies: to an unheated kitchen that faced east; to the boldness of famishing rats; to oil lamps that flared and candles that guttered; to so much being poised on the edge of going wrong, like the petrol engine that raised or didn't raise the water supply from a brackish well; to the taste of coffee made with semi-salt water; to having to fetch whatever one needed from inland, often from quite a long way inland, and in a gale, and finding the fire out when one got back. Yet, in the main, we were intensely happy; the game dealer in the market town sold the best pheasants I have ever cooked, and we had two bathrooms. At the end of a day of vicissitudes it was a queer Elysium to lie soaking in that brackish water, listening to the assault of the waves and to the steadily screeching wind, and to reflect that the water one lay in (for even the pools on the marsh were whipped into waves by the force of the gale) was the one unvexed surface for miles.

It seemed that the end of such a house must have been laid with its foundations. Sooner or later, it was agreed, the sea would get the Folly; and because its isolation and its battlements gave it a particular air of bulldog panache, it was assumed that the close of the story would be dramatic. There was this much drama. When the people on the real land had struggled out of their share in the general calamity – the tidal inundation of 1953 that swept along the east coast, up the Thames estuary, on over Holland, everywhere drowning and destroying – and found time to look seaward beyond the sea at their doors, the Folly appeared to be still there. They saw what they had always seen – the landward aspect of the house. But the tide, tugging away the northern slope of the hillock, had brought down half the structure. The solid-seeming house was a shell.

That autumn we went to look at it. The marsh was marsh again, the causeway passable; but where it formerly ran out in the fishermen's path down to the beach a mass of heaped-up pebbles blocked it, and we had to clamber over this to get to the house. The door was gone, the windows were gone. Part of the stairway remained. One of the baths had come to rest across the stair foot. What was left of the front of the house stood leaning above its downfall, with the unsupported floor of the upper room dangling like a crazy shelf. Light poured in from above and was reflected upward from the water below. The sea was so still that one would have thought it motionless if the light reflected from it had not danced on the rent walls and the dangling ceiling. Another winter would finish it.

To ALYSE GREGORY 2o:x:1950

... I think Valentine [Ackland] will have told you about Great Eye Folly. I have the oddest impressions of it, since we were only there for about fifteen minutes, and conversing all the time with its owners. But the first five of those minutes was enough to enchant me. It is the sort of house one tells oneself to sleep with, and sometimes I almost suppose that it is really one of my dream-houses, and no such solid little assertion of the rectangle breaks the long sky-line of salt-marsh and sea. But things tether it to earth, again: a post-card, saying, 'I forgot to tell you that the butcher is called Arthur.' An inventory, listing 'seven mugs, one glued.' And such facts as that today I packed the four grey and white cups and saucers Valentine bought to take with us, grey and white to complement the view of the sea from our windows: It looks straight out on the sea: fifty feet of a low wind-bitten cliff, and then the shore. At dusk we shall see the ships' lights passing, and the intermittent fixed stars of the light-buoys: and from the south windows, the small far-away lights of the village, and the few head-lamps travelling along the coast-road of what one must think of as the mainland; for the salt-marshes in between have that equivocal character, one cannot really look on them as solid earth. Next Friday, at this time, we shall be there. I can hardly believe it.

To WILLIAM MAXWELL 3:xi:1950
Great Eye Folly. Salthouse. Holt. Norfolk

... I would like to live here for ever – the owners come back at Easter – but that no one could do, for in five years time the sea will have eaten it. The young man who came out from Holt yesterday to bring another cylinder of gas for the cooking-stove said to me, talking of the rate at which the sea is advancing, that his father could remember loads of corn being drawn inland over the bridge. What bridge? – said I. *I* can remember the bridge, said he. It was there. And he pointed to where our track runs out on the shingle, and the high water mark ribbon of seaweed is.

At the other end of the track is the coast road, and the village of Salthouse, where every one is most humanely solicitous to make our flesh creep. It was unaccountably delightful to be told that I need not worry at all until I saw the cattle being taken off the marsh (there has been nothing on the marsh but geese for the last two days), and to be told by the grocer about underground passages between the pillbox on the beach, which the sea has already undermined, and the pillbox that is fastened to the side of the house, and how, if I go and listen at high tide – but I have, and not an underground gurgle did I hear, so I'm afraid it is the usual monkish underground passage story, but brought a little up to date.

Another remainder of when this was a fortified coastal point is a tight little brick hut, with a door lettered: Bomb Disposal. Private. I like the English moderation of this. The door is fastened, but the cat goes in by a crack in the threshold – and knowing how bombs get left about and over-looked I was rather nervous at first. He is the happiest cat in the British Isles – three pill-boxes, and a whole system of trenches to play in, and the spindrift to chase and the sea-tangle to explore.

To MARCHETTE CHUTE 16:xi:1950
Great Eye Folly. Salthouse. Holt. Norfolk.

... To the seaward we see gulls, and sometimes seals and porpoises; to the landward, there is a heron that lives in the marsh, and a kingfisher, and three horses, out for a tonic bite of pré-salé, I suppose; and in the mornings there is the post-girl, coming on a windblown bicycle. That, really, is all, except for sea and sky, and a long sharp-edged pebble beach, where we go out at low tide to see what may have been cast up for us. The flotsam etc is very odd, one would think that people on this north sea did nothing but eat coconuts and brush their teeth.

To PAUL NORDOFF 31:xii:1950
Great Eye Folly. Salthouse. Holt. Norfolk.

. . . We have been snow-bound and ice-bound for days at a time. It has been strange to look across the marsh, and see the chimneys in the village with slow twirls of frost-bound smoke, and sometimes a lorry or a reeling bicyclist inching along the icy coast road. A devoted baker brought us bread twice a week; we had our woodpile, and the sea kept on adding to it with driftwood; once, when all the water froze, we melted snow (it took hours, and was dark grey when we'd got it, and precious little in comparison with the billows of snow it started as) ... I have not seen Valentine so happy nor so much herself for years, and all her beauty has come back to her, and she walks about like a solitary sea nymph ... a sea nymph who can split logs with an axe and manage a most capricious petrol pump, and cut up large frozen fish with a cleaver.

It was a brilliant idea to come here. It has avoided all the small regretful uneasy niggling ghosts that were still sitting about in our house in Dorset, sights from windows that suddenly present you with how you were feeling when you saw them on such and such a day, latent remarks in the familiar noise of a door shutting or a chair creaking.

To WILLIAM MAXWELL 17:iii:1951
　　　　Great Eye Folly. Salthouse. Holt. Norfolk.

A magnificent ham arrived, and I should have written before to say how wonderful it looked against a background of grey sea; but I hoped to combine the letter with another story, and have been hanging on to that hope. It is all done except for one sleeve, like the nettle-shirt in Hans Christian – but then a lot of noisy things began happening, and now we are packing to go home, so I shall have to put it off until I am unpacked and in my right mind again.

One of the things that happened was that we nearly became an island. There was a wonderful concatenation of new moon and northeasterly gale and telephone conversations with the coastguards at Cley ... the coast-guards asked me, 'What's it like down your way,' and I was proudly enabled to reply, 'About two hours ahead of its usual tide-mark, and coming in very full now.' All this was very much as I liked it, and the sea was lovely to see, I have never seen anything enjoying itself more. But the car is all the car we shall ever have, and it became obvious that we could not keep it dry-foot much longer unless the wind shifted, and when the coastguard finally and rather obscurely remarked, 'Well, I should say that prevention is better than cure,' we made a hasty dusky get-away, with the dog, the cat, and a carcass of chicken – for I was determined not to waste the goodness in its bones; and as the wind bowled us along the causeway we saw the spray jumping up over the shingle ridge like hounds, and the water just beginning to lap across.

We went inland to friends, and I made chicken soup that same night. (The ham? It was in my bedroom, I knew the sea wouldn't get at it there); and when we came back two days later, some morose waves were mumbling away at a completely re-shaped beach, with a lot of gaunt remains of tank traps unburied, and looking like some sort of mineral nettles. You could tell that man had been there.

We leave on Monday; and today I have been going round tearing myself away from fishmongers and greengrocers and bakers, and Mr Morris the saddler. It is very painful for me to leave them because they like me so much. I am much more of a social success in East Anglia than in Wessex, and I don't look forward to being just that peculiar Miss Warner again, after being loved and laurelled all the way down Holt High Street, and knowing the Christian names of every one's cat.

WORLD WITHIN WORLD
Stephen Spender
(from *World Within World*, 1953)

We lived at Sheringham in Norfolk, where we had a house at the extreme edge of the town on the cliffs and adjoining fields. My childhood was the nature I remember: the thickness of the grass in the pasture fields, amongst whose roots were to be found heartsease (the small pansies which are the colour of the iris in a golden eye), speedwell of a blue as intense as a bead of sky. There were scabious and cornflower and waving grasses and bracken which came as high as my shoulders.

Sometimes, stuck as though glued to the stem of a flower, just below the cup of the petals, there was a chalk blue butterfly – milky blue its widespread wings; and pale russet chalky colour the short under-wings, with small copper rings and spots as though stamped on to them by a minute hammer. In the sun the butterflies expanded and then shut close their wings with the exact movement of a hinge. When the hinge was shut the closed wings were of a knife-blade thickness, so that you could not have split them with the edge of a razor.

In the garden I would lose myself in a forest of hollyhocks. The scent of a rose was a whole world, as though when I buried my nose in the petals the day was instantly canopied with a red sky.

Near Sheringham there were woods and the common, covered with gorse and heather. In the woods at spring there were the pale damp primroses with their scent of sublimated mould and a buttery thickness which one could almost taste. Then in summer there was the heather, brittle flowers like tiny purple beads on gnarled charcoal stems, flooding over the burnt-looking soil, on which bees descended in thousands to lift away the honey. Beyond the heather, near blackberry hedges, the gorse lay like gold armour, or like fleece of fire all round me, on bushes of spiky green thorns.

At evening, floating above the flat Norfolk landscape, there appeared range upon range of mountains with gulfs and valleys between high peaks, which stayed motionless, sculptured on the sky out of clouds. Sometimes, also, at midday, in the sky whose blue was as solid and opaque as the flushed green of a field of young corn, perfect white pictures would appear, as on a screen. 'Look, a milk jug, a white milk jug. It is exactly like a milk jug,' I would cry. 'No, silly,' my sister would say. 'It's a cat, a white cat, can't you see?'

In autumn and winter the prevailing winds, which caused the branches of the stunted hedges to bend all in one direction, blew across the cliff-edge fields between Sheringham and East Runton. One day the wind was so strong that I could lean against it like an invisible door in a wall of air, it would yield slightly if I pushed it, and then spring back against me. Then I started singing into the wind. Then I stopped singing, and I heard a very pure sound of choral voices answering me out of the blowing sky. It was the angels.

My father would take my sister and me to Miss Harcourt's school at East Runton. On the way he would tell us stories. There was the story of the Rubber Man who could climb any building and stretch his neck to see over any wall. This I liked even more than the ones about the parrot my father owned when he was a boy.

My mother, a plaid rug over her knees, lay on a chaise-longue, perpetually grieving over I know not what. Sometimes my eldest brother, Michael, used to go out shooting rabbits with my father. I never remember a time when Michael didn't lead a life quite separate from the rest of us, conspiring with our parents that he should not be regarded as a child.

At Miss Harcourt's there was a girl called Penelope, with whom, at the age of seven, I was in love. There was also a boy called Forbes, with whom I used to fight. Forbes had black wiry hair and flashing black eyes behind his steel-rimmed spectacles. One day, when we were rolling over one another on the ground, he got into a passionate rage of the kind known only to a small child, when his mind becomes a scale in which he measures the whole of his strength against the whole of his weakness. The will of Forbes was breaking against my body as though against a gate. Suddenly afraid, I lay on top of him and held him very closely in my arms, and at that moment I experienced a sensation like the taste of a strong sweet honey, but not upon my tongue, and spreading wave upon wave, throughout my whole body.

Sometimes, when I sat indoors in the kindergarten on a very fine day, I felt as though a wall had been raised between me and nature to which I belonged. I had a sensation of the garden, which I could just see through a window, twisted through with bird song as with forking flame, and of the limbs of trees running like veins through the sky, which poured down on earth in an enormous cataract of blue light.

Then, after the end of the class, I would run into the garden to a place where there was a pond, and, lying on the ground beside it, stare down into that strange life in rust-coloured water where stagnating processes had furred its concrete sides, and even the grass leaves of motionless subaqueous weeds. I soon observed that activity which as little disturbed the gelatinous stillness of the pond as a fly or a leaf fossilized thousands of years ago disturbs the amber in which it is enclosed. Newts moved along the pond-floor, and little water boatmen with their tiny jerking oars cut their courses up and down and across, through the water, as sharp as needles, and straight as ruled lines. Slow beetles stirred, and the snails, clinging to the water plants with their mouths, moved a few centimetres up a stalk like a sheep nibbling its way to another pasturage.

The life of the pond was like a theatre whose surface was the front of the stage; and peering down upon this stage I saw naked dramas, glutinous loves, voracious murders, incredibly fertile births, taking place in the utter stillness of unnatural light. ...

CROMER CRUSTACEANS
Ronald Blythe
(from *Going To Meet George*, 1999)

'Going to the edge' – this was how we inlanders used to think of a journey to the coast. Its soaring, confident semi-circle on the map gave East Anglia what looked like a good sound cranium. Even when evidence to the contrary piled up during walks in bitter gales, or in surprisingly burning heat, to prove that our edge wasn't sound at all.

Breached by the North Sea by the day, such softly eroding cliffs were inclined to convey romance rather than anxiety The manner in which over the years houses, towers – everything – ultimately fell off the edge had long been part of our philosophisings regarding transience and human endeavour, a notion which gained in piquancy when a churchyard full of longshoremen and their families dribbled into the waves. Although threatened communities moved back a few yards from this land-hungry sea, there had never been an actual abandonment of the edge – and for obvious reasons. It was, as well as destructive, an eternal provider. It gave so much that those who lived on it allowed for its grabbing and taking appetites. Not that there was any way of stopping them, just as there was no way of diminishing the fish. What the edge had done throughout its human occupation was to acknowledge a tendency to crumble but never that it must become a desolation. Nor even where it petered out in the Wash marshes and failed to draw a line between land and water, had there ever been a giving up of territory to the birds.

But now unprecedented underminings of our watery stoicism have changed all this. The first had nothing to do with coastal erosion and everything to do with the disappearance of the herring. Just imagine if some snatch-all method of arable farming had brought the timeless cycle of the corn harvests to a stop – this is the only way in which the previously unthinkable halting of the North Sea's 'silver harvest' of herring can be felt with all of its traumatic force. And not only along our edge but from Scotland to Cornwall.

I am wandering through the paralysed ports of Norfolk and Suffolk during early blustery autumn. The time when the shoals would appear with the certainty of the season itself. There then being no way of catching more than millions, millions more swam on to multiplicity. Then came the hideous international efficiency which landed the lot, the close-mesh trawling, the suction pipes and the purseseine nets which scraped and hoovered up every mite of this swimming harvest, leaving our sea like an aborted womb. Seated in Henry 'Shrimp' Davies's hut on Cromer sands the two of us worry away at this calamity. 'Shrimp' because of the tiny fisher-boy that he was. He shakes his old head at the black miracle which is the obliteration of a fish which only a few years ago was believed to be only a fractionally less numerous than the grains of sand themselves. It is packing-up time on the front when the holiday-making ceases and the town's own leisure begins. Whether end of season or out of season it is hard to find words which adequately describe tides, winds, shutters and stacked chairs. The latter are all Shrimp's. He is Cromer's chair king. Closed down too as any winter pier are the great herring fisheries from Arbroath to St.Ives.

Shrimp meditates. 'You can't believe the industry out there was in the herring trade! A thousand boats out of Yarmouth, a thousand out of Lowestoft. And all the back-up folk – all gone, all gone. And this because of the bloody over-fishing, and scarce one to breed and come by again! You've heard of seed-corn, perhaps? Coming from where you do you would. Well, think about it. Think about thoughtlessness – or sheer bloody greed more like! They did it to the mackerel, they did it to the sprats, and they'll do it to every living thing – you'll see! Yes, once thousands and thousands of us fishing and making boats and boxes and baskets, and the harbour's a forest of masts, and the herring coming by for ever.'

A single steam-drifter provided a living for upward a hundred workers, they said. Now, should the herrings be tempted or nursed back in their old multitude? Will we eat them as we once did, or will our pets? A folk-connection between this particular sea-food and hard times tends to dismiss their deliciousness and put them rather low on the shopping-list – though never on mine, where they remain a treat. Long ago, making do in a little house on the shingle, writing stories and poems, and practising acute economies, I would crunch along the stones in the early morning and buy a shilling's worth from a boat, and receive as many as two hands could manage, slippery and iridescent breakfasts for the week. *Clupea harengus* whose bone-pattern inspired our brickwork. Will the ancient Fish-churches straddling the edge of East Anglia be the last things to declare the herring's greatness – just

169

as the Wool-churches of the interior go on telling us that sheep once made millionaires too? Let us also remember those Great Yarmouth benefactors, Mr. Bishop the inventor of the bloater and Mr. Woodger the creator of the kipper. Humble glories.

Shrimp, like every old fisherman-cum-lifeboatman, is a mixture of free talk and impenetrable reserve. He is poised, playful and unhurried, having ascended the throne of one of the country's best known coastal families. From the time they emigrated from Wales in the 1820s, the Davieses, Cromer's crab fishery and the town's celebrated lifeboat history have been all one. Since 1872 to the present the family has doubled as local fishermen with an oar, so to speak, in the holiday trade, and as heroes. Had there been a time when Shrimp had fancied another sea? His light-ruined eyes look back on an ad about adventurous boys setting out to fish tuna off Australia. And he would have gone with other Cromer lads, except for that shout from his father. 'Oh no you won't! You'll stay here where you bloody belong!' And he'd stayed, to become coxswain of the *Henry Blogg* lifeboat in 1948 and the inheritor of deckchairs and beach huts. He said that the young no longer hire either. Just strip off on the sand. It was his grandfather, lifeboat coxswain during the 1890s, who had invested in the great cumbrous bathing machines from which Shrimp's daringly flimsy box-tents had descended. These were actually a Davies invention and their bleached colours set against the clarity of the East Beach with its striped bodies caught the palette of Wilson Steer. It struck me that Shrimp and the discreet bathing business were not unhappy to be seeing each other out. The trade had made him an expert in packing-up. He ran a huge hand over a sagging chair. 'Mind you, their frames must be as old as mine!' Like everything else, like muttering, 'In the name of the Lord' every time you cast your net, modern indifference to ritual tends to thin both the splendours and the absurdities of life.

A splendour. 'The Empress Elizabeth of Austria was a sick lady who came to Cromer for the air, you know. They all did then. She changed in grandfather's big old horse-drawn machine and when she came out, there he'd be, trim in his snow-white ducks and marking a special spot for her Majesty to swim around. To keep her safe, you know'

For the Davies family the shoreline is written all over with myriad fantasies and mundane ventures which the sea muddles. One day it is harvesting crabs from the rocks, the next souls from the wrecks, both activities becoming somehow natural concomitants of each other. And so it has been with all the hereditary masters of this capricious circumflex of ocean as it gnaws its way into the Gaps. The Gaps are where, from Lincolnshire to Essex, the North Sea thrusts in. At Cromer the lifeboat lives just behind the Pavilion Theatre, and the thought that the stage curtains and the sea doors are only a few yards away from each other is both exciting and sobering. Small boys stare through knotholes at the churning tide. Davies boys had their first trip in the lifeboat long before they were seventeen – the permitted age. And all were seasick. Being seasick is thought neither a weakness nor a matter of other people's comment by fishermen and sailors. When you grew up you learnt how to be totally sick at the beginning of a run but not to feel ill afterwards. It was an art. 'Once I was cox'n I was never seasick,' grinned Shrimp, trusting that I was getting the drift of this. Like the current lifeboat, the *Ruby and Arthur Reed II*, he doubles as a holiday attraction and a challenger of the North Sea's claim to gorge on men and ships at will. He shares with Cromer a dated, bastioned, don't-think-you-will-ever-wash-me-away quality.

Frenchified once-posh hotels straddle the cliff-top and just beyond them can be seen the grand medieval church. The town has got off lightly where the developers are concerned and hasn't had its heart torn out to make space for shopping malls. It retains its hugger-mugger lanes and courts, its flinty walls and orange pantiles, and hasn't given way to very much since its florid Edwardian summer. But nobody stays in a hotel or a boarding-house for a week any more, nobody parades along the parade. The nice train from Norwich decants just me and a couple of others, and not the seasonal multitude. It is the car and the tour bus, the one-night stayers who eat their way round Britain. A whole week in Cromer? Why not? It could amaze you. But it could be too melancholy, like a street when the band has gone by, although I

171

don't find it so. I find myself tapping into the old resourcefulness and searching for jet, amber and chalcedony along the beach, and sea-lavender, buckthorn, purslane, centaury, vetches and glasswort on the headlands, which blow your head off. I would be thinking about murder or love and the gulls would howl.

Fishermen-lifeboatmen never for one moment take their eyes off what is happening here. It is Richard Davies, Shrimp's nephew, who is now principal watcher in these long linked occupations. He is forty-two and has already been lifeboat cox'n for a decade. 'I was the youngest cox'n in the country when I took over from Shrimp and I'll stay cox'n until I'm fifty-five.' Shrimp, as everybody knows, had the daunting task of having to take over from the immortal Henry Blogg, the R.N.L.I.'s greatest hero, the taciturn little man who served in Cromer's lifeboats for 53 years, during which time he saved 873 lives. Mild yet awesome, Blogg's brilliant seamanship accompanied a kind of constant fearlessness. What to most men is a rush of courage to deal with a crisis was for Blogg his normal state of mind. The illegitimate child of a girl who married into the Davies family, he has become the Titan who towers over it, giving it unchallengeable identity He gave Shrimp both his Christian and nickname. 'What a bloody shrimp!' brave uncle Henry had said, looking at the new baby. Nicknames were once as necessary as proper names on this coast. A roll-call is like an extension to Shakespeare's mechanicals. Squinter, Snouts, Teapot, Pokey, Tweet – and Posh, of course. It seems shocking to fix them to the grave and noble faces on the old photographs. Nearly all the fishermen-lifeboatmen were Nonconformists and their sobriquets, from which there was no escape, are debased versions of the old Puritan nomenclature of East Anglia. 'A nickname is the heaviest stone that the devil can throw at a man', Hazlitt said – a verdict which would have puzzled Yarmouth 'Rednecks', Lowestoft 'Pea-bellies' and the 'Joskins' who were half fishermen-lifeboatmen and half farm labourers. The robustness of these old days still clings to Shrimp, but so too does a different kind of language, that which is learnt from reading very little, but this of the best.

172

Joseph Conrad was taught his first English lessons by men like the Davieses when he worked aboard the Lowestoft collier *Skimmer of the Sea*, and he liked to say that the North Sea was 'the schoolroom of my trade'. When Shrimp was a lad he read a poem about Cromer which he has been trying to find ever since. At last somebody has sent it to him. It is by Jean Ingelow and is much longer and entirely different to what he imagined. Shrimp had been waiting a lifetime for a ballad about a Cromer girl keeping vigil 'on the green downs' for a fisherman who will never return. Drowned. Now it appears that she is grieving for a boy who fell off a mountain. 'There's *The High Tide on the Coast of Lincolnshire*', I suggest, turning it up. But he wants the poem which was never written. Above him 'on the green downs' the bronze sou-westered bust of Uncle Henry Blogg, George Cross, with its long nose and gentle expression, stares down on the crab boats and the crotchety tractors which drag them over the shingle, Cox'n Blogg who neither smoked nor drank, but who knew how to be caustically witty in the local manner when he had a mind to.

Young Davieses have a way of guarding tradition without being old-fashioned. All the same, they are aware, though not self-consciously so, that history, occupation and duty have isolated them from what most people experience. They maintain distinctions of dress – always a jersey under a jacket for a wedding – and of speech. Richard Davies, putting down the crab-pot he is mending; 'Now I wouldn't say the 'last' pot – always the 'finishing one'. We never say last. And I'd never start a season on a Friday if there were a thousand crabs! Wouldn't move house on a Friday neither. Due to it being Crucifixion day, perhaps? When the alarm goes in the night Julie's job is to unlock the door for me to run through. She waits here and never runs with me to watch, though some do. You run from wherever you are – you run! I've tied the dog to a lamp-post – and run! Our gear is in the boat and we put it over what we are wearing, and on the way we discuss what we should do. Sometimes we sail far, once nearer to Holland than to Norfolk. Its bad when you find people who have brought tragedy on themselves. And you have to be tactful with idiots, who are very frightened.

Fortunately, we don't get a silly season like those sailing places. Ours is mostly commercial shipping. Things for us are never as safe as they look, There's still more than one lifeboat lost a year and how many crew, I don't know. We officially practise every six weeks but as we are fishermen we practise every day of our lives. The main danger would be turning over, our new boat is a self-righter, but when I started they were open boats. So there you were, out in the cockpit all the time. Our boat the *Ruby and Arthur Reed II* is one of the most sophisticated in the fleet. We always call her 'our' boat. The strongest things which you see on land which you see from the sea are church towers, although not Cromer tower. It hides. We are inbred to these tasks, to this life. They say the first lifeboatmen were the hovellers. When there was a wreck the best hoveller oarsmen would get there first and so they would get the goods. And the not so fast hovellers would get there second, and they got the crew! That's how we started, they say. They said the North Norfolk fishermen could row best and the Yarmouth fishermen could sail best. They'd race the lifeboats, and we'd have to row ours to the race first. Thirty mile. I'd say before my time!'

No one could ever have imagined that the mighty herring fleets would be annihilated and that the little crabbers would not only survive but flourish. Although the Cromer crab-boats have shrunk from fifty to fifteen, seven of which are owned by the Davieses, their catch is still in great demand. It was the Davieses' foresightedness which preserved the crabs on their rocky ledge, and it was they and their neighbours who got Parliament to make a law which forbade the taking of crabs which were less than four and half inches across, and lobsters under eight inches. These crab-fishing grounds are about three miles off-shore and stretch from Cley to Mundesley, and they are fished from April to September by two men and some two hundred crab-pots per boat. The pots hang together in strings or 'shanks', with an anchor and a buoy at each end. On a good day, or rather a good night, a boat can return to Cromer with a catch of eight hundred crabs. The crab-pots are baited with nice fresh fish, usually from Lowestoft, and are emptied just before day-break. Lobsters prefer bait which is a bit more stinko.

During the winter months crabbers will get a kind of catch-crop by sailing to Palling to set pots for whelks.

Richard Davies makes his own pots in the yard behind his fish shop in Garden Street. His strong hands fly through the scarlet mesh. The pots are very elegant and look as though they would double as bird cages. Each has a massive gridded bottom to steady it against the currents. In Richard and Julie's home between the net-yards and the fish-shop sepia faces from the past fill the picture-frames, as do stiff paintings of heavy wooden boats on fierce seas. Every lifeboatman-fisherman's house in Sheringham, Sidestrand, Caister, Overstrand, Yarmouth and Lowestoft contains a similar brave gallery. The photographs are the kind to which the viewer himself has to add colour. I add azure streaking into dark slate, oyster rifts in the sky, blue to eyes, red-brown to skin.

'Talking of eyes,' says Richard, 'I don't think much of the R.N.L.I. at this moment. It is all this fuss they are making about being colour-blind. Good lifeboatmen are having to go because they are colour-blind. Two stations from here, Wells to be exact, they've lost their second cox'n, the best man they have and the skipper of his own fishing boat, and why? Because they found out he was colour blind! And I had two young boys who were as good as any crew members in England, but now no more! Colour-blind. Supposing Henry Blogg had been tested and found colour-blind – then what? I think the Institution should leave the picking of crews to men like us – I do straight! Men may be bad on reds and greens, but what of that?'

Early the following morning I watched Shrimp rolling towards the East Beach, the only person in sight, his face 'coloured like a postcard' as Joseph Conrad described his shipmates, the North sea flashing in his big spectacles and his navy jersey rucked across his fat belly. Choppy waves ran to meet him.

EXILED IN MUNDESLEY

William Cowper

(from *The Letters of William Cowper Vol.2*, 1912)

[All] To Lady Hesketh, Cheltenham, Glocestershire.

Aug. 27, 1795.

Hopeless as ever, and chiefly to gratify myself by once more setting pen to paper, I address a very few lines to one whom it would be a comfort to me to gratify as much by sending them. The most forlorn of beings I tread a shore under the burthen of infinite despair, that I once trod all cheerfulness and joy. I view every vessel that approaches the coast with an eye of jealousy and fear, lest it arrive with a commission to seize me. But my insensibility, which you say is a mystery to you, because it seems incompatible with such fear, has the effect of courage, and enables me to go forth, as if on purpose to place myself in the way of danger. The cliff is here of a height that it is terrible to look down from; and yesterday evening, by moonlight, I passed sometimes within a foot of the edge of it, from which to have fallen would probably have been to be dashed in pieces. But though to have been dashed in pieces would perhaps have been best for me, I shrunk from the precipice, and am waiting to be dashed in pieces by other means. At two miles distance on the coast is a solitary pillar of rock, that the crumbling cliff has left at the high water-mark. I have visited it twice, and have found it an emblem of myself. Torn from my natural connexions, I stand alone and expect the storm that shall displace me. ...

W. C.

Mr. Johnson is again absent; gone to Mattishall, a circumstance to which I am indebted for an opportunity to answer your letter as soon

176

almost as I have received it. Were he present, I feel that I could not do it. – You say it gives you pleasure to hear from me, and I resolve to forget for a moment my conviction that it is impossible for me to give pleasure to any body. You have heard much from my lips that I am sure has given you none; if what comes from my pen be less unpalatable, none has therefore so strong a claim to it as yourself.

My walks on the sea-shore have been paid for by swelled and inflamed eyelids, and I now recollect that such was always the condition of mine in the same situation. A natural effect I suppose, at least upon eyelids so subject to disorder as mine, of the salt spray and cold winds, which on the coast are hardly ever less than violent. I now therefore abandon my favourite walk, and wander in lanes and under hedges. As heavy a price I have paid for a long journey, performed on foot to a place called Hazeborough. That day was indeed a day spent in walking. I was much averse to the journey, both on account of the distance and the uncertainty of what I should find there; but Mr. Johnson insisted. We set out accordingly, and I was almost ready to sink with fatigue long before we reached the place of our destination. The only inn was full of company; but my companion having an opportunity to borrow a lodging for an hour or two, he did so, and thither we retired. We learned on enquiry, that the place is eight miles distant from this, and though, by the help of a guide, we shortened it about a mile in our return, the length of the way occasioned me a fever, which I have had now these four days, and perhaps shall not be rid of in four more; perhaps never. Mr. J. and Samuel, after dinner, visited the light-house. A gratification which would have been none to me for several reasons, but especially because I found no need to add to the number of steps I had to take before I should find myself at home again. I learned however from them that it is a curious structure. The building is circular, but the stairs are not so, flight above flight, with a commodious landing at every twentieth stair, they ascend to the height of four stories; and there is a spacious and handsome apartment at every landing. The light is given by the patent lamp, of which there are two ranges: six lamps in the upper range, and five in the lower; both ranges, as you may suppose, at the top of the house. Each lamp has a broad silver reflector behind it. The present occupant was once commander of a large merchant-man, but, having chastised a boy of his crew with too much severity, was displaced and consequently ruined. He had, however, a friend in the Trinity-House, who, soon after this was built, asked him if he would accept the charge of it; and the cashiered captain, judging it better to be such a lamp-lighter than to starve, very readily and very wisely closed with the offer. He has only the trouble of scouring the silver plates every day, and of rising every night at twelve to trim the lamps, for which he has a competent salary, (Samuel forgets the amount of it,) and he and his family a pleasant and comfortable abode.

I have said as little of myself as I could, that my letter might be more worth the postage. My next will perhaps be less worth it, should any next ensue; for I meet with little variety, and shall not be very willing to travel fifteen miles on foot again, to find it. I have seen no fish since I came here, except a dead sprat upon the sands, and one piece of cod, from Norwich, too stale to be eaten. — Adieu.

W. C.

Sept. 26, 1795.

... I have been tossed like a ball into a far country, from which there is no rebound for me. There indeed I lived a life of infinite despair, and such is my life in Norfolk. Such indeed it would be in any given spot upon the face of the globe; but to have passed the little time that remained to me there, was the desire of my heart. My heart's desire however has been always frustrated in every thing that it ever settled on, and by means that have made my disappointments inevitable. When I left Weston I despaired of reaching Norfolk, and now that I have reached Norfolk, I am equally hopeless of ever reaching Weston more. What a lot is mine! ...

W. C.

Oct. 23, 1798.

DEAR COUSIN,

... In this country, if there are not mountains, there are hills; if not broad and deep rivers, yet such as are sufficient to embellish a prospect; and an object still more magnificent than any river, the ocean itself, is almost immediately under the window. Why is scenery like this, I had almost said, why is the very scene, which many years since I could not contemplate without rapture, now become, at the best, an insipid wilderness to me? It neighbours nearly, and as nearly resembles the scenery of Catfield; but with what different perceptions does it present me! The reason is obvious. My state of mind is a medium through which the beauties of Paradise itself could not be communicated with any effect but a painful one. ...

—I remain as usual, dear cousin, yours,

WM. COWPER.

A HAPPISBURGH INTERLUDE

John Cowper Powys

(from *The Dorset Year,* 1998)

Sunday 25 November 1934

Had a splendid night sleeping in Blankets <u>very</u> <u>very</u> <u>warm</u> – 3 new blankets. Could hear the Sea but all was dark. Frances had met me at Walsham in an open car; it was very misty – not <u>dense</u> fog – but pretty foggy. ... It seemed very odd not passing through Norfolk scenery in the day. It seemed very unnatural not getting out at Thorpe Station at Norwich & not being met there by Aunt Dora. But I think Aunt Etta is better. Well Norwich is a place of Memory in my life. This morning I woke at 8.45 & walked to the Church [Happisburgh] before breakfast. Here I noted one of those great poetical massive flint church towers & a richly carved wooden screen at the choir & a Norman font. Knocked at the Post Office talked to Mr Easily a man with 3 children who could never leave his post as a postmaster for which he got 33/- weekly but he had to stay in all day. Bought a lot of cigarettes. After breakfast we talked for long. I went over to Mrs Gregg's house & lay on her couch. I went alone for a walk in the twilight along the sand of the sea – no shells – very little seaweed only pebbles here & there – nothing but sands extending as far as <u>Yarmouth</u> where Peggotty's family lived & where Steerforth was drowned. Again had a lovely warm night in blankets.

Monday 26 November
<u>Up</u> <u>at</u> <u>8.45</u>. Walked for half a mile along the Sands. Beautiful Sun the Tide was in. But I came to an old Black Boat where yesterday I had walked with Betty – she telling me of sad stories about children from the newspaper – coming home along the sands among seagulls & little white birds that <u>may</u> be Mother Carey's chickens she told me to write a story for her about children in sad adventures with wrecks and caves. So I began thinking of one with her called 'After the Wreck' about a boy called John & a girl called Josephine & a Baby called Mary & what they did when washed on to an island. How they found a goat & a kid & milked the goat and how they lit their fire. After breakfast today we all three went for a walk along the Sands and gathered driftwood for kindling. I liked well this job. We saw that same Boat called the 'Heart of Oak' that I saw when I walked with Betty. This morning I walked before Breakfast to this black massive boat & last night I walked & saw them launching it in the evening and it must have been a catch of fish in the night. They seem to stay out late fishing in this heavy boat – as heavy as any I have seen – far heavier than the usual Weymouth ones – suitable to the Norsemen of this coast. There are low mud-cliffs here about 20 feet or 30 feet high & further away there are Sand Dunes with long

grasses & Frances showed me how isolated pieces of grass by being blown in the wind made crescents round them in the sand & sometimes perfect circles. This morning I was scared of a barking dog that followed me. Here there are 2 dogs & 2 cats who have more liberty than I have ever seen given to animals. The dogs jump in and out of the windows of these little wooden houses & the cats jump up on everything there is. But scared of this stray dog I went back by the land & I saw no less than <u>Six Church Towers</u> including the one here. This is the sort of country familiar to my mother in her childhood. It is strange that it does not thrill me more than it does! It is Tennysonian country too! F. discoursed with passionate emotion on her mysterious philosophy. We went over in the evening and had tea in the 'Madonna's' bungalow next door. I recited poetry all the evening.

Tuesday 27 November

... Yesterday and today as I walked along these unending sands so easy to walk on I had many stoical thoughts and many thoughts of how to face various things that are difficult; & I noticed that the idea in my instinctive attitude that kept me going in *medias res* & *rebus in arduis* was not the 'Ichthian' Leap or the 'Panergic' Act about wh I make such an ado in my book but the idea of being a Skeleton walking between earth and sun. I did get such great satisfaction in thinking of or to say the truth in worshipping as gods the four elements for here on the sand & where there were no shells, little seaweed, nothing but sand, sea, sky, sun, you had nothing between yourself and these four elements. I tried to put every worrying thought out of my mind & concentrate as a walking skeleton – A <u>'Skeleton in Armour'</u> as Longfellow's verse says – on water, sand & air, & a sun so misted by fog that you could look straight at it. Last night I saw the Moon & the moon on the waves. These wooden little Bungalows are all a stones throw from the edge of the sea. It is bleak weird desolate forlorn country, with these huge flint church towers & high nave-roofs standing up out of the vast flat plain like erratic milestones arranged in a vast circle – few trees, bleak hedges and a great desolation of wasteland round these wooden bungalows. ...

181

Wednesday 28 November

Up at 9 had a long night in new Blankets. Walked to the Village to get the time – bought cigarettes for self & F. Had a pleasant breakfast with F. & Betty. Went across to chat with the Madonna before leaving. She told me of her early life & of her 25 years of teaching. And how she learnt Short hand. Drove into North Walsham alone with F. Had lunch in the 'Blue Tea Room'!!!!!!! Caught the 1.30 through train. Was very interested to look out of the window at the Thorpe suburb of Norwich where Uncle John Patteson & Aunt Elizabeth lived & where I recall quite well going. This Uncle John was curate to Rev. L.C.P. at Bradford Abbas or at Stalbridge & this was how the Powyses first met these Norfolk people. ... I was pleased to see a *Windmill* from the train window making me know I was in East Anglia. It is a wild desolate forlorn county this Norfolk of my distaff ancestors – Donnes and Pattesons & Johnsons – the clumps of reeds & rushes and of dark poplars & of fir trees & the spaces of marsh and dike & estuary (& mere) have a peculiar and romantic desolation so totally different from Wessex. ...

LOVE IN A COLD CLIMATE
Sylvia Townsend Warner
(from *I'll Stand By You*, 1998; *Letters*, 1982 and *Diaries*, 1994)

1931

While we lived in the houseboat on the river Thurne, hearing the slap of water and the windmill's creaking refrain leap its minor seventh and fall back, we agreed that we must postpone our return to Miss Green and spend the winter in Norfolk. Ruth [Valentine Ackland's mother] was proposing to give up her flat at St James's Court and settle economically at The Hill House [Winterton]. She would repine less,

Valentine said, if we were in the garage flat. By mid-October we were there, laying up a stock of wood against the winter. The landscape, stripped for winter, the skies tall as the horizons were wide, was as compelling as a chaconne: one never knew what variation of light would come next.

We were still engaged in learning more about each other, and she had Norfolk to teach me. I had never known a winter sea. I had never encountered the East Coast climate, nor a wind so strong that it blew me off my feet. All that rigging of fishermen's jerseys had prepared me for a stern climate but not for such a fickle one. After an easterly gale which raged for three days and wrecked a ship by driving it up the beach, we woke to a morning so calm, so blue, so mild, that we strolled out in dressing-gowns to walk on the plateau. A south-bound vessel was travelling smoothly through a halcyon sea. I said it was a boat by Shelley. Valentine, whose mind was more positive, fetched her binoculars. The Shelleyan vessel was lettered: *Huntley and Palmer.*

While we were still settling in a succession of women from the village arrived with presents of jam and pickles. I remarked on their kindness. 'We don't want all this jam,' she exclaimed. 'Come on! I'll take you down to the Three Mariners and display you.'

I remembered that Ruth, condoled with on my emergence as yet another of Valentine's loves, was reported to have said, 'Well, at any rate, she's a gentlewoman.' 'Miss Maaalie's latest,' I commented. 'Will you feel embarrassed?'

'Why?'

We sat in the snug. More and more people came in.

Winterton was like no village I had ever seen. It was a small closed community, violent and feuding, where everyone was related, and known by a nickname, like characters in the Icelandic Sagas. It had two public-houses, a church, a chapel, and a sacred stone which only the old men might sit on. During the summer half of the year old men and boys were the only males in the village; the men were away in the herring-fleet. In autumn they put in at Yarmouth, got their money, came home, saw the children born while they were away, begot more, bellowed sentimental hymns at the Fishermen's Thanks-giving Services, put fresh coats of tar on their seaward flint walls. The women, a six-month matriarchy, were as outspoken and upstanding as the men. 'Popularity' is a servile word. At Chaldon, Valentine was conditionally popular. At Winterton, she was unconditionally accepted. ...

The belief that she would inherit The Hill House, rule there and restore the old order derived its conviction from her resemblance to her father. 'Mr Ackland to the life,' said the village. 'Same way of walking. Same way of giving you a look.' He was consistently remembered. Only Ruth seemed to have forgotten him, taking a widow's licence to cut him down to her own size, ignore a formidable perfectionism, and implacable streak of melancholy. But she habitually falsified: it was her expedient of possessiveness. For the first week or so of our stay at Winterton Valentine's presence was pleasure and support to her. But possessiveness cannot accept; it cannot even strike a fair bargain; it has to confer. We lived on the end of a string, incessantly tweaked across to the house for small celebrations – shrimps for tea, a pheasant, some relative's birthday or death-day – or sunk in return hospitalities. The intention of being there so that Ruth should repine less was lost under demonstrations that Ruth was doing all in her power to keep us from repining.

We did not repine. We were together, Norfolk was wide, we were often blazingly happy; but we could not call our happiness our own. Valentine took time more seriously than I did. My casual consent to its wastage exasperated her; she would suddenly lose control and let fly at me. No comfort came of this. Her mechanism was too intricate to receive anything but damage by explosions.

At intervals as if it were something of great importance I hadn't been attending to, I would remember the sea.

'Let's go down to the beach.'

This time – we were nearing the end of our stay, and we both had colds in the head – it was a grey afternoon, stone cold and windless. The sea was so calm that the waves did not break. They travelled to the shore and died on it. During that first visit to Winterton, which now seemed a visit to some quite different place, I had told her she had mermaid blood. I had meant it lightly, a comment on her beauty and beguilingness. But there was more than that to mermaid blood, I thought, looking at the stern quiescence of the winter sea. She picked up a small, pure white, pebble, showed it to me, tossed it high in the air, caught it again.

'Sometimes I love you like that,' she said.

*   *   *

To PAUL NORDOFF 3:vii:1940

The Hill. Winterton. Norfolk

... This place is very beautiful, and you would love it. It is right on the coast. As I look out of the window I see on two sides nothing but pale sand-dunes and pale sea. Inland the country is flat as a chessboard, a thrifty sandy soil, patterned with pale corn and oats and barley, and broken with great stretches of inland water, called Broads. Windmills and church towers stand up all around. One can see for miles and miles, and everything is pale and severe. It is so flat that it might just as well be mountains. No boggy valleys or Walden Ponds.

The people have bony noses, and cunning grey eyes, and talk in snarling rasping voices, like foxes barking. They have obstinate upright characters and violent tempers, and are as proud as Lucifer, and very nice and easy to get on with, because thay are all as good as you are, and better.

To PAUL NORDOFF 13:viii:1940

Hill House. Winterton. Norfolk.

... Valentine and I have rented a very small cottage, built of flint, and exceedingly out of repair: which we shall furnish with a horse hair sofa, and a couple of seicento virgins, and a jampot or two. Where we expect to be very happy. The wooden virgins are mine. They seem rather unexpected, but they have been housed here because Frome Vauchurch is not the sort of house one can put seicento virgins into. In a cottage with no bath they will be perfectly at home.

(Don't worry, by the way, about addresses. This village is so small that the post-office always knows where one is, and distributes the letters accordingly. Meanwhile, *Winterton* Norfolk will do). ...

But it is called Beach Cottage. And we are in now. It is all very much according to plan except that the door was too narrow to admit the horsehair sofa. It is really a very well-contrived little house, and furnished like Mole End with *windfalls from aunts*, and providential last minute looting. Except for a teapot, and a bucket, we've scarcely had to buy anything.

Its name is a misnomer, for it is nowhere near the beach. It is at the low end of the village, where the street peters out into sand dunes, and where the village leaves its tins and broken bottles. The dunes we can look at, but can't walk on, as they are dotted with defensive landmines. One of these went up the other day, when a tired soldier accidentally stepped back on it. There was an enormous stately tree of smoke and sand that hung on the air, slowly dissolving; and presently another soldier came running from far away, stiffly holding at arm's length a boot with a piece of bloodied bone sticking from it. ...

*   *   *

Oct. 5th 1949 [At Warren Farm, Horsey, Norfolk.] After tea, thinking that she [Valentine] would want to write to Eliz [Wade White]: I walked alone along the familiar road to Waxham. It was too familiar to retrace, so I came back along the sands in the dusk watching the tide come up the shelving beach, throwing its cactus blossoms of spray between the sand-colour and the dim hyacinth-blue. When I came in she was pleased because she had begun to write on her Norfolk story again. For a little while I think she was really happy.

Oct. 6th In the morning we again walked on the beach, and brought back a great deal of drift-wood, and cut our toe-nails, on her theory that the sea would mollify them. After lunch we cleaned the car. Then Ruth came to tea – it went off better than I supposed it would. After she had gone we walked out on the fen, and watched an owl set out on its first dusk-flight. It flew low towards us, and right over our heads, so close that we could see its demure mild face and the sharp nose set in it, and the bright eyes; it was above us before it saw us, and wheeled off on a new tack. In the evening, late, we went out to look at the beach, and watched the subsidence of the waves running southward, the white feathering swallowing up the black smooth tunnel. She has a chill in her stomach. Sorrow comes over me like a mist, and I feel myself lost and fading, and at a touch or a word, the mist thins; but then it comes on again. This place is beautiful, and serene, and the air is mild and allaying; but with its evocations of Lavenham, and Winterton, and the time when she loved me as I still love her, and when I felt myself delighting her, it has also an effect of making me a ghost to myself. To feel myself delighting her . . . that is something I think I shall never feel again; and of all the things I grieve for, it is that I grieve for most.

Oct. 11th. After tea she set to copying more of the Norfolk story, and I was reading Michael Howe's Spring Song, when there was a clap of thunder, and a violent rain storm. Suddenly it cleared, I ran out to see if there were a rainbow – there were two, and everything drenched in brilliant low-shafted light, the moss on the thatch, the white ducks gobbling, and we counted seven churches on the horizon, and knew there was an eighth – Horsey hidden in its woodlands, Waxham, Palling, Happisburgh, Ingham, ? Hickling, Somerton, Winterton. And three windmills and two owls.

In the evening the wind blew, the driftwood fire crackled, and I remembered that she had spoken, under that rainbow, of asking for a first refusal of this house. But I remember too, her typewriter crackling before breakfast, and how she left it with a sigh as deep as the Pacific;

and it seems to me that this time the disease of Eliz: is working in her far more deeply than in 1939 ... .

Oct. 12th. And yet, in days between, small sprouts of hope begin to grow. A pollarded tree, so I read today, gives more timber than a straight one.[...] Pheasants were crying and complaining to each other, the sunset had dyed the brown reeds a dull dead rose colour, and she spoke of how we might suggest to Mrs Howlett that we should spend a winter here. I can think of nothing I would love better. This place has enchanted me, slowly, persuasively, as if with an affinity. And could she speak so unless she had it in her heart to remain? And then, seeing her so ill, and so turmoiled with letters and complications of compassion, I wonder if she can remain anywhere, if she can survive. And yet I put out this pollarded growth of hopes.

Oct. 16th. Alas – our last day in this endeared place. And in the morning we made our last expedition towards Waxham for wood; and in the afternoon it rained, and we looked at the annexe – and were personally pained to see that the sea-ward wall is damp – though Valentine says that one could always make out with a damp sitting-room; and in the evening we went up to the hills, and saw the loveliest of all the skies we have seen here – for the s.east was full of clouds, and they were all in relief patterns of pale violet against deep violet, above a dull flint-blue sea: or was it obsidian? a chipped-stone sort of colour, anyway, nothing in the likeness of flower or feather; and on the shore there was a Craske group of men fishing. But the colour of the clouds was such as I have never seen before, and untinged by any whiff of pink or gold – a pure solemn purple.

BOARDING HOUSE BLUES

George Gissing

(from *The Private Papers of Henry Ryecroft*, 1905)

Frid. July 19th. Of course a rainy morning. Left home at 8, and caught the 10.15 to Yarmouth at L'pool St. Reached Gorleston at 2.30 (1 Sunrise Terrace, Mrs. Bunn; two rooms 30/-). Sunny evening, but high wind.

Sat. July 20th. Day of wild wind and rain. Of course the first bad day for many weeks. A little better in afternoon. Boy dug on the sands a little. – Reading [Hermann] Sudermann's 'Es War' [*The Undying Past*, 1894].

Tues. July 23rd. The first fine day. But the sky hung with clouds, and thunder-shower at dinner-time. In the afternoon I walked alone to Burgh Castle, about four miles. The ruins stand amid corn-fields; wheat is growing in the space they enclose; and only by a narrow path on either side can they be walked round. At the SW. corner a huge mass has broken away, and leans threateningly. They are on high ground, overlooking the Yare at its junction with Breydon Water; view over wide plain, with windmills and sails of boats. Very lonely and quiet. – The church of Burgh (pronounce Borough) has a *round* tower, of flints – perhaps taken from the Roman walls. – Home to tea, rather tired.

Sat. July 27th. Boy feverish all night. In morning called in Dr Bately, of High St., who made light of the case. Weather terribly hot. Kept boy in bed all day. Great discomfort here in lodgings; wretched cooking. Arranged to leave at end of second week.

Mon. July 29th. A few bright intervals, but on the whole clouded and gloomy. Letter from Alg, in which he speaks persistently of his hope to earn £150 a year by literature, poor lad! – Sent three stories to Shorter. – E. spent some hours in Yarmouth trying to find lodgings, as this place is intolerable. She got two rooms at last, near the pier, for

189

27/-: an attic and a basement sitting-room. A terrible holiday, this! The woman Mrs. Bunn outrageously coarse and brutal.

Tues. July 30th. Weather fine, but a day of horrors. Arranged to leave the house after dinner. Paid the bill (rent up to next Friday, according to agreement with Mrs Bunn,) and E. and the boy left, whilst I waited for arrival of parcels delivery cart to take the luggage. Presently Mrs Bunn enters room, and begins to be abusive. I walked out; whereupon she locked the door, and refused to allow luggage to leave until I had paid whole of rent for three weeks. I sought a policeman, who could only advise me to see the inspector. Meanwhile F. and the boy returned to see the cause of my delay. Wrangling between E. and Mrs Bunn, who at length refused us admission to the rooms, which we had paid for till next Friday! I then discovered that, on the plea of not being able to write (a lie) she had given E. no receipted bill.

We had to walk about from 3 to 5.45, till we could see the inspector at the police-station. A horrible time; spent part of it in the public reading-room, next door to Police. Poor little chap ate buns there. At 6.45 [sic] found Mr and Mrs Bunn with the inspector, and a tragi-ludicrous scene ensued. The Bunns violently insulting, of course damaging their case. Bunn, whom I had so innocently taken for a plain, honest seaman, turned out rampant rogue and blackguard. Asked me why I had spied after him this morning to see that he was going to be away from home. On my answering that I didn't know but what he was at home all day, he roared 'You're a liar!' – In the end, the inspector gave the case against the Bunns, and advised them to surrender luggage at once. I thereupon demanded safe-conduct of policemen, in whose company I got a fly, and drove up to the house with constable on the box. – F. and the boy walking slowly the while towards Yarmouth, to be picked up afterwards.

At the house an exhibition of ruffiandom. As we drove up to the front door, Bunn comes out shouting: 'Go to the back! We don't want tramps here'. – (It has since occurred to me that he alluded to my walk to Burgh Castle. The fellow thought I *walked* to save money!) Amid jeers and brutal insults, we got luggage onto the cab, and so off, heaven be thanked. Of course I spoke not a syllable. In my flurry, I even forgot to demand the receipt of payments, but I dare say that doesn't matter.

The constable tells me that these Bunns are Salvation Army people, and *therefore* worthless.

I picked up E. and the poor boy, and we reached our Yarmouth lodging about 6.30. A great contrast; decent woman, and nice house, though no view, and might be in Brixton. Address: 15 Paget Road, near the Pier. The landlady, Mrs Squire, has made arrangement by which we have a ground-floor bedroom, and, until Saturday, a ground-floor front sitting-room, generally occupied by a curate – one Frank Eardley, I find.

Wed. July 31st. Bad night in consequence of fleas, but this we felt to be a trifle after recent troubles. Very fine day. All went by the 'Yarmouth Belle' up the river to Norwich, starting at 9.30, and getting to Foundry Bridge about 1.30. For last half hour, boy slept on my lap. Had dinner at restaurant in London Street, then to the Cathedral. Unfortunately, no service till 5, which was too late. Walked to the top of the Castle Hill, and just entered the Museum, where boy was much interested in a stuffed group of a great snake crushing a tiger. Back by train to tea. – Have sent advt for new servant to Hetheringtons.

Wed. Aug. 7th. The sky still burdened with great gloomy clouds, frequently breaking into showers; cold and windy. Afternoon warmer and brighter. Went by the 2.40 to Ormesby, walked back to Caister, and thence home again by train. Caister a rather squalid village, but pleasant shore.

Thurs. Aug. 8th. The first very fine day since we left home. I went alone to Cromer, and spent a few hours there. Quick building going on, and the place crammed with people. Can see how beautiful it must once have been. Letter from Miss Collet and Alg.

Frid. Aug. 9th. Very fine. Morning on pier, afternoon to Caister. Fine sands here, and I decided it shall be our place for a holiday next year.

Mon. Aug. 12th. Fine, but high wind, and thunder in distance. All spent the day at Reedham, a very delightful place. Had dinner (bacon and eggs) at the Station Hotel. Long talk with decent old man who owns a cottage and ground on the shore of the river; he lets lodgings and had, he told us, an artist family named Luker from Notting Hill. A pleasant house to live in, if cooking were decent. The boy enjoyed himself, but on return was rather overtired.

Tues. Aug. 13th. Left Yarmouth by the 8am., and reached L'pool St. at 11.30. Pouring rain.

A SEASIDE TOWN IN WINTER (1989)
Richard Mabey
(from *Country Matters: Selected Writings 1974-99*, 2000)

On a glum winter's afternoon on Great Yarmouth's vast and gusty prom, the red kiosk outside the old Empire Theatre looks like an oasis. 'Take the Health Ray', it urges, 'Check Your Vitality and Heartbeat', be reassured about 'How Old You Look'. No such luck. Like almost every other building on the front, the Health Ray is battened down against the weather, a tantalising Aladdin's cave whose inscrutable rejuvenations must stay under wraps until next spring. Meanwhile you stand out in the east wind, surrounded by empty amusement arcades and knowing all too well how old you look.

When Yarmouth first became a resort two centuries ago, people came principally for their health, to dose themselves with fashionably therapeutic sea water and bracing east winds, and the season stretched to all but the coldest months. Nowadays, the front in winter is less of a tonic. There are no cheering noggins to be had at Captain Flint's Bar, no rounds of novelty golf, not even one last rousing chorus of 'Agadoo' from Black Lace at the Marina Centre. It is a bleak prospect, and it would be verging on the perverse to be a willing off-season visitor to a place so thoroughly devoted to summer fun were it not for the fact that, with the illuminations switched off and the trippers gone, Yarmouth's other business with the sea starts to edge out of the shadows.

I have long been fascinated by shorelines, and the various spells they seem to cast; but the transmutation of this tract of melancholy marshland and fisheries into eastern England's favourite kiss-me-quick resort is surely one of their more remarkable stories.

I arrived in the town on a late November morning, by the road that runs along the front. Yarmouth's prom is one of seaside Britain's famous 'Golden Miles', and is so unnervingly straight and wide that, with barely another soul in sight, I felt in danger of losing my sense of direction. In a brief stab of panic I even wondered whether the whole town had shut down completely. But it is nothing so drastic. For six months, Yarmouth simply turns its back on the beach and, like a migrating salmon, retreats to home base. Old Yarmouth, seafaring rather than seasiding, lies about half a mile inland, clustered around the long harbour that has been formed from the estuaries of the rivers Yare, Bure and Waveney. It has always been a major port, gateway to the Norfolk Broads and once the foremost shipping town in Britain. Less than twenty years ago it was home to a huge herring fleet, and the quay was hectic with packing stations and market stalls. Now the herring is almost fished out, and Yarmouth has become a major European cargo terminal, not quite so amenable to those who simply wish to gaze at boats.

There is little visible evidence of the old fishing port. Yarmouth suffered terrible damage in both world wars, and most of the buildings are no more than thirty years old. It was one of the first towns to be hit during the Zeppelin raid of 1915, as the German airships made their way along the east coast, bound for Sandringham and, they thought, the King. During 1941, Yarmouth was on the receiving end of some of the most severe bombing of any small town in Britain, and by mid-November had been hit in seventy-two separate raids. What was left was bulldozed during the 1960s. Now, as you wander among the neon-fronted cocktail bars and chip shops, you come across little marooned remnants: a Customs house; an eighteenth-century Fishermen's Hospital; a score of chapels and meeting houses that are a testament to East Anglia's Non-conformist history. The fate of the town's spectacular medieval wall perfectly symbolises the changes. Built in 1261 to defend what was already a very wealthy town against land attack (there were iron chains strung out over the river to keep out hostile shipping), it has now become, rather like a redundant but favourite fence, something to lean other things against.

The wind will eventually drive you into Yarmouth's splendid little museums, and you will be able to make some sense of its various rises and falls as working town and resort. It began as nothing more than a scattering of huts on a bank of silt and sand which began to form across the Yare-mouth about a thousand years ago. Migratory fishermen from the Kent coast used to camp there during the herring season. The bank, as one contemporary historian put it, 'waxed in height and greatness'; the herring catch waxed, too, and Yarmouth grew into a large and prosperous mercantile centre.

A beautifully painted topographical map of 1570 shows housing development following the contours of the receding high-water mark. Another, two centuries later, notes a population of twelve thousand and shows the unique labyrinth of narrow alleys known as 'rows' which were built at right angles to the river – and, presumably, to the prevailing wind. A few survived the Blitz, and the Tolhouse museum has one of the slender, one-seat pony carts which were used for transport down them. All this happened at the harbour. The seafront was ignored until the fashion for seaside holidaying began around 1750. Within thirty years the first theatres and bowling greens had arrived, as well as a pastiche of the harbourside 'troll carts', in the form of a special lightweight carriage, drawn by two men, in which holidaying ladies were transported between the entertainment spots and the town. One of the earliest souvenirs has also found its way into the Tolhouse, a tiny labelled bag of the very stuff that has made Great Yarmouth famous:

> *From Yarmouth, where the silv'ry sands*
> *Stretch as far as eye can reach*
> *Accept this little book of views*
> *And SAMPLE OF THE BEACH.*

Yarmouth's sands are still a marvel, even under a dull winter sky, and I was amazed that I virtually had them to myself when I went for a stroll along them one morning. I then went to explore another patch of the littoral, the estuary and marshes from which, so to speak, Yarmouth was deposited. The curious thing about the landward side of the town is that it has a beach of a kind too, a transitional area of jumbled paddocks and allotment shacks before the creeks and waterscapes of the flood-plain begin. Breydon Water is virtually a tidal lake, and was formed after the estuary was sealed off by the sand-bar. It is surrounded by Halvergate marshes, an immense expanse of water meadows and grazing marshes, claimed out of the wetlands by centuries of drainage.

It looked, a few years back, as if drainage would go one stage further, and the whole area might be given over to cereals. But it has now been given a considerable degree of protection, and in winter is a paradise for wetland birds. That afternoon the first flocks of Scandinavian fieldfares were clacking from meadow to meadow. Flocks of golden plover flashed briefly in the distance. A heron flapped heavily in front of a derelict windmill.

Many of these birds fly to Breydon Water to roost, and later, in a brief glow of low sunshine, the low-tide mud was a vista of tens of thousands of gulls, dunlin and clamouring redshank, and an almost continuous stream of lapwing and curlew flying in from their feeding grounds on the nearby fields.

Back in the town that evening, after some while wandering the almost empty streets, I found what seemed to be Yarmouth's only fish restaurant, in a converted pub down among the quayside warehouses. Mr Kikis' whitebait and turbot, caught locally that day, were life-savers, the purest taste of the sea I had in all my stay. But they are getting hard to come by, Mr Kikis told me. Over-fishing and pollution (the Sandoz mercury trail had just about reached the Norfolk coast that day, I reckoned) had drastically reduced the catch; and what fish was available from the nearest port, Lowestoft, mostly went up to London to satisfy the huge new demand. But he had the adopted local son's pride in his own locality: 'The mange-touts are from Kenya, the potatoes from Italy, but the fish is *home grown!*'

There is talk in Yarmouth of a massive new development, a bunded deep-water haven stretching out from the harbour mouth. If it goes ahead, it will be the first time that the earnest commercial world at the town's heart has pushed so conspicuously into the pleasure zone. You will be able to see it from your deck-chair, and through the coin-operated binoculars on the piers. But it might be no bad thing. When Dickens set *David Copperfield* up here, it was the drama of shipping out at sea that brought the town's people down to the front in winter. One would earnestly pray for no more storms of the kind he described. But I have a feeling that the harbour development, and its dramatic views of those who have their business on great waters, might give Yarmouth's now deserted Winter Gardens a new life and a real meaning.

A BACKWARD GLANCE

Norfolk Backwaters

THE FORNCETT LETTERS

Dorothy Wordsworth

(from *Letters of Dorothy and William Wordsworth, Vol.1*, 1999)

7th December 1788

My dearest Jane [Pollard],

... we were anxious to see our destined abode. At our entrance we saw
Norwich to great advantage, as they were celebrating the revolution
and the discovery of the gunpowder plot, the town was very well
illuminated and the illuminations and ringing of bells would almost
have given us spirits if we had wanted them. We had intended going to
Forncett the next day, but were disappointed, however the day after our
curiosity was gratified; Forncett is a little village entirely inhabited by
farmers, who seem very decent kind of people, my Uncle's house is
now very comfortable and may be made an excellent one; the gardens
will be charming. I intend to be a great gardener and promise myself
much pleasure in taking care of the poultry of which we are to have
great abundance. My Uncle has changed his plan since I last wrote to
Halifax, it was then his intention to make the alterations intended at
Forncett this winter; but he now thinks of going there immediately and
we hope to get there on Friday. Since we came to Norwich we have
been very busy making the necessary preparations for beginning
house-keeping such as making linnen, going a shopping, &c., &c. We
have sketched out a plan of the manner in which we are to spend our
time, which I will give you that you may have some idea of my
situation. We are to have prayers at nine oclock (you will observe it is

winter) after breakfast is over we are to read, write, and I am to improve myself in French till twelve oclock, when we are to walk or visit our sick and poor neighbours till three, which is our dining hour; and after tea my Uncle will sit with us and either read to us or not as he and we find ourselves inclined. You can have no idea how much I please myself with the idea of seeing my dear Aunt in Spring. My Uncle and Aunt fully expect her. ...

8th December 1788 Monday morng.

It is a charming morning and my Aunt and I are going a shopping.

I have not I find given you any account of Norwich. It is an immensely large place; but the streets in general are very ugly, and they are all so ill-paved and dirty, as almost entirely to take away the pleasure of walking; we have been introduced to some of the genteelest families in the place but have visited very little on account of business. Their visiting is entirely in the *rout* stile; and they are so ridiculous as to send invitations three weeks or a month beforehand. We had an invitation came on the 26th of November for the 18th of December to tea and cards, can any thing be more absurd? I cannot help thinking how my Gmr and the old ladies at Penrith would stare at this. They claim against the idleness and folly of the age; and say it is impossible to secure company unless you send two or three days before you intend to receive them. Adieu my dear Girl.

Sunday Decr 28th. [1788]

... We are now happily settled at Forncett, and upon a nearer view my prospects appear even more delightful than they did upon a more distant one; we have not however yet been able to put in practice the regular plan of spending our time which I mentioned to you; as we have had a good deal of linnen to make, and the house to put into order;

200

however, we have walked every morning but the two last when it snowed so violently it was impossible to get out. You would laugh to see us wading through the snow in our half boots and spatter-dashes we never go out without them for we find them not only very *comfortable* but *necessary.* Oh! my dear friend if you were with us how happy we should be! I often wish for you to walk with me in the garden; my room is one of the pleasantest in the house. I wish you were here to share it with me, some of the views are beautiful and I frequently wish that you were with me when I am admiring them ... we went in the morning to one of my Uncle's churches which is only a step or two from the house [St Peter], and in the afternoon to the other which is about a mile from us [Forncett St Mary], we drank tea with Mrs Dix, the lady of whom I spoke to you as being the only neighbour we had within two miles of us. She appears to be a sensible woman, but has a good many of the particularities, and some of the bad qualities ascribed to old maids; her appearance is rather remarkable as she always wears long ruffles and a common stuff gown; she is rich, but lives alone and in a very plain manner, I cannot say whether it proceeds from covetousness or not as I do not know what use she may make of her money, she is likely however to be a very useful neighbour and I think in general she has a very good character, her worst fault is censoriousness, of which she seems to be guilty.

25 and 26 January 1790

... Did I ever tell you that I had got a little school; indeed when I recollect, it is not possible that I should have told you, as I have only kept it six months. I will give you my plan. I have nine scholars, I had at first ten but I dismissed one and during the winter I did not think it prudent to supply her place. Our hours in winter are, on Sunday mornings from nine till church time: at noon from half past one till three: and at night from four till half past 5: those who live near us come to me every Wednesday and Saturday evening.

I only instruct them in reading and spelling and they get off prayers hymns and catechisms. I have one very bright scholar, some very tolerable, and one or two very bad. We distribute rewards such as books, caps, aprons &c. We intend in a little time to have a school upon a more extensive plan – so that this of mine is only a temporary thing. We are to have a mistress who is to teach them spinning, knitting &c in the week days, and I am to assist her on Sundays, when they are to be taught to read. Mr. [William] Wilberforce has been with us rather better than a month, tell your Father I hope he will give him his vote at the next general election. I believe him to be one of the best of men.

He allows me ten guineas a year to distribute in what manner I think best to the poor. It is a very nice sum by which I [am] enabled to do more good than perhaps might ever have been in my power – remember all this is between ourselves, therefore don't mention it. ...

April 30th 1790.

. . . Your inquiries about my school I cannot answer so satisfactorily as I could wish; as my scholars have had a holiday ever since little Mary's Birth, on account of the small pox which have never been out of the parrish; we are very fearful she should catch them and we think my little girls likely to bring them. I hope however that I shall in a week or two be able to have them again. Whenever I see any of them I am asked the flattering question, 'Pray Miss when shall we come to school again?' One of them who came to me six months on Sundays and a very few times a part of that time in the week days is able to read exceedingly well in the testament can repeat the catechism and a part of that explanation of it; five or six hymns, the Lord's prayer, the creed and a morning and evening prayer; she can read the church prayer book as well as I could desire and did not know a letter when she came to me – the rest do not do quite so well but however I have no reason to complain. ...

... Our ac[quain]tances don't any of them except Mrs. Dix, live within two miles of us, at that distance there are several pleasant families, particula[rly the] Burrougheses. Mrs B. is a most elegant beautiful and sensi[ble woman,] but unhappily her mind is frequently deranged; she has two daughters, who are accomplished and agreeable girls, and a son who is a very pleasant young man, here I see you draw up and smile but however you have no reason. We have a very respectable and worthy man who lives in the adjoining parish who makes an excellent use of a large fortune; and a very smart little goodtempered fellow his curate – here too you look significant. We visit two families at the distance of 5 miles; they are bo[th] very agreeable – but my dearest Jane how much I wish that *you* lived within two miles of us! ...

23 May 1791

... I have been three times at Norwich lately which is something extraordinary as we stir little from home. These three journeys produced three visits to the theatre, but my principal errand was twice of a disagreeable nature: I went each time to get a tooth drawn; I have been much troubled with the toothache lately so my uncle determined that I should consult a dentist; but however I first went to take the advice of Mr Martineau; he drew me a tooth and as I was fearful of beginning with a dentist I went no farther, I was, however, obliged to make another journey the following week when Mr. M. took another tooth from me, and I have since been perfectly well. I staid at Norwich several days each time. I hope to hear that your dear father's health continues to improve. Pray make my particular Compts. to him, your Mother, and all your sisters. Do you go into the country this summer? We have lately enjoyed ourselves exceedingly, the weather has been so delightful. I rise about six every morning and, as I have no companion walk with a book till half past eight, if the weather permits; if not I read in the house; sometimes we walk in the mornings, but seldom more than half an hour just before dinner; after tea we all walk together till about eight, and I then walk alone as long as I can in the garden; I am particularly fond of a moonlight or twilight walk – it is at this time that I think most of my absent friends. My brother William was with us six weeks in the depth of winter. You may recollect that at that time the weather was uncommonly mild; we used to walk every morning about two hours, and every evening we went into the garden at four or half past four and used to pace backwards and forwards 'till six. Unless you have accustomed yourself to this kind of walking you will have no idea that it can be pleasant, but I assure you it is most delightful, and if you and I happen to be together in the country, as we probably may at Mr Rawson's, we will try how you like my plan if you are not afraid of the evening air. ...

Sunday Morng June 26th. [1791]

... My Aunt and I are at present pleasing ourselves with the thoughts of riding a good deal this summer; she is to ride double, and I upon a little horse of my Uncle's. The country about us though not romantic or picturesque is very pleasing, the surface is tolerably varied, and we have great plenty of wood but a sad want of water. ...

16 June 1793

... It was in Winter (at Christmas) that [William] was last at Forncett, and every Day as soon as we rose from Dinner we used to pace the gravel walk in the Garden till six o'clock when we received a Summons (which was always unwelcome) to Tea. Nothing but Rain or Snow prevented our taking this walk. Often have I gone out when the keenest North Wind has been whistling amongst the Trees over our Heads. I have paced that walk in the garden which will always be dear to me from the Remembrance of those long, long conversations I have had upon it supported by my Brother's arm. Ah! Jane! I never thought of the cold when he was with me. I am as heretical as yourself in my opinions concerning Love and Friendship; I am very sure that Love will never bind me closer to any human Being than Friendship binds me to you my earliest female Friend, and to William my earliest and my dearest Male Friend. ...

10 and 12 July 1793

None of this is to be read aloud, so be upon your guard!

My Aunt is gone to take an airing with my Uncle and Mary. The evening is a lovely one, and I have strolled into a neighbouring meadow where I am enjoying the melody of Birds and the busy sounds of a fine summer's evening, while my eye is gratified by a smiling prospect of cultivated fields richly wooded, our own church, and the parsonage house. But oh how imperfect is my pleasure! I am *alone*; why are not you seated with me? and my dear William why is not he here also? I could almost fancy that I see you both near me. I have chosen a bank where I have room to spare for a resting-place for each of you. I hear *you* point out a spot where, if we could erect a little cottage and call it *our own* we should be the happiest of human beings. I see my Brother fired with the idea of leading his sister to such a retreat as Fancy ever ready at our call hastens to assist us in painting; our parlour is in a moment furnished; our garden is adorned by magic; the roses and honeysuckles spring at our command, the wood behind the house lifts at once its head and furnishes us with a winter's shelter, and a summer's noon-day shade. ...

... The dew begins to fall so I think it not quite prudent to sit upon the grass. I will take a few turns at the bottom of the field where I have a sweet prospect, and I will adorn our little cottage. I shall almost fancy you are with me – alas! this cannot, cannot be; but I will console myself with the idea that that happy period is not far removed. I fear what I have written is quite illegible – a knee is not the most convenient writing desk. Adieu –

PARSON WOODFORDE

Virginia Woolf

(from *The Common Reader*, 1925)

One could wish that the psycho-analysts would go into the question of diary-keeping. For often it is the one mysterious fact in a life otherwise as clear as the sky and as candid as the dawn. Parson Woodforde is a case in point – his diary is the only mystery about him. For forty-three years he sat down almost daily to record what he did on Monday and what he had for dinner on Tuesday; but for whom he wrote or why he wrote it is impossible to say. He does not unburden his soul in his diary; yet it is no mere record of engagements and expenses. As for literary fame, there is no sign that he ever thought of it, and finally, though the man himself is peaceable above all things, there are little indiscretions and criticisms which would have got him into trouble and hurt the feelings of his friends had they read them. What purpose, then, did the sixty-eight little books fulfil? Perhaps it was the desire for intimacy. When James Woodforde opened one of his neat manuscript books he entered into conversation with a second James Woodforde, who was not quite the same as the reverend gentleman who visited the poor and preached in the church. These two friends said much that all the world might hear; but they had a few secrets which they shared with each other only. It was a great comfort, for example, that Christmas when Nancy, Betsy, and Mr. Walker seemed to be in conspiracy against him, to exclaim in the diary, 'The treatment I meet with for my Civility this Christmas is to me abominable'. The second James Woodforde sympathised and agreed. Again, when a stranger abused his hospitality it was a relief to inform the other self who lived in the little book that he had put him to sleep in the attic story, 'and I treated him as one that would be too free if treated kindly'. It is easy to understand why, in the quiet life of a country parish, these two bachelor friends became in time inseparable. An essential part of him would have died had he been forbidden to keep his diary. When indeed he thought himself in the grip of death he still wrote on and on. And as we read – if reading is the word for it – we seem to be listening to someone who is murmuring over the events of the day to himself in the quiet space which precedes sleep. It is not writing, and, to speak of the truth, it is not reading. It is slipping through half a dozen pages and strolling to the window and looking out. It is going on thinking about the Woodfordes while we watch the people in the street below. It is taking a walk and making up the life and character of James Woodforde as we go. It is not reading any more than it is writing – what to call it we scarcely know.

James Woodforde, then, was one of those smooth-cheeked, steady-eyed men, demure to look at, whom we can never imagine except in the prime of life. He was of an equable temper, with only such acerbities and touchinesses as are generally to be found in those who have had a love affair in their youth and remained, as they fancy, unwed because of it. The Parson's love affair, however, was nothing very tremendous. Once when he was a young man in Somerset he liked to walk over to Shepton and to visit a certain 'sweet tempered' Betsy White who lived there. He had a great mind 'to make a bold stroke' and ask her to marry him. He went so far, indeed, as to propose marriage 'when opportunity served', and Betsy was willing. But he delayed; time passed; four years passed indeed, and Betsy went to Devonshire, met a Mr. Webster, who had five hundred pounds a year, and married him. When James Woodforde met them in the turnpike road he could say little, 'being shy', but to his diary he remarked – and this no doubt was his private version of the affair ever after – 'she has proved herself to me a mere jilt'.

207

But he was a young man then, and as time went on we cannot help suspecting that he was glad to consider the question of marriage shelved once and for all so that he might settle down with his niece Nancy at Weston Longueville, and give himself simply and solely, every day and all day, to the great business of living. Again, what else to call it we do not know.

For James Woodforde was nothing in particular. Life had it all her own way with him. He had no special gift; he had no oddity or infirmity. It is idle to pretend that he was a zealous priest. God in Heaven was much the same to him as King George upon the throne – a kindly Monarch, that is to say, whose festivals one kept by preaching a sermon on Sunday much as one kept the Royal birthday by firing a blunderbuss and drinking a toast at dinner. Should anything untoward happen, like the death of a boy who was dragged and killed by a horse, he would instantly, but rather perfunctorily, exclaim, 'I hope to God the Poor Boy is happy', and add, 'We all came home singing'; just as when Justice Creed's peacock spread its tail – 'and most noble it is' – he would exclaim, 'How wonderful are Thy Works O God in every Being'. But there was no fanaticism, no enthusiasm, no lyric impulse about James Woodforde. In all these pages, indeed, each so neatly divided into compartments, and each of those again filled, as the days themselves were filled, quietly and fully in a hand steady as the pacing of a well-tempered nag, one can only call to mind a single poetic phrase about the transit of Venus. 'It appeared as a black patch upon a fair Lady's face', he says. The words themselves are mild enough, but they hang over the undulating expanse of the Parson's prose with the resplendence of the star itself. So in the Fen country a barn or a tree appears twice its natural size against the surrounding flats. But what led him to this palpable excess that summer's night we cannot tell. It cannot have been that he was drunk. He spoke out too roundly against such failings in his brother Jack to be guilty himself. Temperamentally he was among the eaters of meat and not among the drinkers of wine. When we think of the Woodfordes, uncle and niece, we think of them as often as not waiting with some impatience for their dinner. Gravely they watch the joint as it is set upon the table; swiftly they get their knives to work upon the succulent leg or loin; without much comment, unless a word is passed about the gravy or the stuffing, they go on eating. So they munch, day after day, year in, year out, until between them they must have devoured herds of sheep and oxen, flocks of poultry, an odd dozen or so of swans and cygnets, bushels of apples and plums, while the pastries and the jellies crumble and squash beneath their spoons in mountains, in pyramids, in pagodas. Never was there a book so stuffed with food as this one is. To read the bill of fare respectfully and punctually set forth gives one a sense of repletion. Trout and chicken, mutton and peas, pork and apple sauce – so the joints succeed each other at dinner, and there is supper with more joints still to come, all, no doubt, home grown, and of the juiciest and sweetest; all cooked, often by the mistress herself, in the plainest English way, save when the dinner was at Weston Hall and Mrs. Custance surprised them with a London daint – a pyramid of jelly, that is to say, with a 'landscape appearing through it'. After dinner sometimes, Mrs. Custance, for whom James Woodforde had a chivalrous devotion, would play the 'Sticcardo Pastorale', and make 'very soft music indeed'; or would get out her work-box and show them how neatly contrived it was, unless indeed she were giving birth to another child upstairs. These infants the Parson would baptize and very frequently he would bury them. They died almost as frequently as they were born. The Parson had a deep respect for the Custances. They were all that country gentry should be – a little given to the habit of keeping mistresses, perhaps, but that peccadillo could be forgiven them in view of their generosity to the poor, the kindness they showed to Nancy, and their condescension in asking the Parson to dinner when they had great people staying with them. Yet great people were not much to James's liking. Deeply though he respected the nobility, 'one must confess', he said, 'that being with our equals is much more agreeable'.

Not only did Parson Woodforde know what was agreeable; that rare gift was by the bounty of Nature supplemented by another equally rare – he could have what he wanted. The age was propitious. Monday, Tuesday, Wednesday – they follow each other and each little compartment seems filled with content. The days were not crowded, but they were enviably varied. Fellow of New College though he was, he did things with his own hands, not merely with his own head. He lived in every room of the house – in the study he wrote sermons, in the dining-room he ate copiously; he cooked in the kitchen, he played cards in the parlour. And then he took his coat and stick and went coursing his greyhounds in the fields. Year in, year out, the provisioning of the house and its defence against the cold of winter and the drought of summer fell upon him. Like a general he surveyed the seasons and took steps to make his own little camp safe with coal and wood and beef and beer against the enemy. His day thus had to accommodate a jumble of incongruous occupations. There is religion to be served, and the pig to be killed; the sick to be visited and dinner to be eaten; the dead to be buried and beer to be brewed; Convocation to be attended and the cow to be bolused. Life and death, mortality and immortality, jostle in his pages and make a good mixed marriage of it: '... found the old gentleman almost at his last gasp. Totally senseless with rattlings in his Throat. Dinner to-day boiled beef and Rabbit rosted.' All is as it should be; life is like that.

Surely, surely, then, here is one of the breathing-spaces in human affairs – here in Norfolk at the end of the eighteenth century at the Parsonage. For once man is content with his lot; harmony is achieved; his house fits him; a tree is a tree; a chair is a chair; each knows its office and fulfils it. Looking through the eyes of Parson Woodforde, the different lives of men seem orderly and settled. Far away guns roar; a King falls; but the sound is not loud enough to scare the rooks here in Norfolk. The proportions of things are different. The Continent is so distant that it looks a mere blur; America scarcely exists; Australia is unknown. But a magnifying glass is laid upon the fields of Norfolk.

Every blade of grass is visible there. We see every lane and every field; the ruts on the roads and the peasants' faces. Each house stands in its own breadth of meadow isolated and independent. No wires link village to village. No voices thread the air. The body also is more present and more real. It suffers more acutely. No anaesthetic deadens physical pain. The surgeon's knife hovers real and sharp above the limb. Cold strikes unmitigated upon the house. The milk freezes in the pans; the water is thick with ice in the basins. One can scarcely walk from one room to another in the parsonage in winter. Poor men and women are frozen to death upon the roads. Often no letters come and there are no visitors and no newspapers. The Parsonage stands alone in the midst of the frost-bound fields. At last, Heaven be praised, life circulates again; a man comes to the door with a Madagascar monkey; another brings a box containing a child with two distinct perfect heads; there is a rumour that a balloon is going to rise at Norwich. Every little incident stands out sharp and clear. The drive to Norwich even is something of an adventure. One must trundle every step of the way behind a horse. But look how distinct the trees stand in the hedges; how slowly the cattle move their heads as the carriage trots by; how gradually the spires of Norwich raise themselves above the hill. And then how clear-cut and familiar are the faces of the few people who are our friends – the Custances, Mr. du Quesne. Friendship has time to solidify, to become a lasting, a valuable possession.

True, Nancy of the younger generation is visited now and then by a flighty notion that she is missing something, that she wants something. One day she complained to her uncle that life was very dull: she complained 'of the dismal situation of my house, nothing to be seen, and little or no visiting or being visited, &c.', and made him very uneasy. We could read Nancy a little lecture upon the folly of wanting that 'et cetera'. Look what your 'et cetera' has brought to pass, we might say; half the countries of Europe are bankrupt; there is a red line of villas on every green hill-side; your Norfolk roads are black as tar; there is no end to 'visiting or being visited'. But Nancy has an answer

211

to make us, to the effect that our past is her present. You, she says, think it a great privilege to be born in the eighteenth century, because one called cowslips pagles and rode in a curricle instead of driving in a car. But you are utterly wrong, you fanatical lovers of memoirs, she goes on. I can assure you, my life was often intolerably dull. I did not laugh at the things that make you laugh. It did not amuse me when my uncle dreamt of a hat or saw bubbles in the beer, and said that meant a death in the family; I thought so too. Betsy Davy mourned young Walker with all her heart in spite of dressing in sprigged paduasoy. There is a great deal of humbug talked of the eighteenth century. Your delight in old times and old diaries is half impure. You make up something that never had any existence. Our sober reality is only a dream to you – so Nancy grieves and complains, living through the eighteenth century day by day, hour by hour.

Still, if it is a dream, let us indulge it a moment longer. Let us believe that some things last, and some places and some people are not touched by change. On a fine May morning, with the rooks rising and the hares scampering and the plover calling among the long grass, there is much to encourage the illusion. It is we who change and perish. Parson Woodforde lives on. It is the kings and queens who lie in prison. It is the great towns that are ravaged with anarchy and confusion. But the river Wensum still flows; Mrs. Custance is brought to bed of yet another baby; there is the first swallow of the year. The spring comes, and summer with its hay and strawberries; then autumn, when the walnuts are exceptionally fine though the pears are poor; so we lapse into winter, which is indeed boisterous, but the house, thank God, withstands the storm; and then again there is the first swallow, and Parson Woodforde takes his greyhounds out a-coursing.

MEMORIES OF EAST WINCH

Osbert Lancaster

(from *All Done From Memory*, 1953)

There is no silence in the world so overwhelming as that which prevails on a small country station when a train has just left. The fact that it is by no means complete, that the fading echoes of the engine are still clearly audible from beyond the signal-box behind which the guard's van is finally disappearing, that one now hears for the first time the cawing of the rooks, a distant dog's bark, the hum of the bees in the station-master's garden, in no way detracts from its quality. The rattling world of points and sleepers, of gossiping fellow-passengers and sepia views of Cromer beach has been whirled away leaving a void which, for some moments yet, the sounds and smells of the countryside will be powerless to fill.

At Eastwinch station, lost amidst the un-by-passed fields of my Edwardian childhood, this period of suspension was apt to be longer than elsewhere. The platform, though I suppose no higher than most, appeared in the flat East Anglian landscape to be a raised island, isolated way above the surrounding elm-broken cornlands. Nor did it ever, at first glance, exhibit any sign of life, as the solitary porter's immediate duty was to open the level-crossing gates regardless of the passengers, alone with their luggage amidst the shiny tinplates advertising Stephens' Blueblack Ink and Venos Lightning Cough Cure. And it was only just as we were beginning to wonder whether or not this was the right day, that an aunt would suddenly emerge from the waiting-room.

Her greeting never varied. After the usual brisk, no-nonsense kiss and the routine enquiries she would announce that Jones had brought the trap (the Renault was never sent to the station save for my grandfather himself or some guest of more than usual age or decrepitude) and would take Nurse and the luggage, but that she expected that Osbert would like a little walk after all that time in the stuffy train. This was always said with a richly sardonic smile, she

213

knowing full well that there was nothing Osbert so much abominated as little walks, no matter how many hours had been spent in stuffy trains; he, however, had long since learnt the uselessness of protest and would inevitably find himself a few minutes later trudging along the Station Road gazing regretfully at Nurse, comfortably ensconced in the trap, bowling briskly away in a cloud of dust.

Even today Eastwinch is a very small village; at that date it was smaller still. Small, that is, judged by the number of its inhabitants rather than by its extent. Strung out for a mile or more along the Lynn-Swaffham road it started at the Lynn end with the church, a decent enough fourteenth-century Norfolk structure without, but scraped and scrubbed into insignificance within by the late Sir Gilbert Scott, standing on an outlying ridge of the Breckland, that scruffy, sandy waste which runs like some horrid birthmark across the homely face of East Anglia. Alongside, dank and laurel-shaded, was the vicarage; beyond, down the hill, lay the straight village street, hardly differing in character from the rest of the highway, so widely separated were the cottages, the four public-houses (two of them no longer licensed since my grandfather had decided that the needs of the villagers were being, perhaps, too amply cared for), and the solitary village shop. Half a mile beyond the point where it was entered by the Station Road, an ordinary country lane crossing the branch line from Lynn some three-quarters of a mile away, the street ended in a sharp fork, in the apex of which, facing directly up the village to the church, stood the imposing, globe-topped entrance gates of Eastwinch Hall.

The gates, once entered, were generally felt to be an overstatement. On the right lay a croquet lawn screened from the converging roads by a plantation of copper beeches; less than a hundred yards ahead was the house itself. Built a century earlier by some modest nabob who had done well in the tea trade, tradition maintained that it had been deliberately designed on the model of a tea-caddy. Although at the time I never dreamed of doubting this theory, on looking back it seems to me to have been a perfectly ordinary, four-square late Georgian residence with a rather low-pitched roof. Such idiosyncrasies as it displayed were all, in fact, the work of my grandfather; they took the form of terra-cotta masks of Comedy and Tragedy with which he had seen fit to enliven the plain expanse of yellow brick between the first and second storeys, unexpected bow-windows bulging out on ground level, and a vast gabled porch masking the front door. The erection of this last had unfortunately coincided with the height of the old gentleman's genealogical enthusiasm, and the pediment was adorned with a highly baroque version of his coat of arms in terra-cotta. So unexpectedly heavy had this forthright statement of the Lancaster family's inclusion among the armigerous classes proved that the fretted and white-painted wooden supports were already visibly straining beneath their burden of heraldry.

Structurally unsound and decoratively over-emphatic, the front porch nevertheless provided the focal point round which, during the long summer days, the whole life of the house revolved. Here my grandfather would sit reading his day-old *Times*, and to it would come the gardener with his offering of flowers which my aunts would painstakingly 'arrange' in a series of unattractive vases lined up on the tiled floor. As a vantage point from which nurses and parents could keep an eye on the younger children, and sporting uncles could give unsolicited advice to tennis-playing nephews and nieces, it was in constant demand. And always, on arrival, one found there the whole house-party grouped in a welcoming tableau.

I here use the word house-party simply as a convenient noun of assembly, disregarding its overtones. For us, particularly when speaking of the years before the first German war, the term has taken on a certain glamour, suggesting almost exclusively assemblies of the smart and the beautiful pursuing worldly pleasures in a constantly changed variety of expensive clothes. Nothing could bear less resemblance to the gatherings at Eastwinch Hall; no baccarat scandals ever darkened the fair name of a house where the only permitted card games were strictly educational; the conversation was seldom of a brilliance to have fired the imagination of Mr. Henry James; and it can safely be said that never, never did these corridors echo to whispered speculations about the geography of the bedrooms.

The two over-riding interests of my grandfather's life were his family and philanthropy. ... Diligent combing of the further branches of the family tree had revealed the existence of extraordinary survivals from a long-vanished Norfolk of gloomy farmers and manic-depressive yeomen. Unfortunately these had turned out to be exclusively female, and while they afforded many opportunities for the exercise of philanthropy their social gifts were seldom of an order effectively to enrich life at the Hall. They had, therefore, been comfortably installed in small villas on the outskirts of Lynn and in cosy cottages dotted round the country where their maintenance had been made the responsibility of my father and uncles. Deeply and volubly appreciative of their good fortune they were known collectively as the Grateful Hearts but seldom asked to the house.

EDWARDIAN EXCURSIONS
A.C. Benson
(from *Edwardian Excursions*, 1981)

Aylsham is a very pleasant little town of warm red-brick houses, with rather a foreign look. It looks clean, wholesome and comfortable. There are many houses which I wish to inhabit, of course. We walked about a little. The Rectory lies at the further end of the town, in a nice glebe and garden under the Church. A good house and well kept. Nice shrubs and trees and flowers. There is a fine dining-room with white pillars and it is altogether a good substantial house. The Church is long and low, a large grey flint building, low-pitched roof – transepts and aisles, with a very fine tower. The party consists of Stuart and Alba, the

Baroness, Lady Donaldson, St Clair; and Mrs Lawley who has been taking a cure and is rather knocked up. ...

The next day was Sunday and we all went to Church. It is a fine spacious Church, carefully kept and with an air of wealth. Canon Hoare is a rich Evangelical. There was a large congregation of a rather well-to-do kind. A choir, but not surpliced, of men, boys and women, sang briskly – the organ was smartly played. Some nice chants and hymns which I had never heard before. Some windows of the kind which Kempe would detest and I love; laborious, of screaming or rich tints, affected – but somehow showing love and care.

After lunch, we walked out to Blickling. Since Lady Lothian's death it has been kept up elaborately – twenty gardeners – but no one admitted to the house. One Bertram Talbot, a thick-set young man, a cousin of Lady Lothian, lives there, as agent, but more as a kind of gentlemanly policeman, to keep everyone out – even the Meyricks at the vicarage who have been in and out for twenty years, can't get in there now.

The road comes suddenly upon the house, which lies not in the centre of its park, but at the extreme corner, like many of the great houses. You look up about 100 yards, through yew hedges, very splendid and velvety, past a range of great outbuildings on each side, looking like a College Court, at the front, with its lead-capped turrets and balustraded mullions. The effect is somehow not absolutely satisfactory. In the first place it looks a little as if it were sinking into the ground – it has a moat – and in the second place it is either too ornate or not ornate enough.

We walked boldly round and saw the great gardens. At the back stretches away a huge fern-clad park, but it looked sad and deserted, tho' the gardens are all kept up. Vanity of vanities!

Then we went to the Church. There is a fine marble monument by Watts to Lord Lothian. The angels are beautiful at head and feet, looking wistful and yet serene. The figure is a fine one, but the hair and beard too flamboyant. He wore his hair like *Dickens*, I suppose, and this is not adapted for marble. The drapery is very unconventional, and the result is that though it is beautiful, it looks rather as if he had been tossed in a blanket and considerably rumpled. There was a handsome parson, Mr Meyrick Wood, in the church – and his wife – a Miss Meyrick – very pretty and nice. He seemed to know nothing about the church or monuments. We went into the Rectory, a fine house, but dark, ill-kept and second rate. Saw old Canon Meyrick, who sate in a little hot study, with a *fire* (Therm. outside at 70) waiting for the end. He suffers from his throat. His old well-worn books in the shelves; by him a few papers and a cup and plate. He was chaplain to Christopher Wordsworth in '69, with my father, and I remember him at Riseholme. His hair and beard are like floss silk. He was interested to see me, but it made me low-spirited to think of him fading away. He will never leave the house again. We dined pleasantly. Mr Cole, the *locum tenens* came – a nice man but very nervous. He is assistant and curate to Garnier of Quidenham. We talked afterwards about wealth and the duty of tithe. He quoted 'Corban' aptly [Mark, 7, 11]. He called all the ladies Mrs Donaldson with impartial politeness, hoping to be right for once, I suppose.

Tuesday, Sept. 2nd. 1902 ... St Clair had gone off to Barningham to lunch with the Simpsons. After a quiet lunch at home, Stuart and I set off on bicycles to pick him up and to go on to Cley. We rode by Blickling and pleasant farmlands with red houses, and got to Barningham. The park very pretty, but the road ill-kept. It is a very fine tall Tudor house, with curious double dormer windows. As we drew up to the front we saw a party sitting out on a terrace. ...

... Simpson's uncle, a boring old man, with a notebook full of very unimportant and inaccurate information, plied me with questions about an inscription on a bell which he could not remember. We saw the house – not big, but very nice – a fine long drawing room, of rococo Gothic and a good staircase; a few pictures. The house is only taken on lease from one Mott, an odd rich man who lives in town in lodgings and clubs.

This easy, lazy, gentle life is rather perplexing. It looks so beautiful and tranquil, but it seems unfair and unfruitful. The boring uncle took us to the Church, half in ruins – the tower empty, and an odd little stuffy choir used for services. Under the screen is a terrible vault, with long niches, like ovens, for coffins; those occupied closed at the mouth with slabs, where several Motts repose. The smell was awful and penetrating and I nosed Motts, like Hamlet, in the lobby, and I was glad to get out. We rode on, but the rain began to pelt. Saw a nice red house with good porch, at Plumstead, and giving up Cley, made our way home. Walked by workhouse in evening.

Thursday, Sept. 4th. A delicious day. We went off early and caught 9.50 train to Wroxham. Here a difficulty occurred. We were told we might have a steam-launch, and by going to get it, lost the wherry we had provisionally engaged. Stuart was justly annoyed and spoke with tempered indignation to an old man like a clergyman with a chin beard. However we were at last accommodated with a big roomy sailing-boat and sate round. Miss Buxton was with us (S.A.D., St. Clair, May, Algy, Childers and John the footman). We had books and papers and jested innocently.

We sailed slowly down the Bure, tacking from side to side. This broad rushy river, with the great flat on every side, with the low distant rising-ground, with alder clumps and dykes, and opening into still sheets of water on every side, was extraordinarily beautiful. Much meadow-sweet and loosestrife and valerian. But there were many – too many – people about. The river winds very much, and it is beautiful to see ahead of you apparently in the fields the white graceful sails of a huge wherry (a wherry is not a row-boat, but a big, broad sailing-boat) moving silently along. We passed many happy parties – fathers with their boys, undergraduates etc. The dirty flannels and tumbled hair, unbrushed after bathing, betrayed the campers-out. The undergraduate, sullen, conscious, puffing his pipe, is a disagreeable sort of creature, I think.

A nasty regatta was going on at Horning, the bank crowded and boats tacking as they raced. It was more still and silent as we tacked briskly up the creek to Ranworth; a man was mowing sedges underneath a broken pumping-mill which made a pleasant picture. We landed on a quay, covered with sedge-stacks. A little boy proffered me 'beans, peas, potatoes, apples and plums'. Then we walked up to Ranworth Church, by a pleasant thatched house in a trim garden. The bare high flint tower is impressive. It is being restored, with care and love. The great painted screen is fine, but few people seem to realise that it must have been hideous when new and that age is the toning grace. The most interesting thing there was an old pre-Reformation chanting-desk, with a hideous painted eagle, and an old 'Gloria' with musical notation painted on the upper part for the choir to sing from. The foot worm-eaten. We rambled about a little grassy acre, and came back to lunch at the boat a rich lunch of cold meats, fruits and jellies. Then we got slowly under way and went on to a ruined abbey – St Benet-at-holm – which sent an abbot to the House of Lords, and the Bishop of Norwich *still* sits as abbot of this place. It lies in a great green marshy flat on a low island. The gate-house is fairly intact, with a groined roof, but a huge brick pumping-mill has been built in it – very incongruous. The old precinct-wall is visible, and part of the nave and transept of the church among grassy tumbled mounds. It must have been a very lonely place. The two odd ivy-grown towers of S. Wal[s]ham – and many other grey towers – visible far off over the green flat. The barn of a farm close by is the chapel of the hospital.

We embarked again, the wind dropping every moment, and a golden light falling over the lazy ripples and reeds. The sedge in a high wind, such as we had in the morning, is the most delicious thing both to see and hear. We got a little tired, I think, but talked and jested. I should have liked a little more serious feeling talk, I think – more in tune – but perhaps impossible for so big a party (this sounds horribly priggish; but I don't mean it so. What I mean is that all sorts of little gentle thoughts hovered about, and yet one could not speak of them, tho' probably everyone else was feeling the same). There is a sadness about so bright, sweet and happy a day fading slowly to evening. One has not too many of such days. Horning Church tower stood up among its dark trees like

220

an old engraving.

We saw an odd little drama here on returning. A stout lady had just returned from fishing, with one stiff silvery dace in a net. She hobbled to the house with some wraps, and a black cat took advantage of her absence to steal the dace and walk swiftly off with it. The lady returned; the cat went off round a shed; but we could see both; and to see the cat glaring with the dace in its mouth, and the fat lady hunting in an agonised way in all directions for the fish was very funny. She went sadly off at last, thinking I suppose that the dace had revived and skipt away. ...

I can't understand the conformation of this country – its extreme flatness, rising a few inches straight from the water's edge. I think it must have been pushed up by volcanic pressure a little, and the soil is the marsh bottom, the river the deeper channels, the Broads the deeper pools. But it is all rather mysterious. It gave me a sense of seclusion to look from the populous river into the green flat, with its waving sedge and alder thickets. ...

Saturday, Sept 6th. We started about 12 bicycling, through pleasant lanes to Cawston. On the way passed a new house, built by a South African millionaire called *Cawston* who has settled here to be Cawston of Cawston. A large hamlet of nice redbrick houses with Elizabethan gables – over all a huge stone ashlar tower, very dignified – unfinished – no parapet or pinnacles – pierced with a few little quatrefoil windows to light the staircases, like patches on a Caroline court beauty's face. The Church very large and noble: a great chestnut roof, transepts, fearfully uncomfortable little sitting-benches, but all pretty well-kept. The Rectory belongs to Pembroke, Cambridge – £1000 a year – Mr Marsh, a tiresome old parson, who came jawing about, has been there fifty years. On the warm lead roof sat hundreds of martins gathering for their voyage oversea. We toiled up the tower, only to find the trapdoor shut. The tower is huge, like a cathedral – and all built for the glory of God, as there can never have been more than a hamlet here.

Then on to Heydon. ... After lunch we went to see the Church – very neat and trim, with Bulwer monuments ... Into the Hall Park, by a great gate with urns atop, and a grove of sycamores – shimmering turf beyond. The Hall a fine Elizabethan place, very large, but looking neglected – let for years, as the General has a place elsewhere. The present tenant a Managing Director of Collieries, who comes for shooting. He came out upon us – a man like a butler, very fresh and acute – not a gentleman. He took us back – he had a young officer with him, a cub who had come back from South Africa. A fine panelled hall. Here he introduced us to a feeble bearded man, Professor something, whose attempts at conversation were fitful and his bearing highly inadequate. The pictures plentiful and good. A fine one of G.Villiers, Duke of Buckingham, *asleep*. They said he could only be painted by stealth; and on this occasion he was drunk – all stuff! Many Pastons and Bulwers, with fat faces like ripe plums. The Hall panelled with Cromwellian Ironsides and hung with Morions. We went out at the back – stately but neglected – grass in the walks, hedges straggling. Sir Edward looked sadly about, and said 'I was born here – you can't think how I love the place.'

It is heavily mortgaged; and it is rather sad to think of it let to a Colliery Manager! Fine avenues of oaks to Cawston and Salle. We went off at last; and rode to Salle – caught up the Colliery party in a waggonette ... We rode on to see an extraordinary church with two towers recently built by Elwin, Editor of *Quarterly Review* – designed by himself. Hideous in the extreme – towers set lozenge-wise to the Church, all thick where it ought to be thin, and thin where it ought to be thick. I never saw a more pathetic place. It must have cost £50,000 and is designed in a sort of bastard Gothic, part French, part Early Victorian. Munich or Bruges glass. Very carefully furnished within: chairs, wood pavement – all perfect, and all ugly; but it is *well* done, and age will improve all good faithful work. A grim handsome priest in a cassock gave us short answers and seemed to wish us away.

So we went; back through Cawston. I shall always think of Cawston as I saw it then – standing up very square and sober over sycamores and red roofs, gilt by evening light. The swallows flying all about it like swarming bees, and settled in hundreds on the steep under-sill of the louvre windows – age and youth – experience and hope!

September 11th. ... We were to start early on Friday for Ditchingham, where I was invited by the Carrs. ... We ran very pleasantly along by Bolwich and the well known lanes; then through the great still woods of Stratton Strawless – the huge ugly barrack of the house looking comfortable enough, where Birkbeck lives ... Certainly a motor is delightful; I felt inclined to say like Dr Johnson that there could be few pleasures greater. Through St Faith's and then Norwich, smoking and steaming, lay below us. A bad watery morning.

We tore through the streets. A fine glimpse of the huge spire over the houses, and one glance into the Close through the big gate. Many nice houses but smoke-blackened; horrible little courts, dark and smelly, under archways; flint-built churches innumerable. We were detained by a tyre accident. The brake had jammed and planed a long string off. Soon remedied, and we tore on again. Passed through a rich-looking suburb, and then on towards Ditchingham – Bixley Hall, once Lord Rosebery's – Brooke House, a place like Terling in a park, belonging to Lord Canterbury, who lives in a small house at Seething and drinks with his coachman. Then to Ditchingham – some delightful houses left and right, particularly He[den]ham Hall, like Tremans. ...

We got out at Ditchingham House, a nice trim brick-built house. Rider Haggard appeared, tall, stout, amiable. He is pale with a short beard and rather shambles as he walks; dressed in a large pale coat and gaiters. He seemed both overworked and ill. Various women and smart young men lounged around. ...

A nice keeper, like a clergyman, and two of the handsomest boys to beat I have ever seen – in different ways. One roguish, English, with a perpetual smile and large white teeth – a common country boy, but of extraordinarily graceful carriage. Whatever he did looked well. The other, the keeper's son, could have been dressed up to make a really beautiful woman. Also a young soldier, a hussar, who carried my cartridges; had been through Ladysmith and thrice wounded – very smart and modest. He is going back as Sergeant Instructor on £240 a year. He wouldn't talk of his experiences.

We went round pretty country overlooking Bungay, where Clay prints my books; far in the flat the tower of Beccles. Haggard is a great farmer and writes books about it. I never saw so well-farmed a place. He gets just a small return, he says. The property is his wife's. There were few birds, and I began badly but afterwards shot well (5 out of 17 brace). Haggard lounged, smiled, talked – but seemed tired and fell into long silences waking up to amiable smiles. I told him how familiar his portrait was to me – he gave it to Gosse – he asked whether I thought it good, and seemed to regret having given it away.

We lunched well in a cartshed – Haggard very genial. He told us of his strange experiences in touring about inspecting agriculture (he is hard at work writing a book on Rural England): a strange drunken farmer's where he stayed, where you could get anything to drink and nothing to eat; bad eggs etc. 'The fact is, Mr Haggard, I'm a very temperate *eater*.' ...

After lunch, round fields by a House of Mercy and Ditchingham Church. Here I shot a fine rocketing shot which fell into the Convent orchard. Haggard more and more tired. Walked homewords. Ditchingham Park is very beautiful – well timbered with a long lake full of duck. The house a mellow Queen Anne front, white-casemented on a rising ground, with great cedars by it. Went into a big hall, with portraits – Mr Carr of Bolton etc. Old Mr Carr came out, a regular old Yorkshireman, stout, lame, a small tough man – with a keen face and a shaved upper lip; very hospitable; gave us tea and talked about the estate – he is very deaf.

I had a delightful room, big and comfortable – a regular old country-house room, with a dressing-room opening out of it. A nervous genial butler. Changed slowly and read *Pride and Prejudice*. The whole feeling of the place was like Miss Austen. Down to dinner. Young Mrs Carr a pleasant wry lady; old Mrs Carr like a very benevolent and nervous ghost – very frail, large-eyed and nervously twitchy. She is devoted to her husband, and he treated her nicely, rallying her good-naturedly – 'We daren't leave Mrs Carr at home', he said, 'because she is so mischievous – so we have to take her with us.' But he got by her in the drawing-room, and took her hand gently when no one was looking. ...

After dinner Mr Carr took me off and we had a long genealogical talk. He has great collection of interesting papers. He knew all about my relations and their exact fortunes. Seemed rather vexed that Mr Carr of Bolton had left so much to my grandmother ... He read the paper like a philosopher. Then we smoked in the Hall, and he gave me more information. Finally we could find no matches and he went and hunted in the dark – I could hear him tumble about – and conducted me to my bedroom. 'Here's your room – here's your dressing-room – all you want? Sleep well – you are welcome here, as one of the old stock!' I slept well, in a comfortable bed, the great cedar outside softly roaring in a strong S.W. wind.

September 13th. ... Our first task was to walk up long wide pasture fields with thick hedges – a gun and a beater in each field so that for some time we were alone. There was nothing of any kind to shoot – but somehow, what with the bright sun, the flowers of the pasture, the green trees and hedges – the thistles rising softly, like wading men, out of the light brown grass, I fell into a mood of keen, conscious and elated happiness such as I have seldom known since I was a boy. It was all so fresh and sweet, so quiet and lonely, as we walked, like tiny insects in the chequered squares of the wide countryside. So small we must have seemed from above, so busy about nothing. But the peace and glee of the green unvisited land, with its hazel-shadowed lanes, its undisturbed woods – with the clouds flying over it, in a bright blue sky, came into my very soul; and I had a beautiful and happy hour, for which I thank God.

At one gate there was a pleasing sight. A circle of sheep standing round an old merry shepherd – one pushing against his knees to be petted while he pulled its silky ear. His dogs stood at a distance. He had a real old shepherd-crook (which I think Missionary Bishops ought to carry). He had a weatherbeaten face, all wrinkled with good temper and cold, rough, not ungraceful country clothes and a great flapping hat. He talked very pleasantly. 'I'll lead my sheep out over yonder', he said, 'to be out of you gentlemen's way; and send you good sport', and so he took his hat off and went off smiling to himself.

In the middle of one of these fields lived a horse-dealer in a van, beside a lilied pool, who hired the meadows in summer and lived an odd free sort of life – looking at nothing round him, I suppose. ...

Then we went in to tea. Mrs Carr very birdlike and timid. The motor was late, but we took it tranquilly. Then we had a delicious run back. The lamps were lit in Norwich, and we tore through the narrow winding streets. It was like a dream to flash into the centre of a busy peopled town, to speak to no one and yet pass so close – and we must have seemed mysterious passengers too, sweeping in and out again. A good many people stopped to look at us. Then through the grey wolds and woods of S. Strawless. The moon rose, and when we got to Aylsham, the Church tower stood out in incredible beauty, tipped with gold, a few clouds sailing in a dark sky.

FRANKFORT MANOR
Sylvia Townsend Warner
(from *I'll Stand By You*, 1998 and *Letters*, 1982)

It was a beautifully proportioned house, with a Dutch gable and a reed-thatch roof – filled with the noise of trees. Valentine found it, exploring inland, but only because her quick eye caught sight of it behind its rampart of trees: backing to have another look, she saw it was to let. It stood in that stretch of Norfolk where the soil is deep

226

and fertile: a soil for oaks and chestnuts to plunge their roots into. We never found time to count all our trees but there must have been nearly a hundred of them. Whoever planted them planted them very well, allowing space for their growth. The house was sheltered by them, but the sun bathed it, and seemed to have ripened it; its small 17th century bricks were tinted with pale ochre, faint rose, like a ripe pear. In front of it was a stretch of soft dense lawn, which had never been mown except with a scythe. Our lease stipulated that this should continue. . . .

Behind it was a corresponding amplitude of out-buildings: a stable with four loose-boxes, a harness room, a coach-house, a wash-house, several sheds, pigsties, and outdoor privy. One of the loose-boxes was heaped with chestnut logs; in another we found a rusty bayonet; and an apricot was trained on the stable wall. A path between trees led to the kitchen garden. At its entrance was a small vinery. The roof was broken, a renegade vine flaunted out from it. A penny note-book, bleached and cobwebbed, recorded the weather, day by day, for the summer of 1887. Beyond the kitchen garden was an orchard and a paddock. In the orchard was a vast leaning pear-tree, its limbs propped on crutches; it bore quantities of blunt-ended cooking pears, their rind dark as obsidian. I looked for it in Evelyn's *Compleat Gard'ner* – it was a tree of that quality. I never identified it, nor have I ever seen another like it.

William, grown old, failed soon after our arrival and had to be given his quietus. Valentine buried him in the paddock. This was my first experience of her capacity as a comforter: grave and encompassing, it had the quality of music. That evening, we played a long game of chess.

It was after William's death that the rough cats declared themselves. There was an indigenous tribe of them, thick-coated, low to the ground, moving with a swift slouching gait. They preyed on rats and birds, ate acorns and sweet chestnuts and grew familiar enough to come as far as the back door for scraps; but held no intercourse with our housecats, though when we domesticated one of

227

the rough kittens it attached itself to me with intense affection.

... The house was handsome too, its good looks sobered by age and usage – a seventeenth-century house with a long facade and a reed-thatch roof. It gave an impression of slenderness, of being worn smooth and thin like an old spoon. The doorway was narrow and severe, the mullions and transoms of the windows remarkably delicate. Their white paint was worn to a dandelion-clock silver. The house was of brick, it had been coated with a yellowish limewash, and this too was worn thin and the colour of the brick showed dimly through, so the general tint of the house was that of a ripening pear with streaks of vague rose and pale madder flushing its sallow skin.

To HAROLD RAYMOND 17:vi:1933

East Chaldon. Dorchester. Dorset.

... I have just signed a year's lease of a mouldering grange in Norfolk, which I intend to share with Valentine for a year's experiment of rather larger living than we get here.

It is a seventeenth century house, called Frankfort Manor. It has a Dutch gable, a drive, two asparagus beds and a trap for visitors. For having approached, with all suitable enthusiasm, its blonde brick face, and gone in by its reeded and elegant door, they are tossed straight into an intact Edwardian long hall, complete with carved oak staircase and c.1900 beams. We have already tried it on Valentine's brother-in-law, and it worked like a charm. He burst into inarticulate praise, and went on praising louder and louder as his sensibilities became more and more confused and uneasy.

Otherwise the house is nice and intact, except for a remarkable experiment in dining-room fireplaces, where there is a sort of ground-floor oven beside the hearth, faced with a grille: which I can only explain as a cage for salamanders. ...

To LLEWELYN POWYS 16:viii:1933

Frankfort Manor. Sloley. Norwich.

Dear Llewelyn,

... This house looks out on a great rampart of trees; all day they are motionless in the strong sun; But at dusk they seem to creep silently across the lawn, until looking from my window I seem to see their enormous foreheads pressed to the pane.

I have never lived with trees before. They take some mastering; but I think I shall be on good terms with them even before I see them naked.

To LLEWELYN POWYS 3:x:1933

... One evening we heard strange sounds in the house, thumps and heavy boundings. It was dark. We carried a lamp and a gun in search of the sounds, could not for a long while track them down, for they would cease and begin again. At last, in the sitting room we saw, crouched in the middle of the room, what seemed to be a massive fur hassock. The hassock rose into the air, and soared out into the garden, not knowing much more when she landed of the nature of glass than when she started, for she went through it like a cannon ball. A leap of ten or twelve feet, a magnificent leap. But we became rather pensive, and now, at nightfall, we shut the doors.

We have dug up all our potatoes, gathered all our nuts, stored our apples and keeping pears. Now to chop and saw wood for the winter, the lantern hanging on a wooden peg, the stable very dusky and enlarged around us, and rustling with rats. It is rainy weather at last, the blackbirds sing almost as though it were February, and this morning when I woke I saw the air between us and the hanging tapestry of trees laced with straight glittering rods of rain, each separate, intentional, like a rain of spears.

I am glad. The rain is settling me in; though sometimes I have such a passionately distinct homesickness for Chaldon that to remain here is almost more than I can bear.

The straw is ricked, and the ricks have corn-babies on them. One at either end, standing up like weathercocks. They are baubles of plaited straw, made in different shapes, sometimes crosses, sometimes sharp stars, sometimes birds with long tails. It is on the first-finished rick they are put – for ornament we were told.

Mushrooms and a bull have appeared simultaneously in the field behind the house. It is a pity that the same day should always quicken both. However, we had mushrooms for lunch.

The other day we went to King's Lynn. It is a most beautiful town, stately and prim, with seagulls crying through it. And on our way back we drove through the outskirting grounds of Sandringham. Sandy roads, very smooth, with clipped green grass margins and well-kept rabbits ... All the neighbourhood is excessively spruce, covered with model post-offices and tailored hedges. Suddenly, after about a four mile radius, one sees the landscape sinking back into carpet-slippers with a sigh of relief.

We have a library now, all Valentine's books and mine at last assembled and in order. The rest of the house is also furnished, perfectly to our satisfaction; though when I see strangers looking rather wistfully round the very large hall it occurs to me that perhaps one horsehair sofa, two chairs, a bust and two guns is not quite all the furniture they would expect.

But very few strangers come. And so far, all of them are dull. So we hope that a word has gone round about us, and that we shall be avoided as lepers and eccentrics. ...

To LLEWELYN POWYS 16:ii:1934

... My God, we are gardening so hard. At this moment the whole of my back is uttering smouldering growls of fatigue. But we are not entirely given up to virtuous acts. We have eaten cold partridge legs out of doors, sitting on a heap of dry rushes on a heath, and watched, very disapprovingly, by two church towers, one to the east and one to the west. It is impossible to frolic anywhere in this country without a church tower on the horizon to eye one. There they rear themselves, like melancholy teeth from an old jaw.

To LLEWELYN POWYS 24:iii:1934

... Your letter came to me when I was in sad need of a friend's hand. We have been through a week of murrain and pestilence. There is a killing disease here that in six days has slain, to our certain knowledge, over twenty cats and four dogs. Four of our cats, alas, among them, and two of those the house kittens which I had reared up from babyhood. They were extremely dear to us, and it was misery to see them so suddenly blasted and turned from the comely looks and happiness into little bags of bones wrapped in sullied fur. It is a most virulent and mysterious plague, for the vet., even after two post-mortems, cannot account for it. It is not poisoning, it is not any known distemper. The people are waiting most uneasily to see if it spreads to cattle; and even if it does not it is still a calamity; for the rats will be all over us if it is not stayed.

I have given Valentine a small pocket telescope, by which she observes birds and the moon ... It was a hazardous gift to make, because Valentine's grandfather had, among twenty other expensive and devouring passions, a turn for astronomy and an even more marked turn for telescopes; and I have been waiting for the words, 'Sylvia, we must sell the car and the silver and all we have and buy an astronomer's telescope. And then we will fit it up on a cement platform in the garden, and build a little shelter, and I will sit there all night, observing the heavens. I shall be perfectly happy, I shall not wish for anything else. We must get it instantly.'

However, so far she seems content with a fifteen diameter magnified moon, and the pleasure of watching the expressions of the hens in the field across the lane.

A PASSION FOR CHURCHES

John Betjeman

(from *Collected Letters Vol.2*, 1995, and
Norfolk Country Churches And Their Future, 1972)

To Edward Mirzoeff 24 January 1974

29 Radnor Walk London SW3

Dear Eddie,

I am still reeling with delight at the soaring majesty of Norfolk and our tour there with Jane Whitworth. I put down here some preliminary thoughts only.

I think the obvious is the best and that the film [A Passion for Churches] should be our earthly pilgrimage expressed in the sacraments and psalms of the C[hurch] of E[ngland] to which most people belong even though they may have forgotten. It will stir memories. Phrases from the *Book of Common Prayer*, especially the General Thanksgiving, that Norwich invention – the psalms and hymns *A[ncient] and M[odern]* will wander through the script, much of which should be spoken by someone with a Norfolk accent, and a *strong* Norfolk accent. All the time what we look at must be Norfolk and that may help to imply the remoteness of this separate country which Norfolk is, miles from London and miles even from Cambridge and the Midlands.

Having now read most of Colin Stephenson's *Walsingham Way*, I realise we cannot ignore it. The pilgrimage was of European fame before the Reformation and though I don't much like relic worship myself, things do get an extra quality when they have been revered for centuries by thousands. They are something like the monarchy. That well at Walsingham and the water that is sprinkled from it (we might even sprinkle over the lens of the camera to surprise and bless our readers!) are a nice incident on life's journey. I like to think there is illimitable light all round us waiting to press into our lives if we will let it. We come from it trailing clouds of glory, we go into it after death and we see it portrayed in the Resurrection. But one thing we must avoid is solemnity and conscious do-goodery and taking ourselves too seriously. The film must be natural and life-like and full of jokes like Chaucer and some of those carved bosses and bench-ends we saw. All round us are fields and trees and the toil through the seasons. These are shown in glass and wood and stone in the churches. They are going on all round us in the towns whether it's selling second-hand books in Reepham or second-hand cars in the industrial suburbs of Norwich or sitting in a field of turnips having lunch as we saw those two ladies doing at Booton. The C[hurch] of E[ngland] will be taken for granted and Norfolk will be taken as the whole world but what we show must, so far as possible, be essentially Norfolk – gossip in ringing chambers before the bells are rung up or during a pause in the ringing. Tower after tower we will see as we go down unfenced roads, the most dominant things in the landscape now that windmills have disappeared and the towers which gave England the name of the 'Ringing Isle'.

We see them first at the birth of the film which is the hard struggle up the shingle from Cley beach, with a few pulled-up boats and some bits of rusty machinery and then the Saltings where the vegetation is grey and strange and muddy, Crabbe-like ponds abide. And we look up from them to the tower and beacon-tower of Blakeney or maybe the stretch of Horsey Mere and the sand dunes on the seaward side of it or the view of King's Lynn shown in Billa [Harrod]'s *Guide*. All will show, without words being necessary for emphasis, that Norfolk is a fleet of churches on undulating pasture, meadow and breck. We begin church with Baptism in the font at Trunch or we need only film that font and its soaring cover and the pouring of the water or immersion of the baby can be somewhere else. Then we have Sunday School and all over Norfolk in glass and wood and stone are school scenes, the beating of bottoms as in the porch at Cley or in the Cathedral and Bible lessons painted on walls and carved on stalls. Then we can have Confirmation and a Bishop's hand and the words and flaxen or reddish Norfolk hair on boy or girl or adult. Then we must have a village wedding, the coming out from the cottage and all the finery and ribbons on the hired car and illegal confetti and the relations in the pews. That unrestored church at Walsingham or South Creek would be a place for that. The Market Place which is an essential part in the daily life scenes in our film could be that fair Billa mentioned which is held annually outside Worstead, a wonderful Norfolk church and village and this could introduce us to a totter through the traffic-less lanes of Norwich City with a church round every corner and [George John] Skipper's art nouveau shopping arcade as well, and Norwich cattle market and fish being bought from the trawlers in a harbour and carried home straight to the cottages and houses without being sent to Grimsby. And now the keepers of the house tremble and the grinders cease and mourners go about the streets and that will bring us to a village funeral, the motor hearse and professional undertaker. All this is under wide sky in the sound of waves on shingle and bells in church-towers, single bells in dim churches. A ring of ten from big ones and from there we go to the singing angels in Norfolk mediaeval glass as at Bale and Warham-St-Mary. Up and up to the roof at Cawston and down for light relief to those Victorian ladies waiting to go to heaven and queuing in the stained-glass at Booton. And then more feathered angels in glass and wood. Then out into clouds and sky and from that the gold rays of the Resurrection gush to Lady Harrod (Wilhelmine and called Billa by me) and to Paul Paget.

With best wishes for a Happy Christmas and New Year to you, the missus and the kiddiz.

Yours for aye, Iain MacBetje

Candida Lycett Green

As a child my father, John Betjeman, used to come to the Norfolk Broads and the River Bure, sailing and rowing with his father. But it was another aspect of the county which was to enthral him all his life.

He explained in his commentary for the film, *A Passion for Churches*. ... 'I think it was the outline of the church tower of Belaugh against the sky which gave me a passion for churches; so that every church I've been past since I've wanted to stop and look in.'

If the flame was lit then when he was eight years old, it was certainly fanned by Billa Harrod in the 1940s and '50s when we all used to stay with her family at Bayfield Brecks in sandy, gorsy, piny country above the Glaven valley. From there you could see the towers of Blakeney, Wiveton and Cley. On Saturday afternoons, the grown ups used to go 'church crawling', which meant stopping and looking at every single church they passed.

Us children on the other hand, my brother Paul, Dominick and Henry Harrod and sometimes Ned Hamond, all violently anti anything old, used to walk two miles to the cinema in Holt. It wasn't until the Harrods moved to the Old Rectory there, with the cinema right on the doorstep, that my horizons began to broaden and the glory of Norfolk's churches was revealed to me.

One of my favourites is Booton near the small, mellow brick town of Reepham, along the dipping, well-hedged lane which leads to a sparse scattering of houses and the much pinnacled and wildly eccentric creation of the Revd. Whitwell Elwin.

If you look northwards towards the coast you get a spectacular view of perhaps the most beautiful churches in Norfolk – Salle and Cawston, their great towers rising majestically from this mild and gentle East Anglian landscape; Salle's from huge lonely arable fields, and the 14th century Cawston's from the huddling roofs of the little town.

Perhaps it was their inspirational glory in this particularly pretty bit of the county which led Whitwell Elwin to Booton, coupled with the fact that his uncle, Caleb, was already patron and rector there in the 1830s when Whitwell decided to take holy orders.

Booton's houses and church evoke a perfect vignette of Victorian ecclesiastical life, centring around the magnetic character of its incumbent who was a direct descendant of Pocahontas, the native American princess who married an Englishman and died at Gravesend. Elwin's noble profile bore witness to this.

He designed Booton as a complete amateur and took many of the features of the churches and cathedrals he had visited over the years, including Lichfield Cathedral, Temple Balsall in Warwickshire, St Stephen's Chapel at Westminster and Glastonbury Abbey.

Although Booton hasn't got a tower, it tells a story of faith – something my father never found easy to sustain. I think Norfolk's churches particularly gave him an extra strength which helped quell his doubts:

> *What would you be, you wide East Anglian sky,*
> *Without church towers to recognise you by?*
> *What centuries of faith, in flint and stone,*
> *Wait in this watery landscape all alone.*
> *To antiquaries, 'object of research',*
> *To the bored tourist 'just another church'.*
> *But still the faith of centuries is seen,*
> *In those who walk to church across the green.*
> *The faith of centuries is in the sound*
> *Of Easter bells, that ring all Norfolk round.*
> *And though for church we may not seem to care,*
> *It's deeply part of us. Thank God it's there.*

William Rivière

I remember a Norfolk carol service when I was still child enough to be made exceedingly nervous by having to stand up before the congregation and read to them that 'They shall not hurt nor destroy in all my holy mountain,' despite having been exhaustively rehearsed for this honour in the kitchen at home.

I remember a harvest thanksgiving during the preparations for which the sexton, who had fought on the Western Front nearly half a century before, sat on the porch bench and showed me how to bind a sheaf of wheat. But my parents also often took my brother and me to visit churches when no service was to be held. We went to favourites of theirs like Edingthorpe and Oxnead, and to Sloley and Tunstead and Paston, to ferret among the nettles for the graves of people we were descended from. We rubbed the lichen away from the lettering on their headstones to check when they'd been born, who they'd married and when they'd died. I got to know Morston church because one of my grandmothers had a house there. My other grandmother took me to Salhouse where my grandfather was buried at the foot of the tower, and where, she explained to me, she was going to join him.

I must still have been very young, because I found this notion perplexing. She took me to Ranworth where from the top of the church tower I remember looking out with her over the broad and the alder carr and the fen. And so when long afterward I came to write novels, this love of the holy places of my childhood seemed to take its place in them very naturally. By then I had haunted churches in France, Italy, Greece, and in Burma, India, Sri Lanka and Malaysia too, and I'd grown to love temples of other religions also. I never doubted that the mystery and resonance of a beautiful Christian church went beyond Protestant, Catholic or Orthodox doctrines; or doubted that sanctity and peace of spirit may be found in all manner of shrines all over the world, those still used for the celebration of a rite or those fallen into decay.

It's the sort of instinct I'd absorbed from my father on those afternoons when I'd ridden my pony beside his horse up the grassy path to Crostwight with its stumpy tower and commendable lack of electricity.

He'd talk about the different styles of Gothic; about the Church's historic importance as a patron of architects, painters, composers, master-builders, workers in stone, glass, metal; about the beauty of the liturgy; about the seemingly universal need for rituals to welcome the newly born, to wed lovers, to honour the dead and to propitiate the unknown ... before switching back to how vital it was to keep our Norfolk churches in good repair, and not as some of them had been in past centuries, nave roofs gaping, chancels used as byres.

Because what mattered was not church attendance, or even the flourishing or decline of a religion in a country. What mattered – whatever kind of believer, half-believer or sceptic you were – was the preservation of these masterpieces that had been bequeathed to us.

Years later when we'd be back at Crostwight, he now walking slowly and leaning on a stick, we'd rejoice that it had turned out that there were thousands of us all over the county who were happy to band together for the Norfolk Churches Trust. It has been, and will continue to be, a resounding success.

That the hallowed places of our countryside should endure: this seems to me the essence of it. We each have our own loyalties – but I keep walking back to the old paupers' graveyard beside what used to be Smallburgh workhouse, its nave formed not of stone but superb lime trees, and outlasting the injustices its nameless dead suffered.

Then there is magnificent Tunstead church; and beautiful Irstead by the river Ant, where in small congregations, and not always every Sunday of the month, it's been possible to have the use of some of the finest architecture and finest English our forefathers have left us. And perhaps best of all is to sail offshore and see our medieval flint towers lording it over the coast and the sea.

THOUGHTS IN A GARDEN

Elspeth Barker

(The author lives in north Norfolk beside the river Bure)

Mine is a riverine garden, and even indoors one is aware of this, not just by gazing through the window but by simply sitting still, committing words to paper in intense cold, while a great numbness seeps up through feet and lower limbs. Hemlock and the death of Socrates come forward in the mind. The tiled floor is laid straight on the earth in the manner of 17th century folk, and beneath this floor and a thin layer of earth lie the black sullen waters of an underground lake. This is true; I have seen those waters gleaming. Once this garden was fenland, embracing a much wider river, and Norsemen laboured up it in their long boats from the coast, intent on plunder and rapine. I am glad to have missed that.

Now time has modified the river bank, where bramble and hawthorn and snowberry and ivy tangle to forestall small children from a watery demise, and a high beech hedge divides it from the lawn's long slope. This hedge is a source of anger and grievance in postmen, rubbish men, delivery men of all sorts; they claim that its tentacular outreach damages their Vehicles, already woefully menaced by the muddy causeway which curves beside it, and mostly they refuse to come to the house. Which is fine by me, as I don't want to see them anyhow, except for the oil delivery man, who makes a ridiculous point of driving his colossal tanker backwards up the track.

Wet wet wet is the texture of the lawn, currently mounded by molehills of ever more ambitious scale. Wetter still is the stretch of wilderness leading to the pond and the graveyard of the important animals. Bog grasses are growing now, where once in more clement times my children played football or tried to hoist a sequence of angry ponies over jumps. I always chose the highest ground for the graves and I believe these noble beasts still sleep sound and dry; but even in the less sodden past the largest animal you could bury there would be

a Labrador. Any deeper and it was standing water. Consequently, forty-
one years on, space for final resting places is at a premium, and certain
lesser creatures have had to be consigned to the edges of the lawn and
peripheral nettly groves. Desdemona, the cat without character, lies
here, and quite a few hens. I well recall beginning a new flowerbed and
exhuming a dreadful pair of yellow legs complete with claws. 'That's
Joanna,' observed a passing child, unmoved. Sombre, the trees gather
about the upper graves, but in late winter their darkness is offset most
exquisitely by the floating wanness of narcissi, and then wild
primroses.

When we came here, all those years ago, the garden had ceased to
exist. Nettles and brambles and ground elder and cow parsley and dock
revelled luxuriantly through our first springtime. I had three children
under three and was thus preoccupied; soon I had two more. My
husband wrote his poetry in an upper room, looking out into trees, sky
and river, happily removed from earthly concerns. When summer at
last came we began to reclaim the lawn. Children need grass and trees
first of all. Then their animals needed grass, and the hens, disdaining
their run, claimed the trees. Albertine and Madame Alfred Carrière
clambered cautiously up the house and early morning light, refracted
from the river, flickered and shifted through shadowing rose leaves
down our red bedroom walls and danced in the brass knobs of the bed.
Albertine was vigorous and gorgeously pink but died abruptly after
only three years. Madame Alfred, however, continues to thrive and
even this December displayed a scatter of ghostly blooms, whirled to
the sky's four quarters by the bitter Norfolk wind. And as the years
have passed, at last there is the time and chance to give attention to the
flowerbeds, time to alleviate the whelm of greenery.

My husband, the poet, died some years ago and I have tried to make
a six foot garden on his grave; a rowan tree shades his stone and
chequered fritillaries nod amid a profusion of forget-me-nots and
foxgloves. In autumn there come the flaming arches of crocosmia. But
the garden for the living is another matter. I am blessed in having

married again and my husband, although eccentric and American, is a visionary gardener. I have seen him coax a rose, blighted and shrunk through wet and cold, furled tight in deathly pallor, into a perfumed ecstasy of splayed crimson, a performance so charged with eroticism that words must fail me. He has made a vast, overbalancing buddleia into an airy cavern of blue delight, underplanted by cranesbill and campanula; butterflies fold their wings along the silvery boughs and its haunting raspberry fragrance hangs in the air. I take intense pleasure in clambering up inside it and deadheading. There is an unearthly hush about the slow, gentle drift of the spent blooms to the ground, and through the branches I can see birds cross the wide sky, sometimes a swan, or a heron, or a flock of squabbling starlings, and I feel ethereal. But in truth I am a gardener manquée; I participate eagerly in the effect but do little to further the cause. Mostly I have the no-brain jobs, a little basic weeding, the wheelbarrow trundle to the unlightable bonfire, the gingerly poke at the compost heap. I am happy with these simple tasks; I believe myself useful but am without responsibility. Meanwhile, the paragon or paramour creates fabulous small vistas of colour, bells and spires; Saki's 'bewildering fragment of fairyland' glimmers in sudden surprise as you wander past a shrub or around a tree. Look, look, we cry.

He is, however, obsessed with turnips. He grows them everywhere, among cornflowers, and tulips, and beside the miraculous violet sculpture of sea holly. Where e'er your glance may linger, there rears a turnip. No other plant behaves like this. At all seasons they are conspicuous, in leaf, in flower, in white globular roots within whose deep recesses reptiles dwell. There are kindred disruptive elements in this garden; besides the molehills, a number of spiky dead trees present their barren limbs like amputees; still, they give pleasure to woodpeckers. Then there is the oil tank, behind which the junior dog has made a den, furnished by herself with stolen red cushions and Somerfield packaging; and we have the pathetic relic of the duck pen, containing an improvised and unused duck shelter fashioned from an abandoned azure plasterboard bookcase. Those ducks betrayed us. Those ducks went down the river.

Yet we can tell each other that the garden is beautiful, as the low white mist rises from the river and scarves the trees and we hear the sigh and rush of moving water, the toss of aspen leaves. The rainy sounding aspens, Sappho called them, nearly three thousand years ago; the same sound now. And other people tell us that the garden is beautiful as they sit round the lawn table beneath the ancient beech tree. For those summer moments none of us will notice that the great tree is dying from its crown; indeed, to save its life, it is to be pollarded this very month, cut across in half. I absolutely cannot bear to think of this, but I can see that it doesn't want to die. It has already put forth buds for spring and beneath its bark three new trunks are rising from its roots; slim and shining grey, they press with youthful urgency into the aged soft white wood.

At the bleak time of year how tempting it is to lie in bed, cosseted like bulbs; we are aware of the dawn beyond closed curtains and we may consider the virtue of 'maintaining a constant temperature in a dark place,' as recommended so cordially by gardeners and oenophiles. But then, like bulbs and bottles, we must be brought into the light. A garden is idea as much as it is terrain, and now it confers perhaps its greatest blessing; the knowledge that whatever has happened, here we have another chance. Here there will be renaissance. In a garden it is never too late.

PERFECTION THREATENED
John Betjeman
(from *The Daily Telegraph*, March, 1964)

The express train stops at a station high in air and looking over ploughland. We are where the river Waveney meanders between Norfolk and Suffolk.

It is real farming country. The villages have large greens and large flint churches. The older cottages have steep pitched roofs for reed thatch. Elms and willows, abound in this mildly undulating scenery.

East Anglia comes to life in sunlight, especially sharp winter sunlight when colour-washed plaster shines white, pale pink, cream, pale blue, and the knapped flint of the huge, clerestoried naves and elaborate porches of 15th-century churches sparkles like crystal. The red of old brick, the brown of plough and green of meadow and the silhouette of branches against the wide pale sky are so intense and clear that they have the quality of colour in a medieval manuscript.

'Diss' it says on the windy platform. But where is Diss? There is no sign of it, only plough, trees and sky.

All I knew of modern Diss was that it was near to the headquarters of the British Goat Society. Just opposite the station a narrow passage between two sheds had 'The Jolly Porters' over it and down this passage was a country inn, but I was too early for opening time.

Diss is just over a mile from the station. It has a population of about 4,000 which has neither grown nor shrunk through the centuries, an excellent service of trains to Norwich and London, no main road through it to murder pedestrians and take the trade from the shops – in fact, it is the perfect small English town.

Because it is self-contained, prosperous, friendly and contented, it is naturally threatened with overspill on the edges and demolition in its heart.

While we can see it, let us look at it, for Diss has in it the agreeable elements of every old English town.

On the straight road from the station, appropriately called Victoria

Road, are the gasworks, some grey-brick Italianate houses of the eighteen-sixties with bits of country in between. The railway came in 1847.

Of course, there has been more recent 'development' along this road – a cinema, a swimming pool, a miniature Slough trading estate and, just lately, a gaunt row of new shops which might as well be in Southall or Potters Bar. Then, round the corner, is Diss.

Its situation is perfect and unexpected. The colour-washed houses and Georgian brick ones gather on a hill with gardens and orchards sloping down to a mere. This mere is not big enough to be called a lake, yet it is much larger than a pond. Wherever you go in the chief streets you get glimpses of its rippling water, swans and quacking ducks.

Fortunately, nowhere, except at one place called the Mere's Mouth, in Mere Street, the main street of the town, is there any attempt at municipal gardening and crazy-paving. It is all as natural as a Norfolk Broad, but with trees round it instead of reeds, and a hill with houses on, instead of flatness.

It is easy to trace the story of Diss from its buildings. You can see the prosperity from wool and cloth trades of the late Middle Ages in the large, timber-framed houses near the market place. Narrow alleys, steep winding hills and the market place itself, all give views of the great flint Church to which they lead the eye.

The piety of the Middle Ages is still seen in the streets – an archangel carved in wood on the corner of the bookshop where the local paper is printed: the Annunciation and the Nativity on the corner of a corn chandler's shop This was the kingdom of which John Skelton, the poet of love, hawking and laughter and the tutor of Henry VIII, was rector.

The carved staircase and Jacobean plaster work inside the Greyhound Inn are a post-Reformation survival of the old gaiety.

As in all East Anglian towns, there is an abundance of old, Nonconformist chapels, the older hidden away down side streets – Quaker meeting house in dark red brick, with its burial ground: 'The tabernacle', with weatherboarded sides, red-tiled roof and white-painted interior and its burial ground; and, simplest and stateliest of all these Puritan places of worship, the Unitarian Chapel, now a Masonic hall in a field beside the Mere. Nonconformist thrift and industry built many of the dignified late Georgian private houses with their walled gardens, notably Mount Pleasant, the seat of the Taylor family.

Come into Diss on a market day, on Friday, when the Greek Revival Corn Hall is rumbling with the talk of Norfolk farmers and salesmen at their wooden Greek Revival stands. Or notice the handsome Georgian and mid-Victorian shop fronts, particularly the two chemist shops and the charming pair of shops in The Shambles in the market place. One of these is the local museum. See the Victorian classic fittings inside Bobby's, the local drapers, the elder branch of the firm in the south coast towns.

Diss is proud of itself. Its shopping streets have been prettily re-painted under a scheme of the Civic Trust, but what makes Diss so attractive to live in and walk in is its variety and informality. Here a house juts forward, and a tree hangs over a garden wall. There old houses curve up a hill.

Little bits of country come right into the town. Mount Street must be one of the pleasantest country town streets left in England, a mixture of brick and plaster, garden and park, ending with the flint tower of the church. In other parts of the town, there are glimpses of the Mere, some from water level, some from high above. Nothing is conscious planning, yet it all holds together, the old and the less old.

And all this is threatened. The rot has started. Old cottages in the centre of the town, in back streets and on the Fair Green are left to fall to pieces and their inhabitants have moved out to council estates which are, like all council estates, hygienic and harmless but neither town, suburb nor country. How much more far-sighted it would have been to have spent the money used for new estates, on repairing and enlarging the old cottages in the town itself.

Even The Shambles in the market place is threatened, to provide parking for about six more cars.

And over all, like a rising cloud, hangs the threat of an overspill. When that comes this prosperous and happy agricultural community will change. Supermarkets will take the place of old shops; thousands of industrial works from the North of England via London will be housed on agricultural land between the town and the station. The place will be filled with strangers. Neighbour will not know neighbour.

Those who think that this will mean more trade, must not forget that it will mean no more Diss.

CROW COUNTRY
Mark Cocker
(from *Crow Country*, 2007)

Landscapes impose their own kind of relationship. In Derbyshire I was used to getting up high on some commanding rock or eminence and surveying the surrounding moors and fields. ...

The Yare valley demanded a massive adjustment. There are no dramatic contours in this place, aside from its fantastical levelness. For the naturalist it imposes a different mode of operation. In the Yare I've got used to scanning the great sweep of flat country and watching things at range. Unimpeded views have come to compensate for the greater distance. I ceased to be concerned with fine detail or being near to things; instead it is the length of observations that counts. Since the creature I'm watching has nowhere to disappear to, what determines the duration is my own attention span. I've learned to be patient and to wait for things to come to me. I set up my telescope and sit in the same place so that it feels like – it is – a kind of ornithological fishing.

In time I've also learned to love a different register of features. Subtly and unconsciously they have become embedded in my experience. For instance it is a first task on arrival at any point of the marsh to scan the five-bar gates and their curious adjunct in this incised landscape, the fence extensions that lean into the dykes at an angle and prevent the cattle rounding the gateway through the water. The complex architecture of posts and cross-beams, which recede through foreshortening in a seemingly inter-linked network across the marsh, is the external oasis for sparrow hawks, peregrine, merlin, harriers and barn owls that hunt here. I have learned equally to treat each dyke like a hidden valley that you inch towards and, as the full length of the longitudinal strip comes into view, to scan the water quickly for anything that might be resting there.

One other aspect that required a fundamental adjustment was the central feature of this landscape: the river. The Yare is a modest body of water. Looking at its course on the map, you can see that in parts its flood plain is over eight kilometres across, but in comparison with the extensive flats the river itself looks trivial: no more than a single blue wrinkle across an entire face. It's Norfolk's biggest watercourse but it would be difficult to pretend that it's significant in national terms. It's a short river, inherently provincial as well as narrow and slow-flowing. In the 45 kilometres it takes to reach the North Sea after leaving the outskirts of Norwich it falls less than five metres. Twice every day the whole stretch ebbs and flows with the tide and in Norwich it's so saline I've seen cormorants surface with fair-sized flounder.

However insignificant it may seem, it still asserted itself with subtle power. I quickly found that it held sway over an awkward, inaccessible landscape. In the entire stretch from Norwich to Yarmouth it's bridged at either end in the two towns themselves, but in between there is no physical structure across it. I routinely meet people who live on the one bank and who have never visited the village opposite, although they may look upon the place every day of their lives. Once I even encountered a couple during a walk at

Buckenham who'd lived all their lives in a village on the north side of the river, and didn't even know the name of the village on the other side. The Yare has become a psychological borderline.

Halfway between the two bridges in Norwich and Yarmouth is Reedham where there's a small private ferry, which maintains a long venerable tradition and reflects the historical answer to the Yare's hindrance. In previous centuries there was far more contact between the two sides. On either bank the recurrence of 'ferry' place names – Ferry Road, Ferry Lane, Ferry Farm and various Ferry inns – speaks of a community that looked to the water as the main means of communication. Yet to cross from side to side was one thing; to leave the valley itself was another matter entirely.

I soon found that I too was being hemmed in by the river. Places I used to visit routinely during our Norwich days slipped inexorably beyond reach. Old favourites like the magnificent north Norfolk coast involved a one-way journey of an hour and a half. Much of it was spent mired in Norwich, whose entire diameter had to be crossed each way. I sometimes wonder whether, in my passion for the Yare and its rooks, necessity wasn't the mother of invention. The real origins of my obsession were those regular slow-flowing crocodiles of cars, traffic light to traffic light, through the heart of the city.

One by one, old haunts were abandoned, and strangest of all my 'lost' territories was Buckenham itself, the locality for the rook roost. While it's become the key focus of my present interests, I know it now largely as an exile, looking on from the 'wrong' side of the river. I can see the village and its neighbouring woods just a stone's throw away from our house, but to get there and back is an hour's drive. I can reach Cambridge in the same time. Now I go to Buckenham perhaps three or four times a year.

It isn't just the river making this a place of impediment. All the waters of the valley, over which the Yare exercises its irresistible gravitational hold, hedge me in. Even on my side it's impossible to follow the length of the flood plain directly. To visit a section downstream like Thurlton or Haddiscoe I have to drive almost due south away from the valley, circumvent the single obtruding tributary in this stretch called the Chet, then cut back north to my goal. To reach Haddiscoe, a straight downstream distance of about 11 kilometres, is twice as far by road.

But to walk in the landscape is worse. To the human eye the valley is an extensive plain of grassland interrupted now and then with alluring reed-fringed pools, circled with alder carr or poplar plantations. It seems a gentle, unpeopled, easy place, but its very flatness is the source of the illusion. Bounding every field, and initially invisible to the visitor, is a network of water-filled dykes. Farmers and wildfowlers have bridged many of them with old rotting planks, known as liggers, but many others have no means of access. And memorising the navigable routes takes a lifetime of familiarity. My walks across the open spaces were often reduced to a tedious tour of each field's inner perimeter, made more frustrating by the sight of my goal and the impossibility of its attainment.

The net result was a reaffirmation of the Broadlanders' old conclusion. This was a landscape fit only for boats. In the Broads sailing vessels are still ubiquitous and their serene passage while I was on one of my cross-country meanderings only intensified any feelings of annoyance. In truth, though, I had little grounds for complaint. The merest glance at the map shows you that the Yare valley is depicted as a network of blue rhomboids. The two-dimensional image of the interlacing dykes reminds me of shattered glass, or possibly – and this may be a simple case of projection – an abstract representation of the mental state induced by walking around the fields themselves.

One consequence of the valley's intractability is that I take a map with me every time I go out. No other landscape has made such a demand. Other places I've lived in or known resolve into a complete mental picture relatively quickly. The different facets link up like parts of a jigsaw, and as the last few fragments drop into their unique, logical place there is that sweet sense of completion. But it didn't happen like that in the Yare valley and, once more, its flatness was implicated in the matter. The absence of relief leaves you with no fixed frame of reference. Depending on the angle of view, places isolated from one another can concertina together and merge. Distant trees that form a far horizon at one spot, in another can rush across the intervening space and graft themselves to a far closer skyline. Church spires or windmills, the only tall buildings in the landscape, shift their locality according to one's own position.

Another factor was the difficulty of access. Different spots remained far longer as a sequence of disconnected fragments. I'd stumble on a plantation or a piece of marsh and feel excited to have located some totally new feature. Only slowly would it dawn on me that the neighbouring building or the configuration of trees, the church tower looming over the top, were all vaguely familiar. The penny would drop – I'd been here before. The difference had been the direction of approach.

Almost perversely, the Yare's recalcitrance became part of its appeal and I found myself working at the business of mental connection. The slow mastery of its geography seemed to increase the sense of belonging. As if to reinforce its tightening grip on my spatial imagination, soon after moving to the Yare I supplemented my chart of the Earth, which had been on my office wall for fifteen years, with a map of the valley. It had become an alternative world.

The most inaccessible part is the triangular block formed by Halvergate and Haddiscoe Island. While the former is the more famous and customary name (it was the site of an environmental struggle in the late 1980s that exposed the corrosive, tsunami-like destructive power of excessive grain subsidies flowing from the Common Agricultural Policy), from here on I'll refer to it as Haddiscoe, simply because it's the part of the whole I know best.

All of the county is low and rolling – its highest point is only 100 metres – but this fan-shaped extension best fulfils Noël Coward's famous dictum on the Norfolk landscape. It is indubitably, resolutely flat, with much of it below sea level. Technically Haddiscoe is also an island, isolated from the neighbouring land by the converging Yare and Waveney rivers and a man-made water channel linking the two rivers. It says something about the long human timeline inherent in this landscape that the dead-straight navigational canal was dug in 1835 yet today is still known as the New Cut.

Together with the two rivers the New Cut completes a three-sides moat around Haddiscoe. Within this level expanse there is just a single straight road going nowhere and it is unpeopled apart from three homesteads. Two of them crouch down in the lee of a steep bank that prevents the Waveney reoccupying its old domain. Their roofs are barely higher than the level of the river and all of them have a laager-like periphery of outbuildings as if defending themselves against the vast nothingness of Haddiscoe's sky. Just to the south of the island, from the bridge at St Olaves, about seven metres high, you can look upstream to the west and the view is uninterrupted for 12 kilometres. To the north, across Haddiscoe's entire length, you can see the giant wind turbines at West Somerton slicing the air with great clarity, yet they are 20 kilometres away.

Such a place requires a major aesthetic recalibration from its admirers, a transition many don't care to make and they dismiss it as featureless and boring. It is a result of our utter disregard for the beauty of the open plain that this landscape has been disfigured by a regiment of monstrous electricity pylons. It is inconceivable that the Lakes or the Cotswolds would have been violated in this way, yet Haddiscoe seems not even to have been considered a landscape, more a void to the west of the ports of Lowestoft and Great Yarmouth to be treated any old how.

It's true that there are none of the usual constituents of the picturesque. At its most stark, there are very few buildings, no trees and no contours. The stripping away of customary markers does strange things to one's perception. Perspective is flattened out. Features that lie at some range from one another in a horizontal plain are compressed together. Details in the middle distance – a passing boat, a herd of cattle, the brick cylinder of a derelict mill – swim in an indeterminate way, neither getting any closer nor further away, regardless of how long one walks towards them. And if you keep your eyes fixed on this mid-horizon, near things can then take you totally by surprise. Mounds of slub, the thick black mud lugged from a dyke by mechanical digger, break the horizon like a range of hills. Lines of dead thistles erupt from the ground like the broken tops of dead pines in a landscape of snow. A hare jinking away from your feet, bounding off with that odd, intermittent sideways thrust of the hind legs, can seem as big as a deer.

Yet the sheer emptiness of the place can intensify feelings of intimacy with those things that are close. In autumn as I walk the long road bisecting Haddiscoe, the air is filled with dragonflies and occasionally a hunting individual will fly almost at my face. The chitin snapping together as it manoeuvres is like the crackle of electricity, or a firework fizzing before its explosion. Then it settles on the concrete wall, its weightlessness poised on the needle-tip of its six hair-thin legs. In a few days, weeks at most, you know its life will end. Yet here it is, a scarlet cruciform filling itself with autumn sunlight, savouring the immensity of its existence.

The space all around seems a part of such close encounters. It particularises the moment. Things seem special, I could be wrong. The background conditions may be far more prosaic. It may be that I am simply trapped by the sheer impediment of the river, and I am just making the most of the wildlife that's to hand. But I don't think so. In the Yare valley so many of the things that I had once overlooked or taken for granted were charged with fresh power and importance. It gave rise to a strange and fruitful paradox. I had come home to a place where everything seemed completely new.

Rooks are at the heart of my relationship with the Yare. They were my route into the landscape and my rationale for its exploration. Over the last six years I've learned about the birds and the place simultaneously. I cannot now think of one without the other. Yet when I look back it seems bizarre to recall how little they once meant to me. Before we moved I gave rooks no more thought than any other bird.

Rather, I gave them less. they seemed so commonplace.

In the Yare it would be true to say I didn't go to look for them. They came for me. It happened several months after we'd moved. Slowly I was conscious of them flying over our house about an hour before it was time to get up. The birds' calls fired down every morning almost without fail. They kept up the barrage for five or ten minutes, the notes clattering on to the road and the rooftops of the village like flakes of tin. A little of the sound came in at the part-opened window of our bedroom and was softened in the sepia half-light of dawn. It filtered through to us as we lay in that twilight state of half-wakefulness, and over the weeks a gradual sediment of awareness must have gathered in my unconscious.

Eventually they dawned on me like a revelation. I found myself sitting up simply to catch the sonorous gravely voices as they passed, I'd guessed they were in good numbers and that the calls measured the duration of a flock's movements over Claxton. One November afternoon I caught sight of them for the first time. I was in the garden as dusk was falling. Suddenly there was a long silent procession of birds across the sky, a mixture of rooks and jackdaws heading north, presumably on their way to a night roost somewhere in the valley. But where?

Several days later it seemed obvious that I should go and look for the roost site, just as I'd got accustomed to watching the gulls come in at Hardley Flood. It was a mere transference of focus from one roosting species to another. In the way that one tried out another experience simply because it was one more facet of the novelty thrust upon me by a life change, I set off to the river before three, without expectations of it yielding anything of significance.

The first birds were already heading towards the ploughed fields near a big wood, which I now know as Buckenham Carr, on the opposite side of the Yare. Initially I tried to count rooks and jackdaws separately, but they were so mingled together and they came so thick and fast that I gave up and simply listed them under a single heading: corvids, the genetic word for members of the crow family.

253

The cloud was low and a gentle northerly carried heavy banks of grey slowly overhead, then on across the flood plain towards the southern horizon. I positioned myself with my back to the river and to Buckenham Carrs, looking south and homewards to where the birds appeared in random parties. Loose mobs of several hundred broke into the space above the valley, appearing a few dozen at a time. As quickly as they arrived overhead, I attempted to jot down the total. I don't think I'd ever really noticed how impressive rooks and jackdaws could be in flight.

The two made quite separate impressions. The jackdaws often came in low and hard in small tight knots, a football of birds bounding just above tree height. Otherwise they cruised over, scattered evenly across the sky, wings half closed, each creating a separate, small, missile-like profile and almost invariably completing the short distance to the landing place without a single wing stroke. Then at the last, as they approached their destination – a clump of alders already smothered in roosting birds – they performed a beautiful manoeuvre.

Small groups cohered just before the trees and jinked sideways and up, as if suddenly confronted by an onrushing wall of air. They were like surfers mounting a huge wave and at its apex, with their onward trajectory neutralised by the water's opposing momentum, they were held momentarily still. Then down they came with absolute precision to take a place on a branch or twig among their neighbours.

The rooks were usually a good deal higher when they crossed the Yare. They were less vocal and always flew more slowly. They also lost height in a distinctive fashion. The wings were held at an angle forward from the body and raised above its plane to create a striking dihedral, while the body itself was almost pressed downwards with that weird broken nose of a bill pushed foremost. The posture seemed to spill air from the wings and down they came steadily with curiously light, almost mincing, half-beats of the wings. Compared to the nippy missile qualities of the jackdaw, the rooks looked stately in their progress.

By the time the flow of birds had virtually ceased, I estimated about

5,000, although since it was my first attempt to count large numbers it was really a guess. Whatever the true total, it was the largest flock of crows I'd seen in my life. This was impressive enough, but then something miraculous happened.

It was virtually dark. There was so little light, I was barely sure if my binoculars were focused or not. I'd assumed that the great carpet of birds spread across the fields, and down the wires and over the clump of alders, was actually the roost itself. I surmised that the action had ended. Roosting for these birds meant gathering together in a loose aggregation like this. But no.

Suddenly birds started to fly up in a purposeful jet of black shapes spurting from the trees. The movements of some seemed to act as a detonator on the others. Before I knew what was happening the whole host was airborne and swarming towards Buckenham Carrs. When the flock was centred over the wood it started to swirl and twist. The birds were wrenched back and forth as if each was caught by the same conflicting impulses. When portions of the flock turned in unison through a particular angle the entire surface of the wingspan – measuring about a metre on the rooks – was reduced to a single pencil line. The net effect in the quarter-light of dusk was that whole sections vanished and reappeared a split second later. It was as if a tonne of birds was being conjured and re-conjured from thin air.

The flock was a dense as gnat swarm and yet each dark speck in that fluid drift was a bird weighing half a kilo. Their round-winged shapes were blurred and softened and extended in the dusk light. So at home in the twilight, they resembled an escaping deluge of fruit bats breaking for the cover of nightfall.

Another captivating manoeuvre elsewhere in the flock involved a discrete cauldron of birds that looked as if it were about to break away from the parent body. Yet as the last minute it was as if they were caught in the gravitational field of the main flock. The larger number steadily prevailed, sucking the lesser section back inexorably into its orbit. As it careened home towards the primary group the reunion triggered a separate visual effect. Where they overlapped, the outer birds in each swirl were compressed into a higher density, and this sparked knock-on reactions that eddied through all the birds in a continuous shimmer. It offered insights into the whole airborne manoeuvre. While the flock's globular swirl was shapeless and without purpose, at another level it appeared like an attempt to resolve the spatial discord. It looked like, it was, a paradox: harmonised chaos. It was beautiful, mysterious and completely unexpected.

The rooks and jackdaws, the birds that I had presumed to know and judged unworthy of a second glance, had gone, unsheathed entirely from any sense of ordinariness. In their place was a vision which was nothing less than magical: the smoke of a genie's lamp in sinuous folds. It was as if I were seeing them now for the first time. The airborne gyre was both guiding star and immense question mark rotating in the night sky. I've been following it ever since.

DANGEROUS DELIGHTS

The Suffolk Coast

TRIFLES FROM LOWESTOFT

Ian Collins

(from *The Countryman*, May 2001)

While a heavy outcrop of clay can mean a light harvest, it also fired hopes for enterprising figures in the 18th century who sought a living from the land. Given sufficient quantity of this raw material, kilns might be set up for bricks, tiles and even for rough earthenware vessels – wares which had, after all, been made in East Anglia under the Romans. But only in Lowestoft was the local clay deemed of adequate quality to allow for the fine art of porcelain production.

Myth and mystery still swirl around this creative outpost like a sea mist, though historians, ceramicists and industrial archaeologists have slowly discerned the outline and salient features of the story. Certainly a lot of skill, and not a little skulduggery, attended the porcelain factory's birth.

Ever since the 16th century Europe had been swept by passions for exotic imports from the east such as silk, tea, tulips and china. From 1650 onwards continental potters tried to crack porcelain's secret code and aped Oriental styles of decoration on their own native pottery.

Meissen was the first continental factory to blend the correct ingredients, closely followed by Sevres in France, but many other sites experimented with substitute recipes. Amid cut-throat competition, the common aim was to reproduce the rich translucence of Chinese porcelain at a much cheaper price. In England William Cookworthy discovered the proper components as late as the 1740s, and he was then unable to establish a plant, in Bristol, until 1765. By that point porcelain factories at Chelsea, Worcester and Bow were in full swing. By then Lowestoft was also in its stride, if not quite in on the secret.

The Suffolk saga really began around 1756 when Hewling Luson found a 'fine clay' on his Gunton Estate, just to the north of Lowestoft. One fable suggests that the value of the reserve was pointed out by a Dutch shipwreck survivor familiar with the operations of Delft. Luson then sent a sample for tests – almost certainly to the Bow factory, in what was then a village east of London. According to Edmund Gillingwater, in *An Historical Account of the Ancient Town of Lowestoft*, the landowner was encouraged by the resulting report to set up a temporary kiln and furnace and to instal some trained workers, who also hailed from Bow. The town chronicler accused the incomers of sabotage: their old employer had recognised a potential rival and paid them to 'exercise every art in their power' to thwart Luson's design. Curiously, after bankruptcy had forced a sale of his estate, the failed pioneer was eventually to die at Bethnal Green – a pot's throw from Bow.

But if the Gunton researches were indeed deliberately ruined, then a slight shadow of suspicion might fall on the group of businessmen who founded the Lowestoft Porcelain Manufactory shortly afterwards. The main mover, Philip Walker, was apparently an exemplary citizen – but he was also a tenant of the Gunton Estate. Anyway, brickmaker Obediah Aldred provided the partnership with premises in Bell Lane (now called Crown Street) where the trials continued until, Gillingwater again asserts, they were almost wrecked by another batch of duplicitous staff borrowed from Bow. When the site was excavated in 1903, the discovery of a mass of defective models suggested a major accident, or maybe sabotage, during firing.

Not that Lowestoft folk were necessarily above the low behaviour of Londoners. Family legend had it that founding partner Robert Browne, a former blacksmith who was to manage the Suffolk factory, infiltrated the Bow works and, hiding in a room, and possibly in a barrel, saw how the ingredients were magically mixed. He then memorised the formula and escaped undetected. Alternatively, he may just have had innocent and innovative skills as a chemist. Conspiracy theorists have noted, however, that the Bow factory account book for 1757-8 lists weekly wages of 18 shillings payable to a Mr Brown.

Whatever the truth, the raw materials – china-clay, bone-ash and crushed flint or sand (these additives to clay being in place of the petuntse stone of true porcelain) – were successfully combined. Experiments in paste, glaze and tone of underglaze blue painting were satisfactorily completed. Stock was built up and the Bell Lane factory site expanded. So that, early in 1760, the following advertisement could be run through several issues of the *Norwich Mercury* and *Ipswich Journal*:

LOWESTOFT in Suffolk, Jan 23, 1760. Notice is hereby given to all Dealers in PORCELAIN or CHINA WARE. That by or before Lady next will be offered to Sale, a great Variety of neat Blue and White CHINA, or PORCELAIN, at the Manufactery in this Town. 'Tis humbly hoped that most of the Shopkeepers in this County, and the County of Norfolk, will give Encouragement to this laudable Undertaking, by reserving their Spring Orders for their humble Servants, WALKER & Co.

At the outset decoration consisted of Oriental designs, European rococo motifs or stylised flowers, birds and insects. Cheaper, quicker and more economical transfer printing, and costly painting in rich enamel colours over the glaze (the extra cost caused by the need for multiple firing), would be introduced from the late 1760s. Initially, dishes moulded on leaves or scallop shells were often handled with more confidence than thrown vessels. But over time certain attractive shapes became archetypal Lowestoft – particularly a 'sparrowbeak' cream-jug, with a beak-like pourer and a curling tail to the handle. The glaze remained distinctive, frequently gathering beneath the feet of cups and bowls in blue-green pools. And yet, however dogged the enterprise throughout a four-decade existence, and however serious its achievement in outlasting all its larger rivals save for Derby and Worcester, there was an endearing naivety and an enduring humour in the output.

What's more the project was not just provincial, but avowedly local.

261

Artefacts were embellished with landmarks, scenes, games and family or professional emblems to attract merchants and country people in Suffolk and Norfolk. Punchbowls were inscribed for hunts, weddings and farmers' celebrations. There were celebratory birth tablets, pierced to hang as toys in the cots of the babies of factory workers and fisherfolk (those for Anne, Martha and Mary Redgrave can now be seen in the Norwich Castle Museum thanks to the brilliant 1940s gift of Mrs Russell Colman). There were inscribed pieces for vicars, millers, publicans, grocers, butchers, carpenters, carriers, ships' captains, herring curers and lugger owners. And then there were messages for sweethearts, plus commemorative slogans such as A Trifle From Lowestoft which caught the first wave of seaside tourism in a coastal town noted for its healthy air and aspect. Other recorded place names include Bungay, Beccles, Halesworth, Wangford (where there was a toll gate), Woodbridge, Norwich, Hingham, Holt, Crostwick and King's Lynn. More than 200 dated pieces survive, stretching in a virtually unbroken sequence from 1761 to 1799. All these wares were relatively cheap and undeniably cheerful.

The charm of Lowestoft porcelain lies in the bridge it provides between folk art and fine art – plus a unique record of place and period. In 1782, at the height of the factory's prosperity, the proprietors contributed ten guineas to the building of HMS Suffolk, then being constructed at the county's expense. A unique flask shows just such a vessel taking shape on an East Anglian beach.

Though the bulk of production consisted of table ware, and chiefly of tea and coffee services, there were also ornamental objects such as plaques, vases and cornucopia wall-pockets. There were eyebaths, inkwells, scent bottles, spittoons, spoon trays, candlesticks and cutlery handles. One comic cane handle, now in the Victoria & Albert Museum, looks alarmingly like the displaced head of Marie Antoinette. Occasional figures (putti, musicians), together with a swan, a cygnet, a cat, sheep, pug dogs and a cream-jug cow, were akin to earthy Staffordshire pottery designs masquerading as elegant porcelain. Besides catering for the regional market, the Suffolk potters also plotted outright deception in the search for buyers further afield. They mimicked Chinese decoration; they faked the crescent mark of Worcester or Meissen's coveted crossed swords. The Bow practice of signing pieces with painters' numerals, however, was copied only briefly. Maybe it was a coincidence that the rival factory had become known and shunned for jugs and pots which failed to hold hot water and handles which came off in the hand ...

The diarist Silas Neville, ever a gloomy traveller, wrote of a trip to Lowestoft in 1772: 'After dinner visited the China Manufactory carried on there. Most of it rather ordinary. The painting branch is done by Women.' Twelve years later, a French visitor with connections to the court of Louis XVI was more impressed and far more informative. Maximilien de Lazowski noted that two coal-fired kilns burned for 28 hours at a time, with the china left inside for three days in all to allow for gradual cooling. He also recorded that, among a staff of up to 100, apprentices were paid from seven shillings a week, whereas skilled workers earned 14 shillings and the best painters could top 30 shillings.

Certain families (Bly, Redgrave, Stevenson) dominate the known list of employees – women and children being especially cost effective. Numbers of lesser skilled workers would have ebbed and flowed depending on the state of the order book, with casual staff also putting in time in the staple Lowestoft industries of fishing and rope making, or labouring in the fields.

Authorship of almost all these pictures on porcelain is now poignantly anonymous. In the 1770s an unknown painter, or painters, arose who specialised in floral designs – an art which found its greatest flowering in depictions of the tulip. This prized bulb, which had once caused financial frenzy in Amsterdam, was brought to East Anglia by Flemish refugees, along with gillyflowers, Provence roses and carnations. It was destined for cultivation in the Fens after drainage by Dutch engineers and celebrated at florists' feasts in Norwich as early as 1631. Now the art it inspired in Lowestoft can be attributed only to the 'Tulip Painter'.

Another legend claims that an illegitimate son of Louis XVI fled the guillotine and – leaving behind a fortune – found work as a Lowestoft artist. He took the name Thomas Rose after one of the flowers he became so adept at portraying. In the end the strain of working on his delicate art in poor light is said to have cost him his sight and livelihood.

Richard Powles (1763-1807) is believed to have been taken on as a painter at the age of eight. He proved a talented landscape artist and some of his pen and wash topographical drawings of the Lowestoft area have been tentatively linked to specific scenes on porcelain. A marvellous polychrome mug in the Norwich Castle Museum, with a sea view including Lowestoft High Lighthouse and the arms and motto of Trinity House, resembles a Powles wash drawing (as does a similar vessel in the Victoria & Albert Museum). But the artist was often absent on business interests in Denmark and London – his obituarist claiming he had provided coastal charts which helped Nelson in the Battle of Copenhagen.

Robert Allen (1745-1835) is Lowestoft's best-documented artist. He began as an apprentice decorator in the early days of the factory and ended as manager and chief painter. A line of inscribed and dated pieces from the 1760s to the late 1790s can be traced to his hand. He was probably responsible for most of the local scenic paintings and all the A Trifle From Lowestoft series produced in the factory's final years. By 1793 he also had a High Street shop where he sold his decorated ceramics, some of which had been made elsewhere. In later life he helped to revive the art of stained glass: his finest commission, for the East Window of Lowestoft's St Margaret's Church, in 1819, was to be removed during the pious vandalism of Victorian restoration, but some of it was reinstated in the south chancel window where it still remains.

The Lowestoft porcelain factory probably ceased production in 1799, when several senior workers left for Worcester, but existing stock continued to be sold until 1802. Maximilien de Lazowski had said that half the output was shipped to Holland, and thence to France. Armed conflict with the Dutch having suspended this trade in earlier years, there is a story that the factory was finally sunk by the seizure of a large consignment of exported wares during the Napoleonic Wars. Competition from the Staffordshire potteries, with their access to unlimited local clay and coal reserves, may also have helped to capsize the Suffolk craft.

Of the original partners, only Philip Walker outlived the enterprise and all too quickly memories faded. When Robert Allen died, aged 90, he was best known for his work in stained glass.

THE DECLINE OF LOWESTOFT
W.G. Sebald
(from *The Rings of Saturn*, 1998)

... It was already after six in the evening when I reached the outskirts of Lowestoft. Not a living soul was about in the long streets I went through, and the closer I came to the town centre the more what I saw disheartened me. The last time I had been in Lowestoft was perhaps fifteen years ago, on a June day that I spent on the beach with two children, and I thought I remembered a town that had become something of a backwater but was nonetheless very pleasant; so now, as I walked into Lowestoft, it seemed incomprehensible to me that in such a relatively short period of time the place could have become so run down. Of course I was aware that this decline had been irreversible ever since the economic crises and depressions of the Thirties; but around 1975, when they were constructing the rigs for the North Sea, there were hopes that things might change for the better, hopes that were steadily inflated during the hardline capitalist years of Baroness Thatcher, till in due course they collapsed in a fever of speculation. The damage spread slowly at first, smouldering underground, and then caught like wildfire.

The wharves and factories closed down one after the other, until all that might be said for Lowestoft was that it occupied the easternmost point in the British Isles. Nowadays, in some of the streets almost every other house is up for sale; factory owners, shopkeepers and private individuals are sliding ever deeper into debt; week in, week out, some bankrupt or unemployed person hangs himself; nearly a quarter of the population is now practically illiterate; and there is no sign of an end to the encroaching misery. Although I knew all of this, I was unprepared for the feeling of wretchedness that instantly seized hold of me in Lowestoft, for it is one thing to read about unemployment blackspots in the newspapers and quite another to walk, on a cheerless evening, past rows of run-down houses with mean little front gardens; and, having reached the town centre, to find nothing but amusement arcades, bingo halls, betting shops, video stores, pubs that emit a sour reek of beer from their dark doorways, cheap markets, and seedy bed-and-breakfast establishments with names like Ocean Dawn, Beachcomber, Balmoral, or Layla Lorraine. It was difficult to imagine the holidaymakers and commercial travellers who would want to stay there, nor was it easy – as I climbed the steps coated with shiny blue paint up to the entrance – to recognize the Albion as the 'hotel on the promenade of a superior description' recommended in my guidebook, which had been published shortly after the turn of the century. I stood for a good while in the empty lobby, and wandered through the public rooms, which were completely deserted even now at the height of the season – if one can speak of a season in Lowestoft – before I happened upon a startled young woman who, after hunting pointlessly through the register on the reception desk, handed me a huge room key attached to a wooden pear. I noticed that she was dressed in the style of the Thirties and that she avoided eye contact; either her gaze remained fixed on the floor or she looked right through me as if I were not there. That evening I was the sole guest in the huge dining room, and it was the same startled person who took my order and shortly afterwards brought me a fish that had doubtless lain entombed in the deep-freeze for years. The breadcrumb armour-plating of the fish had been partly singed by the grill, and the prongs of my fork bent on it.

266

Indeed it was so difficult to penetrate what eventually proved to be nothing but an empty shell that my plate was a hideous mess once the operation was over. The tartare sauce that I had had to squeeze out of a plastic sachet was turned grey by the sooty breadcrumbs, and the fish itself, or what feigned to be fish, lay a sorry wreck among the grass-green peas and the remains of soggy chips that gleamed with fat. I no longer recall how long I sat in that dining room with its gaudy wallpaper before the nervous young woman, who evidently did all the work in the establishment single-handed, scurried out from the thickening shadows in the background to clear the table. She may have appeared the moment I put down my knife and fork, or perhaps an hour had passed; all I can remember are the scarlet blotches which appeared from the neckline of her blouse and crept up her throat as she bent for my plate. When she had flitted away once more I rose and crossed to the semi-circular bay window. Outside was the beach, somewhere between the darkness and the light, and nothing was moving, neither in the air nor on the land nor on the water. Even the white waves rolling in to the sands seemed to me to be motionless. The following morning, when I left the Albion Hotel with my rucksack over my shoulder, Lowestoft had reawoken to life, under a cloudless sky. Passing the harbour, where dozens of decommissioned and unemployed trawlers rode at their moorings, I headed south through streets that were now congested with traffic and filled with blue petrol fumes. Once, right by Lowestoft Central station, which had not been refurbished since it was built in the nineteenth century, a black hearse decked out with wreaths slid past me amidst the other vehicles. In it sat two earnest-faced undertaker's men, the driver and a co-driver, and behind them, in the loading area, as it were, someone who had but recently departed this life was lying in his coffin, in his Sunday best, his head on a little pillow, his eyelids closed, hands clasped, and the tips of his shoes pointing up. As I gazed after the hearse I thought of that working lad from Turtlingen, two hundred years ago, who joined the cortege of a seemingly well-known merchant in Amsterdam and then listened with reverence and emotion to the graveside oration although he knew not a word of Dutch. If before then he had marvelled with envy at the tulips and starflowers behind the windows, and at the crates, bales and chests of tea, sugar, spices and rice that arrived in the docks from the faraway East Indies, from now on, when occasionally he wondered why he had acquired so little on his way through the world, he had only to think of the Amsterdam merchant he had escorted on his last journey, of his big house, his splendid ship, and his narrow grave. With this story in my head I made my way out of a town on which the marks of an insidious decay were everywhere apparent, a town which in its heyday had been not only one of the foremost fishing ports in the United Kingdom but also a seaside resort lauded even abroad as 'most salubrious'. At that time, in the latter half of the nineteenth century, a number of hotels were built on the south bank of the River Waveney, under the direction of Morton Peto. They met all the requirements of London society circles, and, as well as the hotels, pump rooms and pavilions were built, churches and chapels for every denomination, a lending library, a billiard hall, a tea house that resembled a temple, and a tramway with a magnificent terminus. A broad esplanade, avenues, bowling greens, botanical gardens, and sea- and freshwater baths were established, as were associations for the promotion and beautification of Lowestoft. In no time at all, notes a contemporary account, Lowestoft had risen to pride of place in the public esteem, and now possessed every facility requisite for a bathing resort of repute. Anyone who considered the elegance and perfection of the buildings recently constructed along the south beach, the article continued, would doubtless recognize that everything, from the overall plan to the very last detail, had been informed and shaped by the principles of rationality in the most advantageous way. The crowning glory of the enterprise, which was in every respect exemplary, was the new pier, which stretched four hundred yards out into the North Sea and was considered the most beautiful anywhere along the eastern coast of England. The promenade deck was made of African mahogany planking, and the white pier buildings, which were illuminated after nightfall by gas flares, included a reading and music room with tall mirrors around the walls. Every year at the end of September, as my friend Frederick Farrar told me a few months before he died, a charity ball was held there under the patronage of a member of the royal family to mark the close of the regatta. ... Frederick had told me that on the evening of the charity ball the common folk, who in the nature of things were not admitted, rowed out to the end of the pier in a hundred or more boats and barges, to watch, from their bobbing, drifting vantage points, as fashionable society swirled to the sound of the orchestra, seemingly borne aloft in a surge of light above the water, which was dark and at that time in early autumn usually swathed in mist. If I now look back at those times, Frederick once said, it is as if I were seeing everything through flowing white veils: the town like a mirage over the water, the seaside villas right down to the shore surrounded by green trees and shrubs, the summer light, and the beach, across which we have just returned from an outing, Father walking ahead with one or two gentlemen whose trousers are rolled up, Mother by herself with a parasol, my sisters with their skirts gathered in one hand, and the servants bringing up the rear with the donkey, between whose panniers I am sitting on my perch. Once, years ago, said Frederick, I even dreamed of that scene, and our family seemed to me like the court of King James II in exile on the coast of The Hague.

I had long left the beach fishermen behind me when, in the early afternoon, I reached Benacre Broad, a lake of brackish water beyond a bank of shingle halfway between Lowestoft and Southwold. The lake is encircled by deciduous woodland that is now dying, owing to the steady erosion of the coastline by the sea. Doubtless it is only a matter of time before one stormy night the shingle bank is broken, and the appearance of the entire area changes. But that day, as I sat on the tranquil shore, it was possible to believe one was gazing into eternity. The veils of mist that drifted inland that morning had cleared, the vault of the sky was empty and blue, not the slightest breeze was stirring, the trees looked painted, and not a single bird flew across the velvet-brown water. It was as if the world were under a bell jar, until great cumulus clouds brewed up out of the west casting a grey shadow upon the earth.

269

Perhaps it was that darkening that called to my mind an article I had clipped from the *Eastern Daily Press* several months before, on the death of Major George Wyndham Le Strange, whose great stone manor house in Henstead stood beyond the lake. During the last War, the report read, Le Strange served in the anti-tank regiment that liberated the camp at Bergen Belsen on the 14th of April 1945, but immediately after VE-Day returned home from Germany to manage his great uncle's estates in Suffolk, a task he had fulfilled in exemplary manner, at least until the mid-Fifties, as I knew from other sources. It was at that time too that Le Strange took on the housekeeper to whom he eventually left his entire fortune: his estates in Suffolk as well as property in the centre of Birmingham estimated at several million pounds. According to the newspaper report, Le Strange employed this housekeeper, a simple young woman from Beccles by the name of Florence Barnes, on the explicit condition that she take the meals she prepared together with him, but in absolute silence. Mrs Barnes told the newspaper herself that she abided by this arrangement, once made, even when her employer's way of life became increasingly odd. Though Mrs Barnes gave only the most reticent of responses to the reporter's enquiries, my own subsequent investigations revealed that in the late Fifties Le Strange discharged his household staff and his labourers, gardeners and administrators one after another, that thenceforth he lived alone in the great stone house with the silent cook from Beccles, and that as a result the whole estate, with its gardens and park, became overgrown and neglected, while scrub and undergrowth encroached on the fallow fields. Apart from comments that touched upon these matters of fact, stories concerning the Major himself were in circulation in the villages that bordered on his domain, stories to which one can lend only a limited credence. They drew, I imagine, on the little that reached the outside world over the years, rumours from the depths of the estate that occupied the people who lived in the immediate vicinity. Thus in a Henstead hostelry, for example, I heard it said that in his old age, since he had worn out his wardrobe and saw no point in buying new clothes, Le Strange would wear garments dating from bygone days which he fetched out of chests in the attic as he needed them. There were people who claimed to have seen him on occasion dressed in a canary-yellow frock coat or a kind of mourning robe of faded violet taffeta with numerous buttons and eyes. Le Strange, who had always kept a tame cockerel in his room, was reputed to have been surrounded, in later years, by all manner of feathered creatures: by guinea fowl, pheasants, pigeons and quail, and various kinds of garden and song birds, strutting about him on the floor or flying around in the air. Some said that one summer Le Strange dug a cave in his garden and sat in it day and night like St Jerome in the desert. Most curious of all was a legend that I presume to have originated with the Wrentham undertaker's staff – to the effect that the Major's pale skin was olive-green when he passed away, his goose-grey eye was pitch-dark, and his snow-white hair had turned to raven-black. To this day I do not know what to make of such stories. One thing is certain: the estate and all its adjunct properties was bought at auction by a Dutchman last autumn, and Florence Barnes, the Major's loyal housekeeper, lives now with her sister Jemima in a bungalow in her home town of Beccles, as she had intended.

A quarter of an hour's walk south of Benacre Broad, where the beach narrows and a stretch of sheer coastline begins, a few dozen dead trees lie in a confused heap where they fell years ago from the Covehithe cliffs. Bleached by salt water, wind and sun, the broken, barkless wood looks like the bones of some extinct species, greater even than the mammoths and dinosaurs, that came to grief long since on this solitary strand. The footpath leads around the tangle, through a bank of gorse, up to the loamy cliff-head, and there it continues amidst bracken, the tallest of which stood as high as my shoulder, not far from the ledge, which is constantly threatening to crumble away. Out on the leaden-coloured sea a sailing boat kept me company, or rather, it seemed to me as if it were motionless and I myself, step by step, were making as little progress as that invisible spirit aboard his unmoving barque. But by degrees the bracken thinned, affording a view of a field that extended as far as Covehithe church. Beyond a low electric fence lay a herd of almost a hundred head of swine, on brown earth where meagre patches of camomile grew. I climbed over the wire and approached one of the ponderous, immobile, sleeping animals. As I bent towards it, it opened a small eye fringed with light lashes and gave me an enquiring look. I ran my hand across its dusty back, and it trembled at this unwonted touch; I stroked its snout and face, and chucked it in the hollow behind one ear, till at length it sighed like one enduring endless suffering. When I stood up, it closed its eye once more with an expression of profound submissiveness. For a while I sat on the grass between the electric fence and the cliff edge. The thin, yellowing blades of grass were bending in the rising wind. The sky was darkening as banks of cloud were piling far out across the sea, which was now streaked with white. All of a sudden, the boat, which for so long had not moved, was gone. ... The sand martins, I now saw, were flying solely at the level that extended from the top of the cliff where I was sitting out into empty space. Not one of them climbed higher or dived lower, to the water below them. Whenever they came towards me, fast as bullets, some seemed to vanish right beneath my feet, as if into the very ground. I went to the edge of the cliff and saw that they had dug their nesting holes into the topmost layer of clay, one beside the other. I was thus standing on perforated ground, as it were, which might have given way at any moment. Nevertheless, I laid my head back as far as I could, as I did as a boy for a dare on the flat tin roof of the two-storey apiary, fixed my eyes on the zenith, then lowered my gaze till it met the horizon, and drew it in across the water, to the narrow strip of beach some twenty yards below. As I tried to suppress the mounting sense of dizziness, breathing out and taking a step backwards, I thought I saw something of an odd, pallid colour move on the shoreline. I crouched down and, overcome by a sudden panic, looked over the edge. A couple lay down there, in the bottom of the pit, as I thought: a man stretched full length over another body of which nothing was visible but the legs, spread and angled. In the startled moment when that image went through me, which lasted an eternity, it seemed as if the man's feet twitched like those of one just hanged. Now, though, he lay still, and the woman too was still and motionless. Misshapen, like some great

272

mollusc washed ashore, they lay there, to all appearances a single being, a many-limbed, two-headed monster that had drifted in from far out at sea, the last of a prodigious species, its life ebbing from it with each breath expired through its nostrils. Filled with consternation, I stood up once more, shaking as if it were the first time in my life that I had got to my feet, and left the place, which seemed fearsome to me now, taking the path that descended from the cliff-top to where the beach spread out on the southerly side. Far off in front of me lay Southwold, a cluster of distant buildings, clumps of trees, and a snow-white lighthouse, beneath a dark sky. Before I reached the town, the first drops of rain were falling. I turned to look back down the deserted stretch I had come by, and could no longer have said whether I had really seen the pale sea monster at the foot of the Covehithe cliffs or whether I had imagined it.

GREETINGS FROM SOUTHWOLD

George Orwell

(from *Collected Essays, Journalism & Letters of George Orwell*, 1968)

To Brenda Salkeld, Sunday night, [July 1931]

3 Queen St [Southwold]

Dearest Brenda,

I assume that your friends *did* turn up today? This morning I went to the Bell, & they told me, 'Some of your St Felix friends have been here having high jinks'. I suppose that was you? I hope you were quite sober. Way showed me a piece of his bergamot, which is now flowering. It is very deep red, & not unlike a thistle head – not at all coming up to its beautiful name, I thought. How important names are. If I have the choice of going through two streets, other things being equal I always go by the one with the nicer name. Yesterday evening there were ten or fifteen swans flying over the sea. I saw them in the distance & thought they were swans, & today I was told they were so – I can't think where they came from; certainly they weren't the local ones.

To Dennis Collings, 16 August, 1931

At 1B Oakwood Rd, Golders Green, N.W

Dear Dennis,

I said I would write to you. I haven't anything of great interest to report yet about the Lower Classes, & am really writing to tell you about a ghost I saw in Walberswick cemetery. I want to get it on paper before I forget the details. See plan below. Above is W'wick church as well as I can remember it. At about 5.20 pm on 27.7.31 I was sitting at the spot marked*, looking out in the direction of the dotted arrow. I happened to glance over my shoulder, & saw a figure pass along the line of the other arrow, disappearing behind the masonry & presumably emerging into the churchyard. I wasn't looking *directly* at it & so couldn't make out more than that it was a man's figure, small & stooping, & dressed in lightish brown; I should have said a workman. I had the impression that it glanced towards me in passing, but I made out nothing of the features. At the moment of its passing I thought nothing, but a few seconds later it struck me that the figure had made no noise, & I followed it out into the churchyard. There was no one in the churchyard, & no one within possible distance along the road – this was about 20 seconds after I had seen it; & in any case there were only 2 people in the road, & neither at all resembled the figure. I looked into the church. The only people there were the vicar, dressed in black, & a workman who, as far as I remember, had been sawing the whole time. In any case he was too tall for the figure. The figure had therefore vanished. Presumably an hallucination. ...

To Eleanor Jaques, Monday, [19 September 1932]
'The Hawthorns', Church Rd., Hayes, Mdx.

Dearest Eleanor,

... How horrible & wintry the weather has turned these last two days. On the whole we had excellent weather at S'wold, & I cannot remember when I have ever enjoyed any expeditions so much as I did those with you. Especially that day in the wood along past Blythburgh Lodge – you remember, where the deep beds of moss were. I shall always remember that, & your nice white body in the dark green moss. ...

With all my love
Eric

To Brenda Salkeld, 27 July, 1934
36 High St, Southwold, Suffolk

Dearest Brenda,

Many thanks for your last letter. How I wish you were here! I am so miserable, struggling in the entrails of that dreadful book and never getting any further, and loathing the sight of what I have done. *Never* start writing novels, if you wish to preserve your happiness. I hope your lecture went off all right. Dennis Collings and Eleanor were married on Monday, but they are not back in Southwold yet. Dennis has got to leave for Malaya in about another ten days. I have had quite a lot of stuff from the garden, but the peas have given out for the time being. We have started eating the cauliflowers, and they are delicious. I am fattening a marrow, but it is a very bad shape and I don't think I shall let it get very large. The beans we sowed have grown to an enormous size, but for some reason there is not much blossom on them, so I have pinched out the tops. I had lunch yesterday with Dr Ede. He is a bit of a feminist and thinks that if a woman was brought up exactly like a man she would be able to throw a stone, construct a syllogism, keep a secret etc. He tells me that my anti-feminist views are probably due to Sadism! I have never read the Marquis de Sade's novels – they are unfortunately very hard to get hold of. Do you remember that afternoon when we had tea with Delisle Burns and I asked him what was the tune of 'Malbrouck s'en va-t-en guerre', and he said it was the same as 'For he's a jolly good fellow'? And the other night I was passing the King's Head, and the Buffaloes, who were holding one of their secret conclaves in there, were singing it – or rather, as they seemed to be gargling it through pints of beer, what it sounded like was:

> *Fo-or*-ee's *ajorrigoo' fellow,*
> *For*-ee's *a jorrigoo' fellow,*
> *For*-ee's *ajorrigoo' fe-ellow –*
> *And toori oori us!*

To Brenda Salkeld, Tuesday night, [late August? 1934]

36 High St, Southwold, Suffolk

Dearest Brenda,

... We are getting delicious French beans from the garden, but I am concerned about the pumpkin, which shows signs of ripening though it is not much bigger than an orange. All my fruit has been stolen by the children next door, as I forsaw it would. The little beasts were in such a hurry to get it that they didn't even wait till it was half ripe, but took the pears when they were mere chunks of wood. Another time I must try a dodge Dr Collings told me, which is to paint a mixture of vaseline & some indelible dye, I forget what, on a few of the fruit that are likely to be taken first & then you can spot who has taken it by the stains on their hands. The town is very full & camps of Girl Guides etc. infesting all the commons. I nearly died of cold the other day when bathing, because I had walked out to Easton Broad not intending to bathe, & then the water looked so nice that I took off my clothes & went in, & then about 50 people came up & rooted themselves to the spot. I wouldn't have minded that, but among them was a coastguard who could have had me up for bathing naked, so I had to swim up & down for the best part of half an hour, pretending to like it. Do come back soon, dearest one. Can't you come & stay with somebody before the term begins? It is sickening that I have to go away just after you come back. Write soon.

With much love
Eric

A COASTAL PILGRIMAGE
Henry James
(from *English Hours*, 1905)

... I defy any one, at desolate, exquisite Dunwich, to be disappointed in anything. The minor key is struck here with a felicity that leaves no sigh to be breathed, no loss to be suffered; a month of the place is a real education to the patient, the inner vision. The explanation of this is, appreciably, that the conditions give you to deal with not, in the manner of some quiet countries, what is meagre and thin, but what has literally, in a large degree, ceased to be at all. Dunwich is not even the ghost of its dead self; almost all you can say of it is that it consists of the mere letters of its old name. The coast, up and down, for miles, has been, for more centuries than I presume to count, gnawed away by the sea. All the grossness of its positive life is now at the bottom of the German Ocean, which moves for ever, like a ruminating beast, an insatiable, indefatigable lip. Few things are so melancholy – and so redeemed from mere ugliness by sadness – as this long, artificial straightness that the monster has impartially maintained. If at low tide you walk on the shore, the cliffs, of little height, show you a defence picked as bare as a bone; and you can say nothing kinder of the general humility and general sweetness of the land than that this sawlike action gives it, for the fancy, an interest, a sort of mystery, that more than makes up for what it may have surrendered. It stretched, within historic times, out into towns and promontories for which there is now no more to show than the empty eye-holes of a skull; and half the effect of the whole thing, half the secret of the impression, and what I may really call, I think, the source of the distinction, is this very visibility of the mutilation. Such at any rate is the case for a mind that can properly brood. There is a presence in what is missing – there is history in there being so little. It is so little, to-day, that every item of the handful counts.

The biggest items are of course the two ruins, the great church and its tall tower, now quite on the verge of the cliff, and the crumbled, ivied wall of the immense cincture of the Priory. These things have parted with almost every grace, but they still keep up the work that they have been engaged in for centuries and that cannot better be described than as the adding of mystery to mystery. This accumulation, at present prodigious, is, to the brooding mind, unconscious as the shrunken little Dunwich of today may be of it. The beginning and the end of the matter. I hasten to add that it is to the brooding mind only, and from it, that I speak. The mystery sounds for ever in the hard, straight tide, and hangs, through the long, still summer days and over the low, dyked fields, in the soft, thick light. We play with it as with the answerless question, the question of the spirit and attitude, never again to be recovered, of the little city submerged. For it *was* a city, the main port of Suffolk, as even its poor relics show; with a fleet of its own on the North Sea, and a big religious house on the hill. We wonder what were the apparent conditions of security, and on what rough calculation a community could so build itself out to meet its fate. It keeps one easy company here to-day to think of the whole business as a magnificent mistake. But Mr Swinburne, in verses of an extraordinary poetic eloquence, quite brave enough for whatever there may have been, glances in the right direction much further than I can do. Read moreover, for other glances, the 'Letters of Edward Fitzgerald', Suffolk worthy and whimsical subject, who, living hard by at Woodbridge, haunted these regions during most of his life, and has left, in delightful pages, at the service of the emulous visitor, the echo of every odd, quaint air they could draw from his cracked, sweet instrument. He has paid his tribute, I seem to remember, to the particular delicate power – the pale Dunwich rose – that blooms on the walls of the Priory. The emulous visitor, only yesterday, on the most vulgar of vehicles – which, however, he is quite aware he must choose between using and abusing – followed, in the mellow afternoon, one of these faint hints across the land and as far as the old, old town of Aldeburgh, the birth-place and the commemorated 'Borough' of the poet Crabbe.

Fitzgerald, devoted to Crabbe, was apparently not less so to this small break in the wide, low, heathery bareness that brings the sweet Suffolk commons – rare purple and gold when I arrived – nearly to the edge of the sea. We don't, none the less, always gather the particular impression we bravely go forth to seek. We doubtless gather another indeed that will serve as well any such turn as here may wait for it; so that if it was somehow not easy to work Fitzgerald into the small gentility of the sea-front, the little 'marina', as of a fourth-rate watering-place, that has elbowed away, evidently in recent years, the old handful of character, one could at least, to make up for that, fall back either on the general sense of the happy trickery of genius or on the special beauty of the mixture, in the singer of Omar Kháyyám, that, giving him such a place for a setting, could yet feed his fancy so full. Crabbe, at Aldeburgh, for that matter, is perhaps even more wonderful – in the light, I mean, of what is left of the place by one's

279

conjuring away the little modern vulgar accumulation. What is left is just the stony beach and the big gales and the cluster of fishermen's huts and the small, wide, short street of decent, homely, shoppy houses. These are the private emotions of the historic sense – glimpses in which we recover for an hour, or rather perhaps, with an intensity, but for the glimmer of a minute, the conditions that, grimly enough, could engender masterpieces, or at all events classics. What a mere pinch of manners and customs in the midst of winds and waves! Yet if it was a feature of these to return a member to Parliament, what wonder that, up to the Reform Bill, dead Dunwich should have returned two?

The glimpses I speak of are, in all directions, the constant company of the afternoon 'spin'. Beginning, modestly enough, at Dunwich itself, they end, for intensity, as far inland as you have time to go; far enough – this is the great point – to have shown you, in their quiet vividness of type, a placid series of the things into which you may most read the old story of what is softest in the English complexity. I scarce know what murmur has been for weeks in my ears if it be not that of the constant word that, as a recall of the story, may serve to be put under the vignette. And yet this word is in its last form nothing more eloquent than the mere admonition to be pleased. Well, so you are, even as I was yesterday at Wesleton with the characteristic 'value' that expressed itself, however shyly, in the dear old red inn at which I halted for the queer restorative – I thus discharge my debt to it – of a bottle of lemonade with a 'dash'. The dash was only of beer, but the refreshment was immense. So even was that of the sight of a dim, draped, sphinx-like figure that loomed, at the end of a polished passage, out of a little dusky back parlour which had a windowful of the choked light of a small green garden – a figure proving to be an old woman desirous to dilate on all the years she had sat there with rheumatism 'most cruel'. So, inveterately – and in these cases without the after-taste – is that of the pretty little park gates you pass to skirt the walls and hedges beyond which the great affair, the greatest of all, the deep, still home, sits in the midst of its acres and strikes you all the more for being, precisely, so unrenowned. It is the charming repeated lesson that the amenity of the famous seats in this country is nothing to that of the lost and buried ones. This impression in particular may bring you round again harmoniously to Dunwich and above all perhaps to where the Priory, laid, as I may say flat on its back, rests its large outline on what was once the high ground, with the inevitable 'big' house, beyond and a little above, folded, for privacy, in a neat, impenetrable wood. Here as elsewhere the cluster offers without complication just the signs of the type. At the base of the hill are the dozen cottages to which the village has been reduced, and one of which contains, to my hearing, though by no means, alas, to his own, a very ancient man who will count for you on his fingers, till they fail, the grand acres that, in his day, he has seen go the way of the rest. He likes to figure that he ploughed of old where only the sea ploughs now. Dunwich, however, will still last his time; and that of as many other as – to repeat my hint – may yet be drawn here (though not, I hope, on the instance of these prudent lines) to judge for themselves into how many meanings a few elements can compose. One never need be bored, after all, when 'composition' really rules. It rules in the way the brown hamlet disposes itself, and the gray square tower of the church, in just the right relation, peeps out of trees that remind me exactly of those which, in the frontispiece of Birket Foster, offered to my childish credulity the very essence of England. Let me put it directly for old Suffolk that this credulity finds itself here, at the end of time, more than ever justified. ...

A WRITER'S RETREAT

Edward Thomas

(from *Letters to Gordon Bottomley*,1968)

15 January 1908   Minsmere, nr Dunwich, Suffolk

My dear Gordon,

Forgive me for not writing before. You will when you know I have been writing hard at Jefferies all day & every day ... And now I have made myself weary with it all. I came here straight from a specialist who messed me about, commanded abstinence from alcohol & sugar & almost abstinence from tobacco ... But the medicine & the air & the lively company of the Aldis family who live in the other coastguard's cottage next door soon made me rotund in spirit if still lean in body ...

Oh Dunwich is beautiful. I am on a heaving moor of heather & close gorse up & down & ending in a sandy cliff about 80 feet perpendicular & the black, peat strewn fine sand below. On the edge of this 1.5 miles away is the ruined church that has half fallen over already. Four arches & a broken tower, pale & airy. Just beyond that the higher moor dips to quite flat marsh with gentlest rises inland with masses of trees compact & dark & a perfect huge curve of foamy coast up to the red light at Southwold northward. In the other direction, just behind us, the moor dips to more marshes with black cattle dim & far off under white sun, & three faint windmills that work a sluice & then trees – inland more gentle rises with pines. No hills (unless you lie down in a dip of the moor & fancy the moorland as part of a Welsh 'black mountain'.) I get my firewood, kindling & logs, from the beach, where we pick up champagne corks, sailors' hats, Antwerp beer bottles, fish boxes, oranges, lemons, onions, banana stems, waterworn timber and the most exquisite flat & round pebbles, black, white, dove grey, veined, wheat coloured. Why does Nature make these beautiful things so carelessly & then one wonders whether all beautiful things are not of this careless inevitableness and yet long wrought out too & then one has to earn one's living. May that funny spirit bless*Gunnar* for you. Tell me how it goes.

I will try to remember Mr. Murdoch.

Accept this hurry & good intention. It is late & I am tired & bad in the back.

Yours & Emily's ever Edward Thomas

7 February 1908   Minsmere

My dear Gordon,

My health keeps good in this bracing air with few worries & a useful medicine. But I believe my specialist is lazy with me: I am too docile a patient & too schoolboyish & unquestioning with him; as soon as I get into his room I relapse & expect him to discover everything – So I shan't go often again even if I couldn't afford it. Among few disturbances here I got very fond of a girl of 17 with two long plaits of dark brown hair & the richest grey eyes, very wild & shy, to whom I could not say 10 words, nor she to me. She used to milk the 2 cows her father owned, but has now gone away to school. She is a clever child who has begun to write verse. But I liked her for her perfect wild youthfulness & remoteness from myself & now I think of her every day in vain acquiescent dissatisfaction, & shall perhaps never see her again, & shall be sad to hear she ever likes anyone else even tho she will never like me. ...

I was at Walberswick today, pestered by inane pretty houses, paintable bits & an elderly aesthetic lady with youthful ankles & neat old cottage furniture. But the dreary intersected marshes & invisible sounding sea in twilight mists repaid me a little – with a hump of woods just visible as culmination of the mist. I met a good name over a shop at Southwold BOGGIS, also several others including ADNAMS. Our combination here of wavering moorland & marshes beats all Walberswick. You should have seen Southwold in mist, an almost wholly new town on the top of a gentle hill, with an old flint-towered church, & approached by a sheep bitten slope with gorse & on the gorse whitest linen strewn.

283

I come home daily with pockets full of the smooth pebbles, often pearshaped (flattish), rosy or primrose coloured & transparent nearly, & in the fresh moistness wonderfully beautiful: others white & round or oval: some split & with grain like chestnuts: not one but makes me think or rather draws out a part of me beyond my thinking. How unprofitable so many of our most genuine likings are, pebbles and seventeen years old, for example. Why was I not an artist to make them abide instead of being a sleeper who greets the old sun stirring his fingers idly & frowning & now & then kicking out & muttering – disturbing a bedfellow, no more? Why? Yet am I Yours & Emily's ever

Edward Thomas

DUNWICH IN WINTER
Geoffrey Grigson
(from *English Excursions*, 1960)

... No one, I think, who sees Dunwich – at any rate in the right conditions both of Dunwich and himself, both of place and receptivity – will ever get its lineaments entirely out of his mind. The way to Dunwich is remarkable, to begin with, especially in winter. I have gone from London on a cold day in February. Along the A12 it is just driving, just white lines, halts, houses, traffic. After turning off at Yoxford, the change is not just from main road to country. It is a change, after Westleton, at any rate, to peculiar country. Westleton Heath in winter turns brown as coffee. This coffee heath gives way to newly planted, very dark-green forest. The road bends and dips slightly, and reaches a furthest point, a furthest sharp turn, at what must

284

be the near-abouts, it seems clear, or the nearest recollection of Dunwich. Alexanders, its leaves shining as they do even in mid-winter, grows everywhere up the bank. But where is the sea? It is invisible; till you climb the bank, and find yourself on the firm grass along the top of the most infirm of cliffs.

Unless you count the grey walls of the precincts of the old monastery of Grey Friars and a fragment or two of the monastery itself, the sea has now claimed and absorbed all the buildings of Dunwich, a fact which I first encountered in the first chapter of one of Rider Haggard's books (was it *She*?). Certainly, as I came out on the cliff, among the broom and the brambles, everything was coloured by the thought of a town, a port, which had crumbled and tumbled, street by street, gable by gable, doorstep by doorstep, church by church, into this North Sea. Everything visible at Dunwich – non-existent Dunwich – was coloured by its old existence.

Yet upon its own account, how fantastic a sweep of land and water! A sweep of grey water, a sweep of chocolate shingle; a curve where the cliffs give out, mile after mile, away to Walberswick and Southwold. Landward, a huge low extent of marshes and commons distantly marked with church towers. Seaward, how extraordinary a grey! And this whole affair, sea and shingle and land, laid across the world, underneath how enormous, how important a sky!

I once paced a low shore in Connecticut. My host showed me some twisted iron pipes in the sand. A row of houses had faced the sea there two years before. The sea and the wind had roared and the houses had gone – in one night. They were modern houses. Here at Dunwich the houses had gone in the course of centuries, the 13th century to the 19th. And my host in Connecticut could not show me what I found here for myself, on this rim of Suffolk – the brown human bones dribbling down the soft cliff into the sea, out of the last churchyard of a church which has now vanished (though a few lumps of it lie down below on the shingle) with all the rest of Dunwich.

There were bones on the shingle, bones half way down, bones at grave level near the top.

I stayed on the cliff and on the shingle at non-existent Dunwich till it was almost dark; and watched a great spreading bank of dark blue snow cloud advance towards me over this North Sea from the direction of Walberswick and Southwold. It turned the sea, which was sucking and sucking at the shingle, into an extent of polished grey mud. From Walberswick a red light twinkled on in this deep dark blue. The cloud arrived and snow began to fall. It began to fall white in the grey sea, on the brown shingle, on the glittering leaves of Alexanders, on the last few gravestones of All Saints graveyard, and on the dull human bones. Flake by flake, but without noise or drama, the snow made a grand slam out of doubled and redoubled desolation. Two skulls, side by side, as in the marriage-bed of lifetime, occupied a transitory ledge on the cliff. The flakes gently covered each smoothness, till the skulls were wigged. The snow turned to rain. The wigs melted, the rain washed the pates for their new sea-burial.

Before it became so dark, before the snow began falling, I had peered a good deal into non-existence. I had climbed down and walked on the pebbles, against which the sad North Sea rose and fell, noticing bones and the tumbled oddments of the church. I re-lived an emotion felt long ago by two of the connoisseurs of Dunwich, Henry James and Charles Keene. Dunwich, Henry James wrote, 'is not even the ghost of its dead self; almost all you can say of it is that it consists of the mere letters of its old name', which is a proper exaggeration. He saw 'all the grossness of its positive life' at the bottom of that sea below the cliffs, 'which moves for ever, like a ruminating beast, an insatiable, indefatigable lip'; and at Dunwich he defied anyone 'to be disappointed in anything'.

When he knew it, nevertheless, and when Keene scratched a few copper plates on the hot evenings of his Dunwich holiday, the nothingness was less absolute than today. There were more bones, more gravestones. There was more of All Saints, on the edge of the cliff. The shaft of a well or two protruded like factory chimneys, like the well-shafts of the eroded city of Mohenjo-daro.

Charles Keene also preserves the somethingness and nothingness of

Dunwich. He came here in the 'seventies, enjoying the company of old Edward Fitzgerald; a grave artist, said Fitzgerald, 'a man who can *reverence*, although a droll on *Punch*'. He felt the past of Dunwich, he eyed the space and the absence, the 'sandy cliffs, striped with layers of rolled pebbles', the bones, the tower and nave of All Saints so close to oblivion; and then drew with his etching needle some of the most economical, most air-filled of English landscapes.

Keene liked the phraseless melancholy of bagpipes. At night he stalked the hard sand under the cliff skirling laments over man and time to that North Sea which is so much more extensive, and so much sadder, than you would expect from the atlas.

Farther along the cliff, past the last gravestones (the last I could read was sacred to the memory of John Brinkley Easey, who died on September 2nd, 1826, aged twenty-three years) where the retreating land narrows between the edge and the flint wall of the Grey Friars, beyond sycamores, ilexes and pines bent with the wind, I traced the line, at any rate, of a single street of ancient Dunwich. It was Midgate Street, leading to Duck Street, half a mile out in the waves. A houseless lane, it now advanced direct to the sea and broke off into air. Duck Street, its ancient continuation, had curved round – out to sea – past the monastery of the Black Friars, and past St Peter's Church.

This St Peter's, the shrine, I suppose, of the fishermen and sailors of Dunwich, was the fourth of the medieval churches to go. It stood just over three hundred yards seaward of All Saints, seaward of the last few tilting, drunken gravestones and the bushes of broom by the edge of the present cliff. In 1702 the sea had come so near that St Peter's was stripped and abandoned. Its churchyard was swallowed up in the seventeen-thirties, also re-committing its dead to the scour and the roll of the tides.

Since then the sea has relentlessly eaten more than a yard a year.

People older than myself will remember the last naked bit of the flint and freestone nave of All Saints, and its tower, which was the focal object in Keene's drawings and etchings; and which at one time had an archangel at each corner, Gabriel, Michael, Raphael, and Uriel, powerless to halt destruction, their faces every year more whipped,

287

more salted by the spray.

Let me add, though, that if Dunwich of today derives some of its power over the senses from the Dunwich-that-isn't-there, the Real Thing is not bones or tombstones, is not associations or recollections.

It is position. It is coast and sweep and sky and sea and shingle and sand and colour.

By the time I left Dunwich the February clouds had blown away, and a pale three-quarters moon was out over the North Sea.

GEORGE CRABBE AND PETER GRIMES
E.M. Forster
(abridged from *Two Cheers For Democracy*, 1951)

Before I come to George Crabbe or to 'Peter Grimes' the poem, or to *Peter Grimes* the opera, I must speak of Aldeburgh.

The situation of this place is curious. A slight rise of the ground – I'll call it a hill, though the word is too emphatic – projects from the fenlands of Suffolk towards the North Sea. On this hill stands the church, a spacious Gothic building with very broad aisles, so that it has inside rather the effect of a hall. At the foot of the hill lies the town – a couple of long streets against which the sea is making an implacable advance. There used to be as many as five streets – three of them have disappeared beneath the shallow but violent waters, the house where Crabbe was born is gone, the street that has been named after him is menaced, the Elizabethan Moot Hall, which used to be in the centre of the place, now stands on a desolate beach. During the past twelve months the attack has been frightening. I can remember a little shelter erected for visitors on the shingle. Last autumn it was at the edge of a cliff, so that fishermen at the high tide actually sat in it to fish. This spring it has vanished, and the waters actually broke into the High Street – huge glassy waves coming in regularly and quietly, and each exploding when it hit the shore with the sound of a gun. This sort of attack went on a hundred and fifty years ago, when Crabbe was alive, but the zone of operation lay further out. Today only the hill is safe. Only at the church, where he preached, and where his parents lie buried, is there security and peace.

North and south of the hill lie marshes. The marshland to the north requires no comment, but that to the south is peculiar, and I had it in mind when I called the situation of Aldeburgh 'curious'. It is intersected by the river Alde, which flows due east – but when it is within fifty yards of the sea it turns due south, and does not reach the sea for twelve miles, being divided from it by a narrow ridge of shingle. Here again the waves are attacking, and are trying to break through the barrier that keeps them from the river. If they succeed – and they have had some success – Aldeburgh will be menaced on its flank, and the valuable town grazing-lands will disappear into the slime of the estuary.

It is with this estuary of the Alde that we are mainly concerned today. It is here, and not on the open sea or the sea-front, that the action of the poem of 'Peter Grimes' takes place. There used to be a little port on the estuary, Slaughden Quay. It was important in Crabbe's day, and was well defined even in my own earlier visits to the district. It is now battered and derelict, and the sea may wash across into it at the next great storm. Here Crabbe worked as a boy, rolling casks of butter about, and much he hated it. Hence Peter Grimes set out to fish. The prospect from Slaughden, despite desolation and menace, is romantic. At low tide the great mud flats stretch. At high tide the whole area is a swirl of many-coloured waters. At all times there are birds and low woodlands on the further bank, and, to the north, Aldeburgh sheltering among a few trees, and still just managing to dominate her fate.

I wanted to evoke these sombre and touching scenes as best I could,

289

in order to give a local habitation and a name to what follows. Crabbe without Aldeburgh, Peter Grimes without the estuary of the Alde, would lose their savour and tang. Now for my story, and the first point I have to make is that Crabbe disliked his native town. Born here in 1754, he grew to manhood in straitened circumstances. He was afraid of his odd rough father who made him roll the casks about; then he was apprenticed to an apothecary; he hated that too, he couldn't even handle a boat properly, he was no use at all. One grim day in the winter of 1779, he walked to the bleak and cheerless Marsh Hill, gazed at a muddy stretch of water called the Leech Pond, and decided to clear out. Leaving 'these shores where guilt and famine reign', he set out to seek his fortune in London as a poet. He nearly died of starvation first, and he was rescued not by his fellow townsmen, but by the generosity and insight of Edmund Burke. Burke recognized his genius and had faith in his integrity. From that moment his fortunes were assured; he abandoned medicine and turned to the Church for his profession, took orders, and returned to Aldeburgh three years later in the unexpected role of a triumphant curate.

Again he was unhappy, and no wonder. For he had not concealed his opinions on his home-town, and had indeed described it to Lord Shelburne as a venal little borough in Suffolk. He knew what he thought of his parishioners, and they, for their part, regarded him as an ill-tempered intellectual who, having failed to heal men's bodies, proposed to interfere with their souls. The emotions are recorded with which he mounted the pulpit of Aldeburgh church for the first time. 'I had been unkindly received in the place – I saw unfriendly countenances about me, and, I am sorry to say, I had too much indignation – though mingled, I hope, with better feelings – to care what they thought of me or my sermon.' The tension only lasted a few months. He got transferred. He was appointed domestic chaplain to the Duke of Rutland, and moved away inland into Leicestershire, where he was happy or anyhow cosy. But his distaste for his native town had been confirmed. Everything seemed to incommode him there. Even his hopes of discovering a new species of trefoil on the beach were dashed. 'If I can once more shake off my complaints,' he writes, 'and gain a little life and spirit, I verily believe that I shall publish an account of my plant.' But Sir Joseph Banks reported that the trefoil had been catalogued already. And when, towards the end of his life, he indulged in a visit of sentimentality what were the results?

> Beccles is the home of past years, and I could not walk through the streets as a stranger. It is not so at Aldborough: there a sadness mixes with all I see or hear; not a man is living whom I knew in my early portion of life; my contemporaries are gone and their successors are unknown to me and I to them.

Beccles, Leicestershire, Wiltshire – anywhere else. It is rare to discover in his writings a reference to his native town that is neither melancholy nor satirical.

Crabbe's antipathy to his birthplace was to play an essential part in the creation of 'Peter Grimes'. It was not a straightforward antipathy. It was connected with a profound attraction. He might leave Aldeburgh with his body, but he never emigrated spiritually; here on the plane of creation was his home, and he could not have found a better one. This Borough made him a poet, through it he understood Suffolk, and through East Anglia he approached England. He remains here, however far he seems to travel, whatever he says to the contrary. His best work describes the place directly – *The Village, The Parish Register, The Borough* – and its atmosphere follows him when he attempts other themes.

> *The few dull flowers that o'er the place are spread*
> *Partake the nature of their fenny bed;*
> *Here on its wiry stem, in rigid bloom,*
> *Grows the salt lavender that lacks perfume;*
> *Here the dwarf sallows creep, the septfoil harsh,*
> *And the soft slimy mallow of the marsh;*
> *Low on the ear the distant billows sound,*
> *And just in view appears their stony bound;*
> *No hedge nor tree conceals the glowing sun . . .*

Dull, harsh, stony, wiry, soft, slimy – what disobliging epithets, and yet he is in love with the scene. And the love becomes explicit in a prose footnote which he appends to the passage.

Such is the vegetation of the fen when it is at a small distance from the ocean; and in this case there arise from it effluvia strong and peculiar, half-saline, half-putrid, which would be considered by most people as offensive, and by some as dangerous; but there are others to whom singularity of taste or association of ideas has rendered it agreeable and pleasant.

The sights and the sounds are not beautiful, the smells are putrid, yet through the singularity of his taste and the associations they bring to him he loves them and cannot help loving them. For he had the great good luck to belong to a particular part of England, and to belong to it all his life.

This attraction for the Aldeburgh district, combined with that strong repulsion from it, is characteristic of Crabbe's uncomfortable mind. Outwardly he did well for himself, married money and ended up as a west-country pluralist. Inwardly he remained uneasy, and out of that uneasiness came his most powerful poems. It is natural to remember Wordsworth in connection with him. They were contemporaries, and they had this in common, that they were regional and that their earliest impressions were the most durable. But there the resemblance between them ends. Wordsworth – his superior genius apart – had a power of harmonizing his experiences which was denied to Crabbe. He could encircle them with the sky, he could overawe them with tremendous mountains. Crabbe remains down amongst them on the flat, amongst pebbles and weeds and mud and driftwood, and within earshot of a sea which is no divine ocean. Thus based, he is capable of considerable achievements, and the contradictory impulses possessing him generated 'Peter Grimes'.

We know how this sombre masterpiece originated. When Crabbe was trying to be a doctor he came across an old fisherman who had had a succession of apprentices from London and a sum of money with each. The apprentices tended to disappear, and the fisherman was warned he would be charged with murder next time. That is the meagre material upon which a poet's imagination worked. According to Edward Fitzgerald – who was a persistent student of Crabbe – the fisherman's name was Tom Brown. Anyhow, he is transformed into Peter Grimes.

The poem occurs in the series of *The Borough*, which was written for the most part away from Aldeburgh, and finished there in 1809. As a narrative, it is one of the best of the series, and it is prefaced by quotations from *Macbeth* and *Richard III* which fix the emotional atmosphere and warn us that the murdered apprentices will live again. It opens with a father-motive; like Crabbe himself, Peter Grimes hates his own father – a pious old fisherman who makes him go to church – and breaks away from him abusively, on one occasion striking him on the head and felling him. Murder is not done, but the wish to murder has been born.

> *The father groan'd – 'If thou art old' said he,*
> *'And hast a son – thou wilt remember me.'*

Peter was indeed to beget sons, though not in the flesh. For the present he gets drunk, and when his father passes away indulges in maudlin grief. It is a prelude to the main tragedy.

Freed from control, the young fisherman proposes to enjoy life – 'the life itself' he has called it exultantly – and gambles and drinks. But money is required for such joys, so he develops into a poacher and trespasser, a rustic Ishmael. Then come the sadistic lines:

> *But no success could please his cruel soul,*
> *He wish'd for one to trouble and control;*
> *He wanted some obedient boy to stand*
> *And bear the blow of his outrageous hand;*
> *And hoped to find in some propitious hour*
> *A feeling creature subject to his power,*

and the first of the apprentices arrives, a product of the eighteenth-century workhouse system. Everyone knows he is being mishandled and starved, no one protects him,

> *and some, on hearing cries,*
> *Said calmly, 'Grimes is at his exercise'*

a phrase which is effectively introduced into *Peter Grimes* the opera.

> *Thus lived the lad in hunger, peril, pain,*
> *His tears despised, his supplications vain:*
> *Compell'd by fear to lie, by need to steal,*
> *His bed uneasy and unbless'd his meal,*
> *For three sad years the boy his tortures bore,*
> *And then his pains and trials were no more.*

The second apprentice follows, also with premium, and he too dies. Peter's explanation is that he was playing on the main mast at night, fell into the well where the catch was kept, and hit his head. The jury exonerate him. The third apprentice is a delicate well-mannered child, who rouses the townsfolk to pity and charity and whom Peter dares not beat too hard. He disappears during a voyage at sea. Peter had his fish and wanted to sell it in the London market. They encountered a storm, the boat leaked, the boy fell ill, and before Peter could make harbour both the fish and the boy had died. Such anyhow was Peter's account. But

> *The pitying women raised a clamour round,*
> *And weeping said, 'Thou hast thy 'prentice drown'd.'*

The mayor forbade him to hire any more apprentices (as in the opening of the opera) and none of his neighbours would help him, so henceforward he carried on his trade alone, and melancholy invaded him.

Now begin the depths and, I would add, the flats of the poem – using 'flat' in no derogatory sense, but to indicate the glassy or muddy surface upon which the action now proceeds and through which at any moment something unexpected may emerge. Nothing is more remarkable, in the best work of Crabbe, than the absence of elevation. As a preacher, he may lift up his eyes to the hills. As a poet, he was fascinated by

> *The bounding marsh-bank and the blighted tree;*
> *The water only, when the tides were high,*
> *When low, the mud half-cover'd and half-dry;*
> *The sun-burnt tar that blisters on the planks,*
> *And bank-side stakes in their uneven ranks;*
> *Heaps of entangled weeds that slowly float*
> *As the tide rolls by the impeded boat.*

That is what attracts him – flatness – and upon it the most tragic of his poems deploys. The idea of regeneration, so congenial to Wordsworth and the Lake District, does not appeal to this son of the estuary. Those who sin on the lines of Peter Grimes must sink and sink – incapable even of remorse, though not of fear, incapable of realizing the sun except as a blistering heat, and incapable of observing the stars.

> *When tides were neap, and, in the sultry day,*
> *Through the tall bounding mud-banks made their way . . .*
> *There anchoring, Peter chose from man to hide,*
> *There hang his head . . .*
> *Here dull and hopeless he'd lie down and trace*
> *How sidelong crabs had scrawl'd their crooked race;*
> *Or sadly listen to the tuneless cry*
> *Of fishing gull or clanging golden-eye . . .*
> *He nursed the feelings these dull scenes produce,*
> *And loved to stop beside the opening sluice . . .*

The hanging of the head, the dullness, the nursing of dullness, the lying down motionless in a motionless boat, the dreary contemplation of nature in her trickling exhaustion, the slow downward-bending paralysis of the once active man – they present what the poet too had experienced and the clergyman had combated or ignored. They spring from the attraction and from the repulsion exercised on Crabbe by the surrounding scenery, from the dual feeling which I analysed earlier.

We must consider Crabbe's sensitiveness to dreams in a moment – we are not quite in the world of dreams yet. Peter is still sane and awake. The only sign of abnormality is that he avoids three particular places in the estuary of the Alde; when near them he rows away whistling until they are out of sight. It would seem that here and there the surface of the water is thinner than elsewhere, more liable to be broken from below. He becomes a solitary, seeks men and curses them, and they curse him and he retires to his boat. For a whole winter no one sees him. Next summer he is afloat as before, but no longer fishing. He is gazing, hypnotized by the three places in the stream. 'Dost thou repent?' he is asked. The words have a crystallizing effect and shatter him. Quitting his boat, he goes raving mad, rushes over the countryside, and is caught and carried to the parish infirmary. Here, half nightmare, half vision, the story culminates. ...

Crabbe is explicit on the character of Peter Grimes, and appends an interesting note. 'The mind here exhibited is one untouched by pity, unstung by remorse, and uncorrected by shame.' And he shrewdly observed that 'no feeble vision, no half-visible ghost, not the momentary glance of an unbodied being, nor the half-audible voice of an invisible one, would be created by the continual workings of distress on a mind so depraved and flinty.' Grimes is tough, hard and dull, and the poet must be tough with him, tougher than Shakespeare had to be with Macbeth, who possessed imagination. He must smash him up physically with penury, disease and solitude, and then place indubitable spectres in his path. Physical sufferings have their effect on any nature:

and the harder that nature is, and the longer time required upon it, so much the

296

more strong and indelible is the impression. This is all the reason I am able to give why a man of feeling so dull should yet become insane, and why the visions of his distempered brain should be of so horrible a nature.

The poet sees his literary problem very clearly. A sensitive Grimes would mean a different poem. He must make him a lout, normally impervious to suffering, though once suffering starts it is likely to take a strange form. ...

As for Peter Grimes. He has gone to Hell and there is no doubt about it. No possibility of mercy intervenes. A simple rough fisherman over whom some would have sentimentalized, he is none the less damned, the treacherous flatness of the estuary has opened at last. He will sink into the fire and the blood, the only torments he can appreciate. His father has brought him to disaster – that is his explanation, and the father-motive which preluded the tragedy has re-emerged. To push the motive too hard is to rupture the fabric of the poem and to turn it into a pathological tract, but stressed gently it helps our understanding. The interpretations of Freud miss the values of art as infallibly as do those of Marx. They cannot explain values to us, they cannot show us why a work of art is good or how it became good. But they have their subsidiary use: they can indicate the condition of the artist's mind while he was creating and it is clear that while he was writing 'Peter Grimes' Crabbe was obsessed by the notion of two generations of males being unkind to one another and vicariously punishing unkindness. It is the grandsire-grandson alliance against the tortured adult.

The other motive – also to be stressed cautiously – is the attraction-repulsion one. Peter tries to escape from certain places on the stream, but he cannot, he is always drifting back to them. Crabbe is always drifting back in the spirit to Aldeburgh. The poet and his creation share the same inner tension, the same desire for what repels them. Such parallels can often be found between the experiences of a writer and the experiences of a character in his books, but the parallels must be drawn lightly by the critic, for the experiences have usually been transformed out of recognition and the moral climate changed. To say that Crabbe is Peter Grimes would make that prosperous clergyman indignant and would be false. To say that Crabbe and Grimes share certain psychological tensions might also make him indignant, but it would be true.

And now let us consider *Peter Grimes* the opera; or rather the libretto, for we shall not be much concerned with its music.

The circumstances of its creation are remarkable. The composer, Benjamin Britten, a Suffolk man, was away in the United States, and read there with feelings of nostalgia the poems of Crabbe. They recalled his own country to him, they inspired him, and commissioned by the American conductor Koussevitzky he wrote the opera. It has been accepted as a great work; it has become a national possession and been performed all over the world, and it is a work for which I myself have deep affection.

Now since it bears the same title as the poem people often assume that it is Crabbe set to music. This is not the case. The opera diverges widely from its original, and it is interesting to examine the changes which the composer and his librettist, Mr Montagu Slater, have thought fit to make. They had every right to make them. A composer is under no obligation to stick to his original; his duty is to be original himself. Sometimes he chooses to stick. Verdi's *Otello*, for instance, follows Shakespeare closely – the only addition being the credo introduced for Iago. Bizet's *Carmen*, on the other hand, diverges from Prosper Mérimée's story of the same name, and Donizetti's *Lucia di Lammermoor* owes only the mildest obligations to Sir Walter Scott.

The plot of *Peter Grimes* and the character of its hero are closely interwoven. The curtain rises on the trial of Peter for murdering an apprentice. The scene is the Moot Hall, and the date is 1830 – about fifty years later than the presumable date for the action of the poem. Peter is let off with a warning, and we gather that he was innocent. Ellen Orford, the schoolmistress – who is introduced, with much alteration, from another poem – believes in him, and he hopes to make good and marry her; he hates being an outcast. Then the scene changes to the beach and to that music of the workaday sea which always brings tears into my eyes, it is so lovely, the townsfolk gather, the pleasant time-serving rector (borrowed from another poem) passes, Auntie and her dubious if desirable nieces appear out of another poem at the entrance of the Boar. Peter cannot get help with his boat, people shun him, but he hears of a possible apprentice in the Ipswich workhouse, and Ellen goes off to fetch the boy. The weather turns to storm and the scene to the interior of the Boar. There, in a terrific moment, Peter bursts in on the riotous company. There is silence and he meditates aloud on the Great Bear, the Pleiades, the impossibility of deciphering fate upon the revolving sky. He is revealed as the exception, the poet. The uproar resumes, Ellen enters with the new apprentice, and Peter takes him 'home' amongst cries of derision.

'Home' is an upturned boat on the edge of a cliff. Much has happened by the time we reach it – much gossip about Peter's brutality and some evidence of it. The ill-assorted pair enter – the boy terrified, Peter now irritable, now gentle, trying to make friends, dreaming of marriage with Ellen. The neighbours are heard approaching to look into the rumours of cruelty. Peter, enraged, hurries the boy off to their fishing, pushes him out through the cliff door, he slips, falls, and is killed. The next act is a manhunt; there is evidence of murder, voices shout through the fog. Peter realizes that all is up. He launches his boat, sails out into the darkness in it, and sinks it. The new day begins and with it the music of the workaday sea. Someone sights a sinking boat, but it is too far off to be rescued or identified, and no one is interested, and all is as if nothing had ever been. The chorus gathers, the curtain falls slowly, the opera is over. ...

You remember the words in which Crabbe describes his hero. He is hard and dull, flinty, impervious to sensations, and it was a problem to Crabbe to make such a character suffer. 'The mind here exhibited is one untouched by pity, unstung by remorse, and uncorrected by shame.' And he gazes downward. Whereas Grimes in the opera is sensitive,

299

touched by pity, stung by remorse, and corrected by shame; he needs no apparitions to remind him of his errors, and he lifts up his eyes to the stars. We leave him with the knowledge that it is society who sinned, and with compassion.

The community is to blame. That is one implication of the opera, and Mr Montagu Slater in his Introduction suggests that the implication is to be found in Crabbe himself and that the poet-clergyman was ahead of his times. And the date of the action is put forward into 1830, the year of revolution, and extracted from the placid eighteenth century where it was originally embedded. There is benefit in this operatically, but it cannot be justified from Crabbe. Crabbe satirized society. He did not criticize it. Doctrinally he was a Tory parson, equally averse to idleness and to enthusiasm, and he ascribed human miseries to human frailties and to fate. As his biographer Huchon remarks, 'he had nothing of the radical or rebel in him. To make him a sort of early Cobbett is to take a strangely mistaken idea of his character and his ideas ... He remained essentially bourgeois.' The implication of a social problem combines with the changes in the action and the transformation of Grimes's character to make the opera very different from the poem. The first time I heard it, this worried me rather. I knew the poem well, and I missed its horizontality, its mud. I was puzzled at being asked by Grimes to lift up my eyes to the stars. At the second hearing my difficulty disappeared, and I accepted the opera as an independent masterpiece, with a life of its own.

It is time to leave both the opera and the poem behind. I would like in conclusion to go beyond them and revert to the obscure person who lived at Aldeburgh about two hundred years ago, and whose name was perhaps Tom Brown. He got apprentices from London, they kept disappearing, and he was warned. That is all we know. But he caught the attention of a young surgeon who afterwards specialized in poetry and turned him into Peter Grimes. Two centuries pass. A young musician out in America reads 'Peter Grimes'. It catches his attention, and inspires him to create an opera.

Is that how works of art are born? Do they all depend on a Tom Brown? No, they depend on the creative imagination which will find a Tom Brown somewhere or other, and will accrete round him until he is transformed. So I do not suggest that Aldeburgh need raise a statue to this obscure and unattractive citizen. Still, the fact remains that he happens to be genesis in the whole affair. He is the first step in a series of creative events which has produced your Festival, and if he could ever see anything and if he can see anything now he is feeling surprised.

ALDEBURGH: THE VISION AND THE REALITY
Susan Hill
(from *The Lighting of the Lamps*, 1987)

There are two Aldeburghs, and yet they are one. Yet not one. Separate and distinct. The first may belong to anyone; certainly to those who live there, and to its visitors, festival and fishing people and families on holiday, to all who enjoy it for a day or for years, who work and play there. I lived and worked there for spells, made friends, felt both at home and not so, and now, occasionally, and less often than I would like, I go back. I was not born there, I do not belong to the county of Suffolk at all, but much farther up the same coast, in Yorkshire. My ties with Aldeburgh are all of a different order. Yes, there is that real small town, what is left of it after hundreds of years of storm and tide have washed into it and it has crumbled and fallen, so that the Moot Hall is at the very edge, where once it was in the very centre. There is that visible, visitable place; from Liverpool Street to Saxmundham and then take to the road, and there are fast dual carriageways, now, converging upon it from three directions, and the sea at the other door. There are people who live in houses painted fondant Suffolk pink and cream and grey, or else in terraces cut into the hill like tiers of a cake; people who shop for bread and gloves and aspirin, in and out of the long, surprisingly broad High Street, where small shopkeepers still flourish, for this is one of the last places which does not look like every other place.

This is the real town, yes, with the church at the top of the hill and the sea at the bottom and lanes like fingers of a spread hand poking out to reach it here and here and here, so that you only need to follow any one of them along, to fetch out before and beside its great greyness, only need to follow the salt wind in your nostrils and the hiss and boom and suck of it in your ears.

It is a place much favoured by the energetic retired and for holidays by the intellectual middle classes and a place of boats, pleasure boats, leisure boats, and the working fishing boats, dragged up on to the shingle. It is the music town, with a Festival every year since 1948, well known the world over and in summer, thronged with drummers and pluckers, bowers and blowers, a busy town of golf and whist, Red Cross and Royal National Lifeboat Institution.

Yes, all that, and it is indeed real enough and very pleasing.

But for me, there is another Aldeburgh, and perhaps it is not real. It is as though I open a door in my mind, a door that leads into my own past and to parts of my inner self, a place of my own imagination, which I have written about under different guises in different books, and I am still haunted by it, dream of it.

It was Britten, of course, who brought me to Aldeburgh, he was the Pied Piper and I followed his music until I came to it and heard it, at the heart, on the moan of the wind and in the cries of the curlews, in the thunder of the sea, and the stillness of it, too, as the moonlight lay over it on quiet, clear nights. The beach, the marshes, and the names of all the places around and about, and in, and in between, was like a country invented by his genius.

I find it impossible to be detached about Aldeburgh. I could not write of it plainly and baldly for any guide book, as 'short history, principal buildings, climate, special attractions'. For not only did I first come to it already brimming over with emotion about it, a sense of the place and a passion for it ready formed, not only was it even then partly unreal. I also spent much time in it at a particularly crucial highly charged and rare time of my life, so that I know Aldeburgh through my own emotions and my creative imagination, and through each book that I wrote there and which has left its mark upon me. It is the place in which I experienced deep joy and fulfilment and satisfaction, where I worked best of all and most easily and felt free as a bird. I make it sound romantic and unique and significant and so, for me, it was.

Every year I rented a house there from the depths of winter into very early spring, overlooking – almost *in* – the sea. I saw frost on the shingle and it was sometimes so cold I felt I had lost a skin, the wind battered at walls and windows. And there were those beautiful, vibrant days of late February and March, cloudless, cold, which had a piercing clarity in the air, and there seemed to be sky everywhere, pale sky and silver sea, with the land and houses merely a streak between. Larks spiralled up, the sun shone on the river at Slaughden as on a sheet of metal, the reeds and rushes rattled and shook, dry, dry. On such days, I walked inland for miles and saw no one, I made up page after page in my head, absorbed, concentrated, taut, yet seeing things too, waders in the mud, a heron, still as a tree-stump, the individual blades of grass. There was such a spirit in the air of that place, felt, heard, sensed, glimpsed, in the water and the sky and in the cries of birds.

I wrote all morning, looking up to see a fishing boat or the trawlers that sailed slowly in the far distance, and always the sea, moving about within itself, ruminative, grey, blue, violet, silver, it sang in my ears all day, all night.

I tramped the shingle, too, a noisy walk, head down into the screaming wind, and the gulls shrieked and reeled crazily about, and at night, I was sometimes afraid, and pulled the cat up on to my lap for comfort. For I was always alone there, and alone inside myself, too, that kind of life and work is necessarily utterly lonely. I would not have had it otherwise, and alone, you see and know what is hidden and blurred to you. In company you live on a different level, sensations, ideas, truths, the ghosts of the place, rise up and crowd your consciousness. I could never have been as I was, or written just what I did, in any other place in the world.

Then, sometimes, I would open the window wide on early March mornings, and sit with the sun full on my face and laugh to myself, it was so lovely, and then go out for fish, fresh caught, and dip my toes in the icy sea, and run, run over the stones, or throw them, ducks and drakes, or simply stand, watching some ship break the line of the horizon.

I knew, also, extreme, shattering grief there and the experience, the memory of it, are bound up with my view of the town, too. I remember how I stood and stared, stared down at the sea lapping over one patch of shingle, and could neither believe nor understand the appalling thing that had happened. That day changed my view of the place forever.

Then, I stopped going there to live alone and work. I have visited since, for days and weekends, but when at leisure and accompanied and so it has been the real, outward, everyday Aldeburgh that I have come to, and my presence there has been somehow superficial. Yet the other town is still there. It must be. I would only have to turn a corner and stand alone in wind and rain, to listen, remember.

For the one place I feel warm affection, and friendship, I enjoy it, recommend it, look it up in guide books and history books, I should like my family to remember it as the unspoilt town for happy seaside holidays.

And the other place ... Ah, that Aldeburgh I hold within me, set as in the amber you may find on the beach there, it is a landscape of the spirit.

SHORELINE SECRETS
W.G. Sebald
(from *The Rings of Saturn*, 1998)

From Woodbridge to Orford, down to the sea, is a good four-hour walk. The roads and tracks pass through dry, empty stretches of land which, by the end of a long summer, are almost like a desert. This sparsely populated part of the country has hardly ever been cultivated, and, throughout the ages, was never more than a pasture for sheep reaching from one horizon to the other. When the shepherds and their flocks disappeared in the early nineteenth century heather and scrub began to spread. This was encouraged as far as possible by the lords of the manors of Rendlesham Hall, Sudbourne Hall, Orwell Park and Ash High House, who had in their possession almost the whole of the Sandlings, in order to create favourable conditions for the hunting of small game, which had become fashionable in the Victorian age. ... As their rights were curtailed, the rural population not engaged in rearing pheasants, breeding gun dogs, as gamekeepers or beaters or in any other capacity connected with shooting, were forced to quit the places where they had lived for generations. As a consequence, in the early years of the twentieth century, at Hollesley Bay, just inland from the coast, a labour colony later known as Colonial College was established, from which those for whom there was no future went out to New Zealand or Australia after a given time. The Hollesley Bay premises are now a borstal, and young offenders can be seen at work in the fields nearby, always in groups and wearing luminous orange jackets.The pheasant craze was at its height in the decades before the

First World War, when Sudbourne Hall alone employed two dozen gamekeepers, and a tailor for the sole purpose of keeping their livery in trim. There were times when six thousand pheasants were gunned down in a single day, not to mention the other fowl, hares and rabbits. The staggering scores were punctiliously recorded in the game books of the rivalling estates. One of the foremost shooting domains in the Sandlings was Bawdsey, with more than eight thousand acres on the north bank of the Deben. In the early 1880s, Sir Cuthbert Quilter, a business baron who had risen from the lower classes, had a family seat built on a prominent site by the river estuary, reminiscent both of an Elizabethan mansion and of a maharajah's palace. Erecting this architectural marvel was a demonstration for Quilter of the justice of his claim to status, a demonstration quite as unyielding as the choice of his heraldic motto, *plutot mourir que changer*, which refuted all bourgeois compromise. At that time, the craving for power in men of his kind was at its most acute. From where they stood there seemed no reason why things should not go on in this vein forever, from one spectacular success to the next. It was no coincidence that the German Empress was taking a convalescent holiday across the river in Felixstowe, which had become a desirable resort in recent years. For weeks, the royal yacht Hohenzollern lay at anchor there, a visible token of the possibilities now open to the entrepreneurial spirit. Under the patronage of their imperial majesties, the North Sea coast might become one great health resort for the upper classes, equipped with all the amenities of modern life. Everywhere, hotels mushroomed from the barren land. Promenades and bathing facilities were established, and piers grew out into the sea. Even in the most abandoned spot in the entire region, Shingle Street, which now consists of just one wretched row of humble houses and cottages and where I have never encountered a single human being, a spa centre by the grandiose name of German Ocean Mansions designed for two hundred guests was built at the time, if one can believe the records, and staffed with personnel who were recruited from Germany. Today there is no trace of it. Indeed, there seem to have been all manner of ties across the North Sea between the British and German Empires at that period, ties that were expressed first and foremost in the colossal manifestations of bad taste of those who wanted a place in the sun no matter at what cost. Cuthbert Quilter's Anglo-Indian fairy-tale palace in the dunes would doubtless have appealed to the German Kaiser's artistic sensibility, since he had a pronounced penchant for any kind of extravagance. Likewise one can picture Quilter, who added another tower to his beachfront castle for every million he added to his fortune, as a guest aboard the Hohenzollern. One imagines him, say, together with gentlemen from the Admiralty who had also been invited, at the gymnastic exercises which preceded Sunday service at sea. What daring plans might not a man of Quilter's ilk have evolved, egged on by a like-minded man such as Kaiser Wilhelm – envisaging an open-air paradise extending from Felixstowe via Norderney to Sylt, to keep the nations fit; or the foundation of a new North Sea civilization, if not indeed an Anglo-German global alliance, symbolized by a state cathedral, visible far and wide across the waves, on the island of Heligoland. In reality, of course, history took a quite different turn, for, whenever one is imagining a bright future, the next disaster is just around the corner. War was declared, the German hotel employees were sent back home, there were no more summer visitors, and one morning a zeppelin like an airborne whale appeared over the coast, while across the Channel train after train with troops and equipment rolled to the front, whole tracts of land were ploughed up by mortar fire, and the death strip between the front lines was strewn with phosphorescent corpses. The German Kaiser lost his Empire, and the world of Cuthbert Quilter too went into a gradual decline. His means, which had once seemed inexhaustible, dwindled to such an extent that maintaining the estate no longer made any sense. Raymond Quilter, who inherited Bawdsey, entertained the holidaymakers at Felixstowe, who were now of a somewhat less superior breed, with sensational parachute jumps onto the beach. In 1936 he was obliged to sell Bawdsey Manor to the nation. The proceeds were sufficient to cover his tax liabilities and to finance his passion for flying, which meant more to him than anything else.

307

Having surrendered the family property, he moved into the former chauffeur's quarters, but would still stay at the Dorchester when in London. As a token of the special esteem in which he was held there, the Quilter standard, a golden pheasant on a black ground, was hoisted alongside the Union Jack whenever he arrived. He was accorded this rare privilege by the establishment's reserved staff because of the reputation for chivalry he had enjoyed ever since he had parted, without regret, from the estates his great-uncle had acquired, since which time, apart from a modest amount of independent capital, he had owned nothing but his aeroplane and a runway in an isolated field.

In the years following the First World War, countless estates were broken up in the same way as Quilter's Bawdsey. The manor houses were either left to fall down or used for other purposes, as boys' boarding schools, approved schools, insane asylums, old people's homes, or reception camps for refugees from the Third Reich. Bawdsey Manor itself was for a long time the domicile and research centre of the team under Robert Watson-Watt that developed radar, which now spreads its invisible net throughout the entire airspace. To this day, the area between Woodbridge and the sea remains full of military installations. Time and again, as one walks across the wide plains, one passes barracks, gateways and fenced-off areas where, behind thin plantations of Scots pines, weapons are concealed in camouflaged hangars and grass-covered bunkers, the weapons with which, if an emergency should arise, whole countries and continents can be transformed into smoking heaps of stone and ash in no time. ...

When at last I reached Orford, I climbed to the top of the castle keep, from where there is a view over the houses of the town, the green gardens and pallid fenlands, and the coastline to north and south, lost in the shimmering distance. Orford Castle was completed in 1165 and for centuries was the foremost bastion against the constant threat of invasion. Not until Napoleon was contemplating the conquest of the British Isles – his engineers audaciously planning to dig a tunnel under the Channel, and envisaging an armada of hot-air balloons advancing on the English coast – were new defensive measures taken, with the building of martello towers along the seashore, a mile or so apart. There are seven of these circular forts between Felixstowe and Orford alone. To the best of my knowledge, their effectiveness was never put to the test. The garrisons were soon withdrawn, and ever since these masonry shells have served as homes for the owls that make their soundless flights at dusk from the battlements. In the early Forties, the scientists and technicians at Bawdsey built radar masts along the east coast, eerie wooden structures more than eighty yards high which could sometimes be heard creaking in the night. No one knew what purpose they served any more than they knew about the many other secret projects then being pursued in the military research establishments around Orford. Naturally this gave rise to all manner of speculation about an invisible web of death rays, a new kind of nerve gas, or some hideous means of mass destruction that would come into play if the Germans attempted a landing. And it is a fact that until recently a file labelled *Evacuation of the Civil Population from Shingle Street, Suffolk* was in the archives of the Ministry of Defence, embargoed for seventy-five years as distinct from the usual practice of releasing documents after thirty, on the grounds that (so the irrepressible rumours claimed) it gave details of a horrifying incident in Shingle Street for which no government could accept public responsibility. I myself heard, for instance, that experiments were conducted at Shingle Street with biological weapons designed to make whole regions uninhabitable. I also heard tell of a system of pipes extending far out to sea, by means of which a petroleum inferno could be unleashed with such explosive rapidity, in the event of an invasion, that the very sea would start to boil. In the course of the preparatory experimentations, an entire company of English sappers were said to have met their deaths, inadvertently as it were, in the most appalling manner, according to eye witnesses who claimed to have seen the charred bodies, contorted with pain, lying on the beach or still out at sea in their boats. Others maintain that those who died in the wall of fire were German landing forces wearing English uniforms. When access to the Shingle Street file following a lengthy campaign was finally granted in 1992 in the local press, it revealed nothing that might have justified the top-secret classification, or substantiated the stories that had been circulating since the end of the war. But it seems likely, one commentator wrote, that sensitive material was removed before the file was opened, and so the mystery of Shingle Street remains. – Presumably part of the reason why rumours like this one concerning Shingle Street endured so obstinately was that, during the Cold War era, the Ministry of Defence continued to maintain Secret Weapons Research Establishments on the coast of Suffolk, and imposed the strictest silence on the work carried out in them. The inhabitants of Orford, for example, could only speculate about what went on at the Orfordness site, which, though perfectly visible from the town, was effectively no easier to reach than the Nevada desert or an atoll in the South Seas. For my part, I well recall standing down by the harbour when I first visited Orford in 1972 and looking across to what the locals simply called 'the island', which resembled a penal colony in the Far East. I had been studying the curious coastal land formations at Orford on the map, and was interested in the promontory of Orfordness, which seemed to have an extra-territorial quality about it.

Stone by stone, over a period of millennia, it had shifted down from the north across the mouth of the River Alde, in such a way that the tidal lower reaches, known as the Ore, run for some twelve miles just inside the present coastline before flowing into the sea. When I was first in Orford, it was forbidden to approach 'the island', but now there was no longer any obstacle to going there, since, some years before, the Ministry of Defence had abandoned secret research at that site. One of the men sitting idly on the harbour wall offered to take me over for a few pounds and fetch me later after I had had a look around. As we crossed the river in his blue-painted boat, he told me that people still mostly avoided Orfordness. Even the beach fishermen, who were no strangers to solitude, had given up night-fishing out there after a few attempts, allegedly because it wasn't worth their while, but in reality because they couldn't stand the god-forsaken loneliness of that outpost in the middle of nowhere, and in some cases even became emotionally disturbed for some time. Once we were on the other side, I took leave

310

of my ferryman and, after climbing over the embankment, walked along a partially overgrown tarmac track running straight through a vast, yellowing field. The day was dull and oppressive, and there was so little breeze that not even the ears of the delicate quaking grass were nodding. It was as if I were passing through an undiscovered country, and I still remember that I felt, at the same time, both utterly liberated and deeply despondent. I had not a single thought in my head. With each step that I took, the emptiness within and the emptiness without grew ever greater and the silence more profound. Perhaps that was why I was frightened almost to death when a hare that had been hiding in the tufts of grass by the wayside started up, right at my feet, and shot off down the rough track before darting sideways, this way, then that, into the field. It must have been cowering there as I approached, heart pounding as it waited, until it was almost too late to get away with its life. In that very fraction of a second when its paralysed state turned into panic and flight, its fear cut right through me. I still see what occurred in that one tremulous instant with an undiminished clarity. I see the edge of the grey tarmac and every individual blade of grass, I see the hare leaping out of its hiding-place, with its ears laid back and a curiously human expression on its face that was rigid with terror and strangely divided; and in its eyes, turning to look back as it fled and almost popping out of its head with fright, I see myself, become one with it. Not till half-an-hour later, when I reached the broad dyke that separates the grass expanse from the pebble bank that slopes to the shoreline, did the blood cease its clamour in my veins. For a long while I stood on the bridge that leads to the former research establishment. Far behind me to the west, scarcely to be discerned, were the gentle slopes of the inhabited land; to the north and south, in flashes of silver, gleamed the muddy bed of a dead arm of the river, through which now, at low tide, only a meagre trickle ran; and ahead lay nothing but destruction. From a distance, the concrete shells, shored up with stones, in which for most of my lifetime hundreds of boffins had been at work devising new weapons systems, looked (probably because of their odd conical shape) like the tumuli in which the mighty and powerful were buried in prehistoric times with all their tools and utensils, silver and gold. My sense of being on ground intended for purposes transcending the profane was heightened by a number of buildings that resembled temples or pagodas, which seemed quite out of place in these military installations. But the closer I came to these ruins, the more any notion of a mysterious isle of the dead receded, and the more I imagined myself amidst the remains of our own civilization after its extinction in some future catastrophe. To me too, as for some latter-day stranger ignorant of the nature of our society wandering about among heaps of scrap metal and defunct machinery, the beings who had once lived and worked here were an enigma, as was the purpose of the primitive contraptions and fittings inside the bunkers, the iron rails under the ceilings, the hooks on the still partially tiled walls, the showerheads the size of plates, the ramps and the soakaways. Where and in what time I truly was that day at Orfordness I cannot say, even now as I write these words. All I do know is that I finally walked along the raised embankment from the Chinese Wall Bridge past the old pumphouse towards the landing stage, to my left in the fading fields a collection of black Nissen huts, and to my right, across the river, the mainland. As I was sitting on the breakwater waiting for the ferryman, the evening sun emerged from behind the clouds, bathing in its light the far-reaching arc of the seashore. The tide was advancing up the river, the water was shining like tinplate, and from the radio masts high above the marshes came an even, scarcely audible hum. The roofs and towers of Orford showed among the tree tops, seeming so close that I could touch them. There, I thought, I was once at home. And then, through the growing dazzle of the light in my eyes, I suddenly saw, amidst the darkening colours, the sails of the long-vanished windmills turning heavily in the wind.

MEN OF LETTERS

Suffolk Backwaters

COUNTRY MATTERS
Edward FitzGerald
(from *Letters*, 1910)

BOULGE HALL, WOODBRIDGE,
21 April, 1837

DEAR ALLEN,

... Ah! I wish you were here to walk with me now that the warm weather is come at last. Things have been delayed but to be more welcome, and to burst forth twice as thick and beautiful. This is boasting however, and counting of the chickens before they are hatched: the East winds may again plunge us back into winter: but the sunshine of this morning fills one's pores with jollity, as if one had taken laughing gas. Then my house is getting on: the books are up in the bookshelves and do my heart good: then Stothard's Canterbury Pilgrims are over the fireplace: Shakespeare in a recess: how I wish you were here for a day or two! My sister is very well and cheerful and we have kept house very pleasantly together ...

BOULGE HALL, WOODBRIDGE,
Sunday, Dec. 10/1843.

DEAR FREDERIC,

Either you wrote me word yourself, or some one told me, that you meant to winter at Florence. So I shall direct to the Poste Restante there. You see I am not settled at the Florence of Suffolk, called

Ipswich, yet: but I am perhaps as badly off; being in this most dull country house quite alone; a grey mist, that seems teeming with half formed snow, all over the landscape before my windows. It is also Sunday morning: ten of the clock by the chime now sounding from the stables. I have fed on bread and milk (a dreadfully opaque diet) and I await the morning Church in humble hope. It will begin in half an hour. We keep early hours in the country. So you will be able exactly to measure my aptitude and fullness for letter writing by the quantity written now, before I bolt off for hat, gloves, and prayerbook. I always put on my thickest great coat to go to our Church in: as fungi grow in great numbers about the communion table. ...

MARKET-HILL: WOODBRIDGE:
May 22/61.

My DEAR COWELL,

... My chief Amusement in Life is Boating, on River and Sea. The Country about here is the Cemetery of so many of my oldest Friends: and the petty race of Squires who have succeeded only use the Earth for an *Investment*: cut down every old Tree: level every Violet Bank: and make the old Country of my Youth hideous to me in my Decline. There are fewer Birds to be heard, as fewer Trees for them to resort to. So I get to the Water: where Friends are not buried nor Pathways stopt up: but all is, as the Poets say, as Creation's Dawn beheld. I am happiest going in my little Boat round the Coast to Aldbro', with some Bottled Porter and some Bread and Cheese, and some good rough Soul who works the Boat and chews his Tobacco in peace. An Aldbro' Sailor talking of my Boat said – 'She go like a Wiolin, she do!' What a pretty Conceit, is it not? As the Bow slides over the Strings in a liquid Tune. Another man was talking yesterday of a great Storm: 'and, in a moment, all as calm as a Clock.'

WOODBRIDGE,
June 8/63.

My DEAR GEORGE,

Your sister wrote me a very kind Letter to tell of her safe Return home. I must repeat to you very sincerely that I never recollect to have passed a pleasanter week. As far as Company went, it was like Old Times at Bredfield; and the Oak-trees were divine! I never expected to care so very much for Trees, nor for your flat Country: but I really feel as one who has bathed in Verdure. I suppose Town-living makes one alive to such a Change.

I spent a long Day with Thompson [at Ely]: and much liked the painted Roof. On Thursday I went to Lynn: which I took a Fancy to: the odd old Houses: the Quay: the really grand Inn (Duke's Head, in the Market place) and the civil Norfolk-talking People. I went to Hunstanton, which is rather dreary: one could see the Country at Sandringham was good. I enquired fruitlessly about those Sandringham Pictures, etc.: even the Auctioneer, whom I found in the Bar of the Inn, could tell nothing of where they had gone.

MARKET-HILL, WOODBRIDGE.
Sat. July 18/63.

My DEAR DONNE

... I can hardly tell you whether I am much pleased with my new Boat; for I hardly know myself. She is (as I doubted would be from the first) rather awkward in our narrow River; but then she was to be a good Sea-boat; and I don't know but she is; and will be better in all ways when we have got her in proper trim. Yesterday we gave her what they call '*a tuning*' in a rather heavy swell round Orford Ness: and she did well without a reef etc. But, now all is got, I don't any the more want to go far away by Sea, any more than by Land; having no Curiosity left for other Places, and glad to get back to my own Chair and Bed after three or four Days' Absence. So long as I get on

317

the Sea from time to time, it is much the same to me whether off Aldbro' or Penzance. And I find I can't sleep so well on board as I used to do thirty years ago: and not to get one's Sleep, you know, indisposes one more or less for the Day. However, we talk of Dover, Folkestone Holland, etc., which will give one's sleeping Talents a *tuning*.

FELIXTOW FERRY: *July 25 [1868]*

Mv DEAR COWELL,

I found your Letter on reaching Woodbridge yesterday; where you see I did not stay long. In fact I only left Lowestoft partly to avoid a Volunteer Camp there which filled the Town with People and Bustle: and partly that my Captain might see his Wife: who cannot last *very* much longer I think: scarcely through Autumn, surely. She goes about, nurses her children, etc., but grows visibly thinner, weaker, and more ailing.

If the Wind changes (now directly in our Teeth) I shall sail back to Lowestoft to-morrow. Thompson and Mrs. P. propose to be at the Royal Hotel there till Wednesday, and we wish, I believe, to see each other again. Sailing did not agree with his bilious temperament: and he seemed to me injudicious in his hours of Exercise, Dinner, etc. But he, and she, should know best. I like her very much: head and heart right feminine of the best, it seemed to me and her experience of the World, and the Wits, not having injured either.

To C. E. Norton.

WOODBRIDGE.

August 21/77.

My DEAR SIR,

... I had my house all ready to entertain him [Mr Lowell] as best I could; and had even planned a little Visit to our neighbouring Coast, where are the Village remains of a once large Town devoured by the

Sea: and, yet undevoured (except by Henry VIII.), the grey walls of a Grey Friars' Priory, beside which they used to walk, under such Sunsets as illumine them still. This pathetic Ruin, still remaining by the Sea, would (I feel sure) have been more to one from the New Atlantis than all London can show: but I should have liked better had Mr. Lowell seen it on returning to America, rather than going to Spain, where the yet older and more splendid Moors would soon have effaced the memory of our poor Dunwich. If you have a Map of England, look for it on the Eastern Coast. If Mr. Lowell should return this way, and return in the proper Season for such cold Climate as ours, he shall see it: and so shall you, if you will, under like conditions; including a reasonable and available degree of Health in myself to do the honours.

I live down in such a Corner of this little Country that I see scarce any one but my Woodbridge Fellow-townsmen, and learn but little from such Friends as could tell me of the World beyond. But the English do not generally love Letter writing: and very few of us like it the more as we get older. So I have but little to say that deserves an Answer from you: but please to write me a little: a word about Mr. Lowell, whom you have doubtless heard from.

[August 1882].

My DEAR MRS. KEMBLE,

I have let the Full Moon go by, and very well she looked too, over the Sea by which I am now staying. Not at Lowestoft; but at the old extinguished Borough of Aldeburgh, to which as to other 'premiers Amours' I revert: where more than sixty years ago I first saw, and first felt, the Sea; where I have lodged in half the houses since; and where I have a sort of traditional acquaintance with half the population: Clare Cottage is where I write from; two little rooms, enough for me; a poor civil woman pleased to have me in them. ...

319

WOODBRIDGE.
Tuesday, [June 12, 1883].

Mv DEAR LAURENCE,

... If I do not write, it is because I have absolutely nothing to tell you that you have not known for the last twenty years. Here I live still, reading, and being read to, part of my time; walking abroad three or four times a day, or night, in spite of wakening a Bronchitis, which has lodged like the household 'Brownie' within; pottering about my Garden (as I have just been doing) and snipping off dead Roses like Miss Tox; and now and then a visit to the neighbouring Seaside, and a splash to Sea in one of the Boats. I never see a new Picture, nor hear a note of Music except when I drum out some old Tune in Winter on an Organ, which might almost be carried about the Streets with a handle to turn, and a Monkey on the top of it. So I go on, living a life far too comfortable as compared with that of better, and wiser men: but ever expecting a reverse in health such as my seventy-five years are subject to. ...

To-morrow I am going (for my one annual Visit) to G. Crabbe's, where I am to meet his Sisters, and talk over old Bredfield Vicarage days. Two of my eight Nieces are now with me here in my house, for a two months' visit, I suppose and hope. And I think this is all I have to tell you of.

Yours ever sincerely
E. F. G.

MENDHAM MEMORIES

Alfred Munnings

(from *An Artist's Life*, 1955)

From the days of governesses to those of school I am unable, as I recall earlier years, to place important happenings. There is only one familiar background with its leading feature, the river, for we never went farther away than Norwich, and a journey there was only a rare event. When I did go I was so frightened at the traffic that I daren't cross a street. ...

... I went twice or more a week for drawing lessons at the vicarage under Miss Kate Brereton, a daughter of the parson. These lessons opened up fresh paths. I forget when they ended; but at some time after this I began drawing the trace-horses, taken from the farmers' wagons which came with four-horse loads of wheat to the mill. They were tied to the white meadow gate in front of our house windows, while the shaft-horses pulled the wagon under the lukem platform, and the sacks of corn were unloaded, being drawn up by a bright, shining chain from the wagon.

Early wagons would sometimes arrive in front of the dining-room window as we were at family prayers. Springing up, leaving us there, maids and all kneeling against chairs, my father went through the glass door into his office for the sample of wheat bought at market. Then, through the window, we saw him put his foot on a spoke of the front wheel of the wagon, mount the shaft, open the first sack and compare the wheat with the sample. This having been done, he climbed down with the words, to the wagoner, 'Alright, Cocky. You can drive on.' After which he rejoined us, still on our knees, and resumed prayers where he had left off.

Often there were several wagons with grand teams of horses, their manes and tails done up with red and blue or yellow ribbons and straw plaiting. The journey to the mills with the corn was, next to harvest, the event of the year on a farm. The teams of chestnut Suffolk Punches with brass-mounted harness from Lord Huntingfield's farms were a magnificent sight. Some time after harvest, when the wheats were threshed out, a long line of horses and wagons reached all the way up the lane and round the corner, for over a quarter of a mile. The wheat was shot into the large bins in the upper stories of the mill, until there seemed to be no space left for more – yet more went in. What beautiful flour and wheat meal we used in the house then; and what home-made brown loaves we ate, with the most perfect butter, salted exactly as it should be. I could shed a tear now at the thought of the indescribable flavour of both.

Chestnut-trees stood along the south side of the lane, and horses from the foremost lot of wagons were tied underneath them. The more the wagons the longer the horses had to wait, and I remember the great amount of brass on the harness. Two men were with each wagon as a rule, the wheat, in many cases, coming long distances – fifteen or more miles. I can smell the sweet, curious scent of the horses in the lane now: a scent of pastures coming through the pores of their skin. A glorious smell, the very opposite to that of petrol. ...

But I must not forget the feature of our home – of our lives – the river. In summer and winter alike this was really our true playground, and great happenings were enacted upon its surface and upon its banks, for we had cousins and other lads to join in these doings. As we grew older, devouring the works of Fenimore Cooper and Rider Haggard, reading of pirates and bush-rangers, our adventures took us about, up and down stream. In between I revelled in drawings of Indians on mustangs, trappers and scalp-hunters. One large coloured pencil drawing was of Indians attacking a fort, the air being filled with flying tomahawks and arrows.

What really made these days was our gradual mastery of an old two-ended, flat-bottomed boat which was used for getting weeds from the river after the summer cutting. Our imaginations turned this old boat into a wonderful craft. We not only made a mast and sail; we put heavy flint stones in the boat for ballast, and to do this stripped a rockery on which blue periwinkle grew. And there was trouble with those rockery stones! Imagine us in a strong March gale, with bending mast, stayed by a taut, stolen linen line, with straining, bulging sail, roaring down the long reach of river, leaving a wake on either side like that of a steam launch. The wake as it followed fast lapped over each bank. We sped onwards to the end, which was the overhanging bough of a great tree at the bottom of the orchard. The crash was frightful as mast and sail fell, while we were thrown on our backs by the impact.

How often each one of us fell in the river and escaped drowning I cannot say, but such adventures were rewarded with a thrashing. Then we were sent to bed, no longer skull-and-crossbone pirates, but mere misunderstood, unhappy boys. But who can beat the spirit of youth? Or even begin to understand it in all its phases?

What didn't we do on that peaceful river? When shoals of cut water-weed lay against 'the rack', as we called it, which stretched across from bank to bank above the weir and kept all floating weed from going down to the mill, we fished for perch from that old boat, gazing down into the dark amber depths as the worm swung in the current below. We fished for roach and dace, we found moorhens' nests with their eggs, and in the reeds, small nests of reed warblers. Their continual song was a background to our frolics and adventures.

On the meadows men with horses harrowing and rolling, moving slowly across and back; making wide, velvety tracks on the sunlit grass, as the custom had been on all Good Fridays ever since I could remember.

Whitsuntide followed, with the willows in fresh, new green; and we made our yearly walk to South Elmham Priory. Fences and thorn-trees white with May blossom. The marshes, as far as you could see, one blaze of buttercups; and daisies, as well as buttercups, covered the home pastures. There were horse shows in small towns, where flags festooned the streets. A large flag flew from the church tower as the bells rang out all the afternoon, their sound mingling with the neighing of mares and foals in the show-ground. Tents with lunch or tea and a strong, sweet scent of trodden grass, while a band played waltzes and old tunes, instead of an amplifying van with records.

Hay-making time came round too quickly. All hands were called in for this, for my father made good hay. There were the rows made by

323

the drag-rake, the cocks, the carting, the creaking of the wagons, and the making of large stacks in the stackyard. Tall poles stood at each end of the stack-in-making, so that at night the stack-cloth was stretched across. The cleared hayfields still scented the air as we played cricket on the pitch now open to us.

Later, I remember, there was in the old, tarred boathouse above the mill a new, varnished boat from Beccles. It was a good stiff boat, with plenty of room in the stern. My mother's great joy was a picnic, and as we now had one boat above the mill and one below, we could go either up or down the river to the scene of our spread. If I were in the bows, I trailed my fingers in the tepid, soft water, plucking up the yellow lilies from their stubborn hold, looking down into the clear current with waving weeds below. Homewards again, with cattle standing above on the meadow, their reflections showing below the line of water-moss bordering banks grown with forget-me-nots and scented with meadowsweet. The clatter of oars at the finish, the getting out tea-things and baskets, the chaining-up of the boat and the lap of water in the boathouse as the last one steps ashore. All these memories of the river crowd thickly in my mind.

Opposite the boathouse the kitchen garden bordered the clear-running mill-stream. Close to the path stood an old apple-tree which came into all our doings, and was called the Doctor Harvey tree. On warm days scents came from raspberries and a still richer aroma from black currants hanging in dark clusters where startled blackbirds flew away with a full-throated cluck! cluck! – the same yesterday, today and always. Down the stream by the mill were wooden steps, with a handrail to the waters edge, where men filled buckets of water for the horses in the stables. The sound of the mill was the background to our dreams. ...

Hot days in July and August, and bathing. Learning to swim on bundles of bulrushes. I recapture the smell of the river as we revelled about in our depth where there was a gravel bottom. Our diving grew wonderful in deeper water. Fast-running dives we took, and if any watcher were there, how we loved showing off! We swam long distances underwater; we made great jumps from the bank far out into the river;

and when it was over, we lay sunning ourselves, then dressed and went to tea in the arbour under the weeping ash in the garden. For tea we had small, brown loaves, sometimes a new ham, eggs, jam, beautiful butter, buns and cake, all home-made, the work of our good mother. When everything had disappeared, more took their place next day.

Let me picture afresh the floods when the marsh up and down the river was one vast, desolate sheet of water, studded with island gateways and rows of pollard willows with their inverted reflections. An alder or poplar here and there traced the course of the yellow flow of the stream as it grew swifter and stronger, like a broad moving floor nearing the weir, and, farther on, the flood-gates. White spume-flakes hurried by and disappeared down the yellow slide of weed-smelling waters of the weir, roaring in turbulent masses of foam and, racing on, carving out great slices from banks, pouring through the orchard and by pig-sties, meeting the other maelstrom from the floodgates, where eel-nets, taut and stretched, were submerged in the weight of the flow.

The floods were a great adventure while they lasted. How sure was I that I could paint all this sky and water! What pictures I set out to do! Alas! when I tried, the wide stretches of flood would look like snow.

There are yet the frosts and snow to tell of, which were often the cause of floods and which lasted for weeks and weeks together. Lanes drifted up level, and there were snow-ploughs with horses and men who were given hot, mulled beer to drink. Then a thaw, followed by floods and more frosts and hosts of folk all skating. Some skating and pushing others on chairs; some cutting figures on the ice; skating all hours of the day and in the moonlight. Sharp, hard, sparkling frosts, and a church cold in spite of stoves on a Sunday.

In the mornings, our towels, like Mr Jorrocks', were frozen stiff, and the water in the ewer was a block of ice. As we lay in bed we heard the bang of cracking ice on the river, and hated getting up and going to school.

During these passing years we three brothers had, one by one, left the wings of a governess and walked daily to a grammar school, two miles away, at Redenhall.

We liked the walk, carrying our satchels; loitering if early, hurrying if late. We liked that school with its headmaster, Christopher C. Hall. He made history interesting to us. He encouraged me to draw. We had football and cricket, and a drill sergeant, a bathing-pool and lessons in swimming, at which I won a prize for swimming in the best style. We had canings and Speech Days and we were happy. We even liked the French verbs.

In these days of school and home lessons we nevertheless had evenings of reading during the winter. If it were Scott, my mother was chief reader, one of us occasionally taking a turn, the rest listening to the adventures of Ivanhoe and Front de Breuf, and Sir Brian de Bois Gilbert. We pictured the storming of Torquilstone, seeing Framlingham Castle in our minds. We saw forest glades of oak, and deer sheltering in the bracken.

IN CONSTABLE'S COUNTRY
Adrian Bell
(from *My Own Master*, 1961)

Coming back into Suffolk from our Chiltern interlude, Marjorie and I found an old house in what the house agents call 'Constable's Country', that is to say, the country along the Stour Valley, which may be said to terminate at Sudbury, where the barges of 'The Leaping Horse' and 'Flatford Mill' then lay rotting underwater on the river bed beside Sudbury's once busy, but now deserted, wharves and quay. The house we found was a farmhouse, and around it lay its farm, an ideal little holding of thirty acres, south-sloping, with water meadows beside the Stour. I coveted the farm too. I hoped within a few years to be able to acquire it, since the farmer was young, and farmed it along with another small farm two miles away; and I thought that he would want to get married soon, and then would prefer to farm one good-size farm rather than two small ones separated from one another, necessitating long journeys with tackle, and this would be worth waiting for.

The house was rather a wreck when we first saw it; and we were at first for turning away. Then we found some marigolds blooming in a corner beside the house: it was the first of March. I think it was the marigolds' sun-faces which tipped the balance of 'Shall we, shan't we?' as we stood looking at them, wondering about it.

The house had a roof of jumbled red-brown tiles, like a mountainside in a sunset glow. It was nearly all roof, and fertile roof: a houseleek thrived on it, and several sorts of mosses, not to mention a young ash tree rooted in a compost of plaster and old birds' nests in a hole in the wall. It looked such a hopeless proposition to the superficial eye that I refused to divulge its whereabouts to my mother in Sudbury. But she found out its address and got a cousin to drive her over there, and explored it. Coming out, as she divested herself of cobwebs, she said (the cousin told me), 'Adrian has always been mad, but this is the maddest thing he has done yet.'

But it turned out beautifully; even the bath water ran away – unlike that of a friend of mine, which came back at him under the front door within three minutes of his pulling out the plug.

And after I had dug up several desiccated prams and bicycles from the garden, the garden was beautiful too. When I pass that house today I look in and have tea with the owners, and make friends with it all over again. It has been cherished for thirty years, and looks as good as ever it did, with its oak mullions. I feel then that whatever I have misdone or failed to do, I did on that first of March take a decision which saved that house; which, in spite of its apparent decay, must have been structurally sound, since there it stands with its weird roof intact, in spite of jarrings from land-mines in the war, which cracked newer brick-built houses in the district.

This 'Constable's Country' is a region of small hills and treasured churches, of lanes as numerous and crooked as the boughs of an oak. It belonged to Constable yet, to the great grand oil paintings; 'Flatford Mill', 'The Hay Wain', 'The Leaping Horse'.

Now I hear the Stour Valley is a fashionable region: business men commute daily to and from London. In a way I am glad: they alone have the money needed to preserve its somewhat fragile plaster facades. When we lived there, it belonged to farmers, poor artists and certain fierce old shepherds. It had touches of fantasy: there was a farm named Guinea Wigs. The horse-brake proprietor had swum from Sudbury to Bures in his youth. His son ran buses. The last horse brake stood in a cherry wood, its brackets full of birds' nests.

Our house was of oak and plaster. Its shape was rather that of a crate damaged in transit. The parlour ceiling was twice as high at one end as at the other. It had also a wealth of tiny old red tiles, which the builder dare not touch lest he started an avalanche.

Through this country the Stour burrowed secretly, bearded with willows; stubby pollards or tall willows with silky tresses. In the fields were superstructures of broken locks, beside which we rested on our walks, and listened to water spouting through breached floodgates, which elsewhere was slow, silent and paved with lily-pads. By July water-hens no longer swam the river; they walked it.

Our neighbours were a study in contrasting types. There was dear John Green, generous and easy-going. He and his wife walked foxhound puppies for the hunt, had two pet cows, a great mellow old house, ivy-clad barns and three hundred acres. I can see pans of milk outside the back door for hound or hen or porker to refresh itself. We bought Jersey butter from Mrs. Green for a shilling a pound. She made luscious cakes and biscuits, using Jersey butter. They loved life more than money, and seemed to require no holiday beyond walking around their acres. Their boundaries were woods of wild cherry.

John said that when he tidied his yards the artists came and complained. Mostly the artists inhabited cottages which were too decayed for the farm workers. But there was also an erudite minority of super-artists who were super-gardeners. These even disliked roses. The

328

only roses they would admit into their gardens were those which are termed 'rose species'. I once dropped a brick among them by saying I liked a rose called Golden Ophelia. There was an embarrassed silence.

Et in Arcadia ego ... Yes, we too once dwelt in Arcady, that Arcady of the Stour Valley; but we did not try to understand the Higher Gardening: for us it was a life of cabbages and candles. Away off the beaten track we would find a lane bordered with cherry trees full of tinkling bells; those coiled spring bells which had once summoned parlour-maids, and were now hung in trees to keep off birds. There, an old man brought out very old wooden scales, and weighed us out inaccurate pounds.

The residents, as distinct from the farmers and impoverished artists, were chiefly the now middle-ageing 1914 generation, often childless. They made children of their houses, which were rickety-looking but very beautiful. One man had an emotional crisis because his porch had developed a crack whose progress he measured by sticking stamp paper across it. We knew by the look of him if the stamp paper had been found torn again that morning.

There were also the autocratic old shepherds: they lived in a time and a world of their own, among snows, under stars, looking out from the hatch doors of their wheeled huts on the far uplands of Guinea Wigs – men for whom there was neither antique nor modern but only sheep.

Farming was still in the doldrums: ditches were blocked, hedges were high and wild, and before harvest thistle-down was white like a mist over the fields of barley. In winter the valley often flooded. More than once I was confronted by a seemingly illimitable waste of water as I crossed the Stour Valley to Dedham on my way to supper with Alfred Munnings, whom I had come to know – 'A.J.' as we called him.

A gathering of youths would be standing on the bridge at Dedham Mill, and seeing the distant halted headlights of my car, shouted encouragement or warning, I could not know which. But supper with 'A.J.' was an entertainment not lightly to be missed. I advanced into the flood, sticking my head out of the window and watching the water level mounting above the hub-cap of the front wheel, to the sound of mingled cheers and laughter from the bridge. I came through: cars were built higher in those days.

I found Munnings as ever, ebullient. That I had nearly got stuck in the water was nothing. 'Look at that,' he cried, spanning two treads of his stair with one leg and demonstrating upwards with his right hand. It was a Sargent, I think, this time, which hung in the place of honour, to be saluted as he went up to bed and came down in the morning. He expatiated on the finer points of it.

Munnings had a generous enthusiasm for the work of his contemporaries, or near-contemporaries, matching in vehemence his contempt for more recent styles that seemed generated by cold intellect out of bad dreams. His walls were covered with pictures, his own and other painters'. It was difficult to get from the hall to the sitting-room of his handsome homely Georgian house, there was so much to look at on the way.

The dinner-table was lit by candles in two great silver branched candlesticks. Conversation tended to harp on the decay and misuse of the good earth of England; barley ears invisible for thistledown, land-jobbery, villas instead of cottages, boilersuits displacing the old sleeved waist-coats, tractors ousting horses. What an eloquent champion of old England Munnings was. Watching him there at the head of his table, I saw in him both Cobbett and Sir Roger de Coverley at consecutive moments. He gave us a dramatic description of the family at morning prayers in his father's mill house when he was a boy, and Lord Stradbroke's painted waggons suddenly going past the window; of his father leaving them all there on their knees to go and see that the corn was up to sample, returning ten minutes later and continuing the prayers. ...

Years later, I was sitting in the 'White Horse Inn' at Badingham when I read the notice of Munnings's death in the paper. I tried to believe that he was dead. We had sat in this inn together in those days when I lived by the Stour, on one of our excursions through the byways of Suffolk and Norfolk. Ever since those days, names on the map of East Anglia are scenes in my mind; inns, churches, villages among apple trees, with apples glimmering through leaves. Here today was an old man in the bar of the 'White Horse' telling me how he had mowed his two acres a day of barley, and his one of wheat and tied it up; a man after Munnings's own heart, one such as we used to meet in these country inns. He went on talking of his mowing with the scythe, and his driving of the tall loads as a boy; trace-horse, shaft-horse and the long harvest waggon, and how the 'unpitcher' would swear if he left a gap between the load and the stack, and how the stacker would swear if he let the load brush against the stack. I kept telling myself, yes, this is what we used to listen to, and here is the oak-ribbed bar of the 'White Horse', and the sunlight filtering in through summer leaves as it used to do, but Munnings is dead.

A promising morning, and the telephone would ring. Through the receiver would come a vocal noise, articulation drowning in feeling: 'Nowhere to ride my horse ... barbed wire ... bricks ... must get out ... move ... back where I belong'.

'All right,' I would reply, interpreting; 'I'll be with you in half an hour.'

Soon we would be setting off in his high, yellow open car, a young chauffeur driving and Munnings and I in the back, rugs round our knees, old hats dragged to shield our eyes: we really needed goggles.

If he liked the look of a house, he would tell the driver to stop, get out and conduct me up the drive as though it were his own home, pointing out admirable features. When just about to lead me round to view stables of the best Adam period, he would be intercepted by the owner, striding out from his portico red-faced and ferocious: 'You, there, what the devil do you want?'

Munnings would look at him, screwing up his one good eye, for all the world as if he were judging the irate squire's paintability. Just as flash-point between them was reached, they would discover they had a Norfolk cousin in common, or grand-uncle, and the clenched fist would suddenly be extended in welcome.

Or it might be a family of gipsies we chanced to meet, as in an inn at Boxford in high summer. Munnings was the same to all men. Again pints round, and gossip of So-and-so, and old So-and-so. He seemed to know half the gipsies of England personally. A man would pass the inn window on a cob. Munnings would stride out. 'I'm looking for just such a cob as that you're riding,' and fetch him a drink, and they would talk pint mugs to the bottom about horses they had known.

One of his favourite calls was on a man who at their first meeting had struck him with a stick, as he leaped for a third time into his field, hunting the fox on a day when it did clay soil no good at all to be trampled by hooves. In the altercation which followed, Munnings discovered that this long-suffering small farmer had formerly been a groom to a London veterinary surgeon. Interest in horses made them friends on the spot. Afterwards, whenever he was in that neighbourhood he would walk the mile along the green, bottomless lane where the ex-groom and his wife lived on their heavy-land holding, and sit gossiping for hours.

On the day after Munnings's death I retraced some of the old routes. Green byways were his hobby. I stopped at Dennington church, where he had given a woman half-a-crown to wash the face of the effigy of Lord Bardolf. It was sad to see how generations had scratched their initials on the alabaster body. In Stradbroke church he got up in the pulpit and preached me a sermon on Life and Art.

At Worlingworth we admired the font cover spiring to the roof, and the roof itself. But now I found the chancel barred off and a notice warning that the roof was in a dangerous condition. Worlingworth was peaceful still among propped apple trees, with intervals of silence between the passing of one vehicle and the next; time enough for a toad to cross the road, luxuriating in a dance of raindrops hitting the surface like small crystal explosions as a storm pelted down.

The sun gleamed again: there was a field of praying shocks: a child skipped past the 'Three Horseshoes', and a woman attended to a rose, a cigarette slanting from her lips.

In Brundish church Munnings had become subdued. 'How short life is. We toil at our art, and then we are gone. What is it all for, Bell?' An indomitable sparrow in the roof chirruped in answer. We roused, reopened the heavy door; and suddenly again all the birds of heaven were singing and the sun fell on us warm.

Immediately Munnings revived, and started one of his ballads. So we rollicked along in the old yellow car, with occasional imprecatory gestures at some herds of Friesian cows, those 'damned unpaintable cattle', till we came to Halesworth. There he bought a pint of shrimps. Thence we continued along the Roman road to Bungay, shrimp heads flying, ballad still going strong.

That may have been the day when we went to view Kirstead Old Hall, which Munnings had a fancy he might buy, to get back into his native Norfolk. On that occasion I was cast for the role of intending purchaser, Maurice Codner, the portrait painter, who was out with us, was co-opted to impersonate an architect, Munnings himself to pose as a mere friend, because he said that if his name were revealed the price would probably be stepped up sharply. ...

A wych elm leaned almost over our roof in the Stour Valley, going up all in a rush of boughs and curling over like dark hair. Too lovely a tree to be allowed to live, I have thought, remembering it; and sure enough, when last I passed that way it had gone. I remember looking out of my mullion window in summer dawns which flushed the myriad small leaves of that tree, which the first breeze made rustle. The valley floor stretched level, clouded blue with woods crowding the horizon. The river among its reeds revealed itself at a zigzag bend, like a flash of lightning where the sun struck. I would slip through the reeds in my canoe, hearing the first scratchings of men's hoes from behind a hedge, and perhaps meeting old D., a farmer of an ancient local stock, living out the depression alone in his ruinous, beautiful ancestral home by the river.

It was a strange interim, in that house of ours called Creams; the decaying farms on the one hand, and the city man's new craze for the rustic on the other. Farmers' houses were being bought up by settlers who came for the scenery, then found that a Tudor gem was a full-time job.

THE SECRET RIVER
Roger Deakin
(from *Waterlog*, 2000)

Suffolk, 4 August

Next day I met an otter in the Waveney. I swam round a bend in my favourite river in Suffolk and there it was, sunning itself on a floating log near the reed-bed. I would have valued a moment face to face, but it was too quick for that. It slipped into the water on the instant, the big paddle tail following through with such stealth that it left hardly a ripple. But I saw its white bib and the unmistakable bulk of the animal, and I knew I had intruded into its territory; knew also that it was underwater somewhere close, sensing my movements. It hadn't paused to puzzle over my unconventional mode of approach. It just went. It didn't miss a beat. We can scarcely be said to have communed, yet I can replay every frame of the brief encounter in slow motion, right down to the just-vacated wet log rolling back into balance, oscillating slightly, and my own emotions, a mixture of elation at a rare moment's audience with the most reclusive animal on the river (Ted Hughes called it 'a king in hiding') and shame at having interrupted its private reverie.

That otters came within a whisker of extinction in England and Wales during the late fifties and early sixties is well known. It happened suddenly and insidiously. But there are hopeful signs that they are now gradually returning to many of their traditional rivers. It has taken thirty years for the powerful poisons that killed them, organochloride pesticides like aldrin, dieldrin and DDT, to flush out of our rivers, and for people to realise that otters will only thrive in waters

334

that are left wild and untutored, as well as unpolluted, with plenty of wet woodland, untidy wood stacks, nettles, story-book gnarled trees full of hollows, and as few humans as possible.

I was swimming ten miles from the moat, where the Waveney defines the border between Norfolk and Suffolk. It is a secret river, by turns lazy and agile, dashing over shallow beds of golden gravel, then suddenly quiet, dignified and deep. It winds through water meadows, damp woods and marshes in a wide basin that was once tidal from Yarmouth to Diss, close to its source in the great watershed of Redgrave Fen, where its twin, the Little Ouse, also rises and flows off in the opposite direction, into the Fens. With its secret pools and occasional sandy beaches, the Waveney is full of swimming holes, diving stages improvised from wooden pallets, dangling ropes, and upturned canoes pulled up on the bank. Every two or three miles you come to a weir and a white-washed watermill.

I swam on beyond the otter pool, under some sort of spell. It struck me that the animal's particular magic does not stem so much from its rarity as its invisibility. It is through their puckish, Dionysian habit of veiling themselves from view that otters come to embody the river spirits themselves. Henry Williamson knew this when he wrote his great mythic poem of Tarka the Otter. In the best traditions of spirits, the otter reveals itself through signs. You hunt for their tracks on sandbars, or for their spraint, the aromatic dung they leave behind to mark their territory, like clues in an Easter-egg hunt, under bridges or on the lowest boughs of willow or alder.

That otters were once plentiful in the Waveney was clear enough until recently if you went to the Harleston Magpie, which used to be a principal meeting place for the Eastern Counties Otter Hounds. Before the pub was altered, there were still otter masks and pads on the walls there, and up the road at the De la Pole Arms in Wingfield they have even installed entire animals, mummified in glass cases. One of my Suffolk friends inherited a red and blue tweed hunting coat that would have been worn by a member of the Eastern Counties Otter Hounds. It must have been hot work, hurrying on foot up and down the river bank, and from pub to pub along the valley, in tweed suits. A student of rural customs, he also once saw an otter pad mounted on a wooden shield with the enigmatic inscription: 'Shanghai Otter Hounds, Wortwell Mill, 1912'. Quite by chance, he stumbled on the explanation in a bookshop the following year, looking through the memoirs of an officer of the Shanghai Police, Maurice Springfield, who, it seemed, had been the Master of the Shanghai Otter Hounds, and bought some of the dogs in Suffolk around 1912 to take back with him to China. He must have been allowed to hunt them with the East Anglian contingent, perhaps by way of a road test, running down the unfortunate otter at Wortwell Mill.

In the autumn of the year before, I had crossed Suffolk to Westleton Village Hall one Saturday morning to attend a training session in animal tracking organised by the Suffolk Wildlife Trust so that we could take part in a survey of the Suffolk rivers for otters, mink and water voles. About forty of us sat in the hall studying slides of their footprints, and learning more about their ways. Small plastic tubs containing otter and mink shit were solemnly passed round. It was a bit like a wine tasting. You waved the poos under your nose, sniffed, then passed on the sample to your neighbour. Our tutor described otter spraint as 'fragrant', with something of the quality of jasmine tea, but perhaps an added nuance of fish oil and new-mown hay. A sample of jasmine tea was also circulated. You need a good nose to be a successful otter detective. We took it on trust from our tutor that otter spraint is also 'tarry and tacky'. Mink, on the other hand, have, or do, 'scats'. Scats look quite like spraint, but smell like burnt rubber or rotten fish. I felt the aesthetics of the matter posed some threat to our scientific objectivity.

That afternoon, we had all gone down to the Eel's Foot at Eastbridge, within sight of the Sizewell B nuclear power station, and walked along the bank of the Minsmere river in a crocodile looking for real live otter spraint. The Minsmere otters, no doubt observing all this from the safety of some hollow tree, would have witnessed the unusual spectacle of forty humans queuing to lie full-length on the bank and sniff small dollops of poo, making appreciative sounds. Someone spotted a bubble and all forty of us froze, bright-eyed and bushy-tailed, but it was just a bubble. I find I have since rather gone off jasmine tea.

I had met my Waveney otter downstream of Mendham Mill, near where I began my swim, diving in from a lush meadow where giant puffballs grow in late summer, once in such profusion that I mistook them at first sight for a flock of sheep, or the naked bottoms of swimmers. The breaststroke had again served me well by being so silent. I swam on downstream, over festive streamers of waving ribbon weed, brushed by the floppy leaves of yellow waterlilies, through endless meandering bends, past swans that hissed, but swam away, and turned off into the still, secret world of one of the drainage channels that run in straight lines across the flood meadows. It was five feet wide, full of moorhens and humming with insect life. Damselflies of all hues and patterns courted each other madly right in front of my nose, quite unconcerned. They even flew about in *flagrante*, performing the extraordinary feat of flying and copulating at the same time; a kind of insect Mile High Club. Huge dragonflies, some blue, some brown, hawked up and down the water right over me, or perched undisturbed on lilies. As I pushed through between the reeds, rows of bubbles rose ahead of me as eels sank deeper into the mud, or where a moorhen had dived and was swimming off underwater. Eels are the favourite food of otters, and the most nutritious of all fresh-water fish. This was just the sort of haunt that would have appealed to the animal I miss most on this river: the coypu. It set me thinking about the different attitudes we adopt towards animals. Like the otter, it was a good swimmer, had luxuriant fur, and was recently driven to extinction on this river by the activities of humans. In its special way, it has also created its own myth; indeed the legend is all that is left of it, for since it became extinct in Britain, no one, apparently, would even dream of reinstating it.

The last coypu on the Waveney was martyred like Hereward the

Wake in some reedy outpost of the marshes in 1989. There used to be plenty of them pottering about incautiously along the river. I saw my last one in July 1986, preening itself on the banks of a stream at Thornham Magna in the headwaters near Eye. I also met several on canoe trips down the Waveney. Like mink, these harmless vegans originally escaped from fur farms. They are a native of South America, and probably suffered from some of the same animal racism now directed at the mink. They lived in the rivers and marshes and had all the usual rodent propensities for breeding and occasionally bingeing on carrots or sugar beet. Another of their favourite activities was to burrow teasingly into the banks of rivers and flood defences, thus whipping up even more paranoia amongst the farmers about the danger of inundating large parts of East Anglia.

The animals were good swimmers and had webbed feet. The females produced quins twice a year, and had their nipples high up on their bellies above the plimsoll line, so they could suckle their offspring as they swam alongside, keeping themselves well hidden in the marsh. Coypu could grow to over a yard long, and twelve stone in weight, so they never really had any natural predators in East Anglia. Being very big as well as very fecund and very greedy, they were too much for the Ministry of Agriculture, who, like Pat Garrett before them, hired a posse of men to hunt down every last coypu in the marshes. Cage traps the size of garden sheds began to appear up and down the Waveney, baited with carrots and sugar beet. Men in peaked caps and white vans buzzed up and down the valley. The operation dragged on for years, until someone at the Ministry twigged that it wasn't only the coypu who were adept at self-preservation. The very last thing the good ol' Norfolk and Suffolk boys at Coypu Control wanted was to see the last of the coypu exterminated. Rumour has it that they were eventually persuaded to finish off the job by the mention of generous coypu-sized redundancy packages.

The Waveney Clarion, community newspaper, voice of the people of the Waveney valley, was quick to recognise the rich symbolism of Coypu Control. If an animal chose to immigrate to the Marshes, why shouldn't it be welcome, whatever country it hailed from? True to its liberal traditions, the newspaper came out in full support of the colourful blend of fun-loving, gourmandising, hard-drinking Latin-American culture and general laid-back rodent mischief-making embodied in the fat-bottomed coypu and its struggle against the dastardly, jackbooted, but gullible Coypu Control. And so Mick Sparksman's Coypu Comix cartoon strip was born.

The Clarion was one of the most successful community newspapers of the 1970s, and circulated amongst the growing colony of romantic, liberal-minded people who lived, or had settled, in the general vicinity of the Waveney and shared the Whole Earth Catalogue ideals of the Woodstock era. Many had come from London, like me, and were working hard at the country life. Coypu was the star of the paper. Dressed in plaid trousers and a knotted scarf, he was a hippie Rupert Bear, getting up to all the tricks the Chums had hardly dared to dream about. Yet he was an innocent too. With his friends Reg Rabbit, Ramblin' Dog and Shiftless Mouse, he was forever having near squeaks with the Coypu Control officers. He had a weakness for Adnams ale, carrots, sugar beet, fresh-water mussels and jugs of home-made sugar beet wine. He was always 'starving' and always escaping by hopping into disguise, as a duck, a rabbit, a scarecrow, even a snowman. He once hitched a lift to London in a Lowestoft bloater lorry, feasting and sipping Adnams all the way. In the Coypu v. Rabbit Annual Cricket Match, the rabbits got all the runs and the coypus were sixteen all out. Coypu was an active member of the bungling Coypu Liberation Army and helped organise their annual Reggae and Cider Bonfire Party. He also staged a successful raindance during one of the East Anglian droughts. His favourite hymn, whistled at times of crisis, was 'All Things Bright and Beautiful'.

I returned through the meadows, swimming upriver against the gentle current to Mendham Mill, where the painter Alfred Munnings spent his boyhood. Munnings's brother, Frederick, eventually took over as miller from their father. His nephew Robert Moss gave me a lively account of his swimming education on holidays there as a child during the First World War.

The young Robert and his cousins learnt to swim in three stages. First, in March, they were driven forty miles in the open back of the mill's lorry to their Great-Aunt Ellen's house at Mundesley, on the north coast of Norfolk. Here, they were taken to the shore clad in striped bathing costumes and totally immersed in the sea. It was believed that wetting their heads protected them from chills. The old lady came in with them in the icy March winds, and the rule was, 'No bathe, no lunch', whatever the weather. Even during a year's sojourn with the navy in the High Arctic at 80 degrees north, Robert Moss was never so cold again.

Swimming lessons were resumed at Mendham Mill, where a huge weeping willow stood by the boathouse, and the river was shallow enough for the children's mothers to stand where the willow branches dipped in the water, but too deep for the children, who supported themselves by holding on to the tips of the willow twigs, gaining confidence from the sensation of actually swimming. Their mothers caught hold of their feet and taught their little legs the breaststroke.

They were then ready for Stage Three, in the confluence of the main river with the mill's by-pass streams. Here they learned to use the traditional technique of the village children. It depended on a bundle of reeds about five feet long and eighteen inches thick, bent into a gentle V-shape and tucked under the armpits to act as primitive water-wings. There was an ample harvest of buoyant reeds in the overflow channel between the floodgates. They feature in Alfred Munnings's painting in the Royal Academy of a young man and woman rowing their boat into the bank of reeds in that very channel. The bundle was tied with hempen yarn, usually scrounged from the man who mended sacks at the mill. It required skill to make it. It had to be tied not too tight and not too loose, so that each time it was used a few of the reeds would escape. The theory was that by the time the bundle had finally disintegrated, the aspiring swimmer would no longer need its support. It worked, too.

That evening, I went to Bungay in search of 'Bungay Beach', one of

the town's swimming holes, across the marshy wastes of Outney
Common, where the river kinks into a two-mile oxbow. The path led
over a slender single-span footbridge of cast iron and concrete that is
only sixteen inches wide; just wide enough to walk. The town reeve had
it built in 1922, and its economy of design is breathtaking. It has a single
handrail on one side only, and spans twenty-five feet. It is like a bridge
on a willow pattern plate, and it can only be there for swimmers. The
path now ran through a densely wooded island to its upstream end,
where rhythmic thwackings I couldn't quite place echoed round eight
giant horse chestnuts that supported several dangling ropes with wooden
handles over a deep, green pool surrounded by polished roots. Two boys
were drying their costumes by flogging them against the trees.
Swimming up to the tangle of tree roots in deep water, I experienced one
of those sudden intimations of dread, known to all wild swimmers, about
what could be lurking beneath the surface. This was a perfect pike pool;
what if a big pike was hiding up in one of the holes in the bank beneath
the roots? I swam quickly for the open water in mid-stream.

BLAXHALL AND BEYOND
George Ewart Evans & Oral History
Peter Tolhurst
(from *East Anglia: A Literary Pilgrimage*, 1996)

Just after the war a young Welsh writer arrived in Blaxhall quite
unaware that his friendship with elderly neighbours in this remote
Suffolk hamlet would change the whole direction of his writing and lay
the foundations of what has become known as 'Oral History'. Over the
next few years George Ewart Evans came to realise that those residents

born in the late 19th century were the last remnants of an ancient agricultural tradition – what he later referred to as a Prior Culture – that was being destroyed by the mechanisation of farm labour. The gradual replacement of horse power by the tractor was the main agent of change and for him 'the true end of the Middle Ages is not the accession of the Tudors but the introduction of the internal combustion engine'.

With the aid of a tape recorder he embarked on a remarkable salvage operation to chronicle this traditional rural culture across East Anglia before it disappeared, a daunting mission that preoccupied him for the rest of his life. His great achievements were to establish the value of personal recollection as a valid historical record and give the agricultural labourer a permanent voice in a series of books on East Anglian life spanning thirty years. The first of these, *Ask The Fellows Who Cut The Hay*, published shortly after he left the village in 1956, remains a celebrated tribute to the people of Blaxhall and a way of life that had survived intact until the outbreak of the Great War.

Unlike his contemporaries, Adrian Bell and Henry Williamson, who were determined to carry through their own practical experiments in farming and write about their experiences, Evans came to the region by chance and with no agenda for life in the countryside. Encouraged by the publication of his first short stories before the war, he had already decided to become a writer when his wife spotted an advertisement for the post of head teacher at a village school in East Suffolk and her successful application presented a solution to their current problems: 'Looking back on our last-ditch escape to Blaxhall, we saw it as a watershed in our lives' Evans concluded.

The village remained rather cut off from the outside world and must have presented a bleak picture to this exile from the Welsh valleys. It was three miles to the nearest railway station at Campsey Ash, there was just one bus each week to Ipswich and most people relied on bicycles to get about. Conditions were still quite primitive with no mains drainage, water from a well in the playground and light from oil lamps; but the promise of a school house which went with the job decided the outcome. Evans would look after the two younger children during the day and fit in his writing when he could. He adjusted well to his new role but growing deafness compounded his sense of isolation and he seldom saw anyone but the tradesmen for weeks at a time.

Out of Evans' predicament grew a friendship with neighbours that proved crucial. His children loved to watch Robert Savage, a retired shepherd, feeding his pigs or collecting ducks eggs in his yard opposite the school house, and as Evans spent more time listening to his stories, he began to discover evidence of a rich folk culture still alive in the village. Priscilla and Robert Savage spoke a pure Suffolk dialect enriched with archaic words and phrases that, from his reading of Chaucer and Shakespeare, Evans recognised to be centuries old. Savage referred to his time as a 'page' or apprentice to a shepherd, he used the word 'tempest' to describe a thunderstorm, 'abroad' for outdoors and a whole range of technical terms associated with agriculture which the Suffolk farmer Thomas Tusser had recorded in his *Hundreth Good Points of Husbandrie* in 1557. Evans continued to visit Robert Savage until his death and was quick to acknowledge the enormous debt he owed the old man who had become his mentor: 'He it was who gave me entry to what was a foreign country.'

As Evans became more involved in the life of Blaxhall, partly through his active role on the Parish Council, he acknowledged the differences between the loose knit pastoral communities he had known as a boy in South Wales and the more rigidly structured and deferential nature of society in the arable villages of Suffolk. But it was, ironically, the aquisition of two technical advances in communication which transformed his life and work. A hearing aid ended years of personal isolation and the loan of a new portable tape recorder enabled him to make a permanent record of his early conversations with Blaxhall residents. His one regret was that Robert Savage died before he was able to record 'the rhythm and colour of his speech' that he so admired but Priscilla Savage's memories of the domestic economy which make such an important contribution to *Ask The Fellows*, were saved.

From this tentative beginning, Evans began to construct a picture of traditional life in Blaxhall. George Messenger who worked on the barges at Snape maltings proved to be another rich source of material, describing how he cut wheat on his allotment using a serrated sickle, threshing it with a flail.

I bound up the wheat in little bunches. Then when it was thrashed I had a straw bed laid down nice and thick on the barn floor. And I got a *frail* and thrashed that. Then I'd take all the straw off the floor. There lay the wheat. I put it in a basket whatever I'd got and then dress it with a 'blower' or dressing machine (if I could borrow one). This would blow the chaff away. I remember the first time I used the *frail* I got a clout o' the skull that I'd remember. An old chap that was there said: 'Never mind that, you'll get plenty o' those.'

Abraham Ling's father had been a member of the Blaxhall company of shearers who travelled from farm to farm clipping sheep with handshears. In both cases hand tools were being used that had survived unaltered since biblical times. Traditional dances and folk songs were still performed at the Ship Inn. The women had a dance of their own: the Candlestick Dance, a ceremony with a very long history.

There were lighted candles in the middle of a ring and the women tucked their skirts between their legs. They danced over and around the candles. And the one that danced the longest without putting the candles out won the prize. The music was: 'Jack be nimble, Jack be quick. Jack jump over the candle stick.' Billy Salmon Prickett, a travelling man [a gypsy] played his fiddle, someone played an accordion and Walter Quinn used to play the tin whistle.

As Evans concluded, 'It is likely that there is here a vestige of an ancient custom of ceremony with fire; which was continued long after the original purpose was forgotten. Beltane fires were lit on May Day, and if there was a maypole it was afterwards burned; and there were fires that had a close connection with the corn harvest. In some places the midsummer fires were lit on St John's Day. It was thought that those who leaped over the fire would not suffer from backache at reaping. It was also thought that the higher you leaped over the flames the higher the corn would grow.'

Evans uncovered vestiges of ancient beliefs adhered to by the older generation that hardly seemed credible in the middle of the twentieth century, notably the origins of the Blaxhall Stone recounted by Lewis Poacher. This large sandstone boulder had been transported from Lincolnshire during the last Ice Age, but to Blaxhall people who knew nothing of glaciation, the only logical explanation was that the stone 'whoolly grew'.

My father-in-law ploughed it out, so he told me, in his time, ploughed it out and brought it up there and placed it down there in the farmyard in Stone Farm. And it's still there now. He brought it up and he reckoned it weighed about half a hundredweight when he brought it up. It weighs about five tons now.

My father-in-law was William Ling. He was a horseman at Stone Farm in Mr Toller's time. ... He lived along o' me after I married his daughter, and he used to tell me all these little things, and I tell Cyril [his son] and that's how he knows. But that stone has been there for years. And that whoolly grew. I haven't seen it lately but they tell me it's a huge size. That stone ha'grew, you see. They say that stones don't grow. They do!

Moving to Needham Market in 1956 Evans reflected:

I left the village [Blaxhall] with mixed feelings, because I sensed it was here I had found my life's work, although I did not fully realise this at the time. It was only some years after I left that I identified the village as my second academy [the first had been South Wales] when I began to learn the technique of what became later known as oral history ... it was here at this time, and with the dressing and elaborating on it later, that I transposed the Blaxhall community in my own mind into its true place in an ancient historical sequence. ... that had lasted well over two thousand years.

By the time the second edition of *Ask The Fellows* appeared in 1961 the break with the old tradition was almost complete. It seemed difficult to believe that within the space of a generation or two the old handskills had been discarded, the beliefs forgotten and the dialect impoverished. The young tractor driver listening to the Light Programme in the comfort of his new council house knew little of his father's skill with heavy horses and cared even less. But Evans understood the advantages of mechanisation and personal mobility well enough to be unsentimental about the passing of the old ways. Isolated rural communities often bred the worst kind of parochialism and he acknowledged the inevitable drift to the towns for work and entertainment.

The withdrawal of public transport, the closure of rural post offices, and the demise of the primary school have turned places like Blaxhall into retreats for Londoners drawn to the peculiar beauty of the Suffolk coast and the concerts at Snape maltings. Internet cottage industries and craft workshops now flourish in those once damp, poorly lit dwellings where, nearly 50 years ago, Evans made his first recordings of Suffolk farm labourers.

From his conversations with elderly Blaxhall residents Evans became aware that the most deep-rooted beliefs, indeed the very texture of dialect, sprang from basic working practices. East Anglia had for centuries been a region of arable farming and in *The Horse in the Furrow* (1960), Evans explored the activities and customs associated with horsepower. Completed at Needham Market with illustrations by the wildlife artist C F Tunnicliffe, it is dedicated to the old horsemen, especially those in and around the Gipping valley whose personal recollections were interwoven with contemporary farm records in this celebration of the heavy horse.

The most intriguing revelations are reserved for the last section which examines the wealth of folklore surrounding the horse. Evans discovered that some old horsemen were renowned for their skill in controlling horses. Furthermore, oral evidence from the Stowmarket area identified the existence of a secret society of horsemen, an elite and powerful group with ancient origins, rather like the Freemasons, that kept alive the old beliefs and passed on the knowledge through esoteric rituals.

Someone round here has been telling you about the horseman's business – about stuff and chemicals, the frog's boon and all thet. Well, you don't want to believe half on it. It's someone who's heard a bit of it and is making the rest up. Now I'll tell you about the frog's boon. First of all not one in ten thousand knows what kind of a frog it comes from, or would be able to recognize the boon if they saw it – not one in ten thousand. I knew only one man in this district who had one. The frog you were after wasn't easy to come by: it were a rare kind. It were a black frog with a star on its back; and you'd be most likely to find one in a wood where they'd been a-felling trees. You'd get one, maybe, under an owd felled log or something like thet. After you'd caught it you had to kill it and hang it up on a blackthorn tree to dry. Then you took it down and treated it till it were all broke up and dismembered. Or you could clean it by putting it in an ant hill: the ants would pick all its flesh off the boons. You then took it to a running stream at mid-night and placed it in the water. Part of it would float upstream; and that's the part you had to keep.

Evidence came to light for the existence of similar sects in other parts of Britain, especially in north east Scotland. Using the horse's highly developed sense of smell, members of the Society would smear a gate post or harness with an obnoxious mixture including the powdered frog's bone that would 'jade' the animal, stopping it in its tracks. Other mixtures of herbs and spices had the opposite effect, giving the horseman the power to 'draw' or call the horse at will.

Having endured the noise of heavy traffic through Needham Market for six years, Evans and his wife moved to the peace of Helmingham in 1962 when Florence found a new teaching post at the village school. Helmingham Hall had for centuries been the ancestral home of the Tollemache family and here in the mid nineteenth century John Tollemache laid out his model village complete with school, smithy and picturesque double dwellers all in the style of 'Tollemache Tudor' and each with its own neatly tended allotment garden. Within this 'closed' village estate workers enjoyed a security of tenure and a standard of living unfamiliar to those in 'open' villages beyond the Tollemache domain. But inevitably the price for improved conditions was some loss of personal freedom. Tenants were obliged by the terms of their agreement to attend church on Sunday, to dress according to their station and acknowledge the presence of Lord Tollemache and Her Ladyship. Despite his ambivalence towards the aristocracy, Evans soon felt at home in this manicured landscape and he consoled himself that at least the school house was rented to the education authority.

In his finest book, *The Pattern under the Plough* (1966), written at Helmingham with drawings by David Gentleman, Evans explored the pagan origins of horse cults together with the widespread survival in East Anglia of those folklore elements he discovered in Blaxhall. He succeeded in gathering together the many scattered fragments of pre-Christian beliefs associated with the home and farm; beliefs that by the late twentieth century had degenerated into superstitions but were still expounded by the older survivors of Evans' 'prior' culture. From his reading of the *The Golden Bough* and *The White Goddess*, Evans was able to set the folklore of East Anglia within the wider context of customs and beliefs once prevalent throughout Western Europe. Impressed by its scope, Robert Graves declared that 'a single page of *The Pattern under the Plough* is worth a wilderness of folk-motifs'.

The first part of the book examines the range of sympathetic magic used to protect the home against evil spirits and Evans returned to the same theme when considering the power of the 'hagstone' to ward off the 'nightmare' or 'hag' that would otherwise ride a horse leaving it 'hagridden' and in a lather the following day. Hung over the stable door, this flint with a hole through it was equivalent to the All-Seeing Eye and gave the stone its power as an amulet. Prior to its domestication the horse had been a sacred totemic animal in Britain, especially among the Celts, and the distaste of horseflesh persists to this day even though its slaughter is no longer taboo. Many folk customs that survived well into the twentieth century were descended from ancient horse cults including the Mari Lwyd, a wassailing tradition still alive in Glamorganshire when Evans was a boy. It was part of his cultural inheritance and helps explain the author's recurring fascination with the subject, a fascination at the heart of his work in East Anglia and one to which he finally returned in *Horse Power and Magic* (1979).

TO GRUNSHAM MAGNA

Adrian Bell

(from *My Own Master*, 1961)

So we found ourselves on a day travelling from South Suffolk into North-east Suffolk. ... We set off after breakfast, and soon came in sight of our new home. It looked bare, square and austere; a brick box built in 1863, and its rooms a series of boxes within the box. It seemed at first to be too prosaic to be anything but a convenient machine in which to bring up children. But there was something mysterious about its lack of charm: it became a home. ...

I found myself once again, after warmer, kinder soils, planted on a tenacious clay, a soil with which I was familiar from the days of my farming in Benfield St. George. So, in one sense, I felt at home; as soon, in fact, as it rained, and I found the soil picking up like damp pastry on my soles.

Some people are wanderers by nature and never strike root. They go through life more easily than those of us who identify ourselves with a particular piece of earth; acres or a fraction of an acre, even of a cold and savage clay. We had bought this house from a Miss Leaf, who decided to move when her brother, with whom she lived here, and who had farmed, had died.

But Miss Leaf did not long survive uprooting herself from her old home in the cold clay parish where I succeeded her. She sold it to me a few years after her farmer brother had died. But for those few years of her sole tenure here, she gave rein to exotic dreams in the garden. Which was curious, since she was a Scotswoman, of austere personal habits. But where her brother had grown potatoes and cabbages, she had made beds of lilies and calceolarias. She had planted rhododendrons and azaleas, that hate clay, and variegated brooms that liked it little better. We inherited that summer a brilliant spectacle. I remember walking up and down a path between flower beds on the first Sunday morning after our arrival, hearing a single church bell sounding from over some trees, and saying to myself, 'Whatever is to be done about all this?' Farming can be made to spare a little time for gardening, if you are interested in it, but not for Miss Leaf's kind of gardening.

There came a sudden piercing frost early in that first winter. It was the moment of truth: the garden's semi-exotic mask shrivelled: I was left with an expanse of dour clay.

Then came February: snow melted. But much of the garden remained white – with snowdrops. They were peeping up in clumps, here, there, everywhere. We picked bowlfuls: they scented the rooms faintly of honey. We transplanted a few to the edge of a rose bed under the windows. In a year or two the whole bed became a white sheet. The children planted a ring of snowdrops round the grave of a robin in the shrubbery. Soon the shrubbery was carpeted with snowdrops.

We learned that this clay, the heaviest, stickiest, most boot-clogging, encouraged an extraordinary mobility – of flowers. Snowdrops marched: they proliferated like a procession of nuns to the beech hedge, where they met a migration of aconites from the other side, and fraternized under its buff leafy winter wall. Thence they moved onward to a sunny bank, where primroses celebrated mixed marriages; wild ones from the paddock and the survivors of Miss Leaf's rarities from the garden. I have never seen such a promiscuity of pollination as went on there around a certain pine tree. There were even crimson cowslips.

As the years passed, the garden asserted its true nature; the clay re-clothed itself. It was no longer Miss Leaf's brilliant showpiece, but scatterings of the humble flowers which inspired England's poets: 'February Fair Maids', 'violets dim' and 'pansies freaked with jet'. (Who ever celebrated a calceolaria?) It was a garden which, released

350

from Miss Leaf, mingled itself with the paddock: wild violets were soon in our rose beds, and daffodils in the orchard. ...

The other small room was my bedroom in our brick home in North-east Suffolk, in the village of Grunsham [Redisham]. Superficially it was the meanest room in the house. It had nothing to recommend it but a cupboard with the hot tank in it. Its floor was splintery, its window shaky, its door three plain deal planks with a small brass knob. This had been the maid's bedroom when the house had been a vicarage, and vicars had kept maids. It was on the wrong side of the baize-covered doors which divided even this miniature vicarage of a living worth fifty-one pounds a year.

When Miss Leaf, showing us over the house, had said, 'As a matter of fact I prefer this room to sleep in myself,' I registered in my mind, 'Perverse old thing, having those other three nice bedrooms to choose from, and two of them facing south into the orchard.' This small room had an excellent view of the slate roof of the stable.

And yet, I too came to inhabit this room, and by choice. It was furnished with our odds and ends, iron bed, fading rug. By placing the bed in a certain spot, I could see past the end of the stable, into the back garden, where four ancient apple trees stood with intervolved boughs, one of them lying almost prone. That narrow glimpse became, I don't know why, more to be desired by me than the whole of the orchard in front. There was a lilac leaning backwards into a ditch, just visible above the stable.

When I think of the Old Testament story of Laban and Jacob eating bread together on a heap of stones, I remember that small room, because it was in there that I read it at the end of a long farming day. I remember that little room not for health but for family sickness, not for peace but for war, for fatigue. Yet there was a peace too. I read those Old Testament stories to get my mind off its concerns. I drank my early tea at six, sitting on the window sill if it was spring or summer, with yesterday's labours still stiff in my back, and the birds' songs half drowned by the drone of bombers assembling overhead for another raid. I read a psalm, not for any innate faith, but to try if I might discover what had been to former

351

men a source of strength. I could not see the sun from the window, which faced north-west, but I woke to that white lilac flashing full in it, and the knowledge that the news from the hospital where Marjorie had gone for an operation had yesterday been better.

In June the sunset lay out there in the north-west. I could lie with the window-sash right up, staring myself to sleep at it, while breaths of air came cool over acres of green corn.

For things read, and sunsets, and the pony stirring in the stable below, I remember that small room more than any of the others. And I remember its glimpse above the stable roof of a hundred acres of clay, of brick-earth, so difficult to farm, flashing in an April shower.

There was that bell ringing every Sunday from over the yew trees of the garden, a single bell, plaintive like a sheep's bell. Beyond a meadow I could see the eaves of a barn and granary gables; and a wooden belfry that seemed to be perched right among them, half hidden by feathery green willow foliage flowing in the wind. It looked like a beehive, painted white, with a gold cock roosting on it. In the meadow a horse stood swinging its tail. There were also stacks over there. The church seemed to be right in the middle of agriculture, a part of it.

One Sunday, soon after our arrival, I crossed the ditch out of my paddock at a spot where an old sleeper lay athwart it. The sleeper had a hole in it, and the hole was covered by a loose piece of tin, slippery to tread on, which clanked as I trod on it. As I went on, I thought, the clank of that loose tin is the sort of sound which becomes part of a person's life. If I live here long enough I suppose I shall hear it in my sleep. And I did.

I crossed a field, and climbed a stile into the churchyard. The churchyard was full of knapweed, clover, hogweed; a wild-flower garden, stuck about with headstones bearing gold medals of lichen. A hen was peering through a fence opposite, where a farmyard was.

The church had a Norman doorway, with zigzag designs framing a door with iron strappings. It stood open. The church was empty as yet of humanity, but crowded with a congregation of round heads and long heads, golden tresses. There were plumped cabbages, and a choir of corn-sheaves, tight-waisted. Heads of oats bowed down, and turnips were in a row like the scrubbed faces of schoolboys. There was a tawny mangold and a scarlet beet, marrows like green hogs. Grey veils of 'old-man's-beard' draped the altar rails. A cluster of lilies were preaching from the pulpit, with vivid tongues.

A man stood pulling on a bell-rope. It had a fat plush grip of twined colours that made me think of swing-boats. The man's face was gentle, and reminded me of T. S. Eliot. I smiled. He smiled back at me, and nodded in time with his ringing.

I was early, so I sat down for five minutes in the porch, looking out at the land, some of it already ploughed. Then I saw approaching up the path a bunch of huge dahlias on human legs. Dahlias always remind me of the flowers we used to doodle at school with a pair of compasses; too precise and perfect. But these that approached were like fog lamps, blazing orange-yellow. A woman completely hidden by them was carrying them, a late contribution to the harvest decorations...

People entered at first in ones and twos, and then in families. Soon the small church was crowded with people, that already had seemed crowded with produce. Some piece of the internal mechanism of the harmonium thrust regularly against the material with which the back was covered, and it fascinated the eye rather, as when somebody's elbow makes a sudden bulge in a theatre curtain before it is due to rise. This palpitation affected the dahlias, so that they nodded like puppets whenever an Amen was played. I seemed to notice it mostly then: A-nod, men-nod: the great silly shining heads.

About half-way through the service an earwig emerged from a cell of a pink ruched dahlia of a bunch of small ones on the window-sill beside me. It crept down the wall, and then along the top of the pew in front of me. It stood waving its feelers about as if undecided whether to climb the neck of the child sitting before me, or to descend on to my prayer book upon the ledge. It chose to descend. The lesson was now being read, and my prayer book lay open at the next psalm. The earwig traversed a page of it, keeping to a line of print, and stopped on the word Lord as if struck by a thought. It set off again in a determined way, straight down the pew to the floor. The man who had read the lesson was just walking back to his place. His right foot missed the earwig by a fraction of an inch.

I lost the creature during the sermon, but in standing up for the last hymn, I caught sight of it again. It had mounted the chancel step, and stood there, as if questing. Decision came: it moved along the edge of a floor-board in the direction of the altar. Loudly all sang the joyful harvest hymn; and I did too, for boots were now all about that tiny black dot on the floor, boots of the parson moving to the altar, and of the two sidesmen bringing up the offertory bags; a sixfold danger.

We knelt for the blessing. I prayed for the safety of the earwig, so nearly at the end of its long long journey from the dahlia. I could still just make it out, a tiny black dot, but still going. It would get under the altar cloth, and lie safe and sanctified in a six-day silence.

When I returned by the field path to my house, I looked up Earwig in the *Encyclopaedia Britannica*. It was as I thought. The diagram of its anatomy showed that it too was an intricate temple of life.

GUMA'S VALLEY
Ronald Blythe
(from *Places: An Anthology of Britain*, 1981)
(The author lives in the Stour valley)

I was about to begin, 'I remember my first sight of this remote old house', only to realize that I do not. It is a wholly unexpected realization. Does it mean that, from now on, I must assume some loss of recall of what happened at the beginning of things, and that I could be one of those people who fail to stock up naturally with initial impressions, whether of places or people? The notion that my brain doesn't start its docketing processes until the importance and necessity of someone or something in my life has been confirmed by subsequent encounters, is a novel one. But a few tests prove the opposite, and so it is just this farmhouse. There was a day when I first saw it, but the day has got lost and since diary-keeping has always been a stop-go affair with me, and those who lived here then had no reason at that time to put me in their journals, no words exist to jog my memory. It would have been summer, certainly, which may be why, even in bare and open January, the site for me retains an all-the-year-round seclusion and density. I never so much as come back from a walk without feeling that I have to break my way into it, although winding grassy paths give access in all directions.

My old friends John and Christine Nash bought it for a few hundred pounds in the middle of the last war. It was quite in character that although he was busy in the Marines and she working endless hours at different ports, there should run parallel the dominant peace-time obsessions of a home from which one need never walk more than half a mile to find plenty to draw and paint, and a garden in which there was a soil for all seasons. They'd actually had their eye on it for a decade or more before they took the plunge and took it off Mr Lewis's hands, as they said. He must have given one of those great heartfelt sighs of agricultural relief, for it had been empty for years and was rapidly becoming, in the way of ancient dwellings of its kind, all of a hummocky, bosky piece with its grounds. Nettles (which always grow at their mightiest best where men have lived for generations) grew all around it by the acre, and fruit trees had impacted themselves with the architecture, so that here and there one could reach up in a room and pick Blenheim Oranges or elderberries. And just as there were boughs trying to get indoors, so there were writhing hanks of convolvulus doing their best to get out. After all these years one still finds a few inches of it curling from the crevasses in the scrubbed floor where the patterns created by moist clay set out to dry on Stuart or Georgian grass show up vividly after a dose of Flash. Brick-floor scrubbing is, of course, a lost art – and a well-lost art at that, most will say. But the colour it brought to the interiors of all sorts of buildings, churches, inns, farms, and cottages, used to be an important element in their aesthetic. The brick floors in this house don't stay wet and brightly coloured for more than an hour or two. One has hardly had time to put the rugs back before the little flattened shapes of plants of centuries ago vanish from their fast-drying surfaces and they take on their parched, anhydrous look, clinking silverly where they are loose. When John and Christine took the house on (I use this phrase judiciously, for its ownership involves one in a running battle of wills between occupier and half a millennium of local building materials) the stream actually ran straight through it, like the stream in Wordsworth's Dove Cottage. It is a few yards to the north of the garden now, I'm relieved to say, but still part of the watery network which culminates in the slow-flowing Stour, Gainsborough's and Constable's river only a mile or two off. At certain moments when the light is caught, this famous river, one of whose little arteries enticed a Saxon farmer to chance his luck in this spot, glitters and winks against the windows, and the sound of the stream running to it never ceases. Neither ice nor drought has ever silenced it.

Although the house had suffered some of the typical vicissitudes of the agricultural depression, having its hundred or so acres annexed by a neighbouring farm, coming down in the world from yeoman independence to squire's tenantry and even to becoming a double-dweller for farm-workers, and ultimately to years of emptiness, it had never been entirely abandoned, for I recently discovered the following pencilled on the inside of a 'Tenner' cigarette-box which had been carefully placed on a ledge under the stairs: 'Feb 19th 1937 painted outside of this House and Distempered inside. H. W. Spooner and B. Welford. NAYLAND & Boxted.' The box also contained a nail and a hazel-nut. But the abandonment of its ancient roadway, barns, piggery and stackyard was another matter. There had been no attempt to keep these in some ticking-over order, and from being the means of access and operation of the place, they had, with astonishing swiftness, reversed their roles and become the chief threat to its future habitation. There is almost no more daunting ruin than a ruined farm, or a more unappealing one. The merciful thing was that neither John nor Christine would have seen the place in such terms. Its past and future laid lightly on their conscience and imagination. They simply had an exciting hunch of the uses it could be put to *now*, even in the middle of a war, and in this respect they were like that great seventeenth-century gardener John Tradescant who, while fighting in a battle, was observed botanizing during the carnage, bending down among the swords and blood and digging up interesting specimens. And so they spent the latter part of their work-filled lives here, and myself the first part of mine. These years running away from and towards the centre have passed slowly and thoroughly, leaving parallel but differing impressions. For quite a long time after their deaths I felt it a compulsion and a duty to let things run on in the way they always had, and which they could have done, because strong personalities and well-regulated lives leave behind them rhythms and patterns which have learnt how to repeat themselves long after those who originally set them in motion have departed, but one morning this need simply wasn't there. It had evaporated, had been overcome like the hoar-frost hanging around in the frost-pocket by the bay-tree when the sun burst in on it.

It is always a problem to know what to do in a landscape where others have done so much. Do nothing, could be the answer. It is finished, so contemplate on what is. But gardens and antiquated water supplies, and banks and medieval tracks, not to mention the view itself, partly exist to keep one on the go, physically and intellectually, and the mere maintenance of what 'is' subtly turns it into what you would like it to be. I doubt if one could so much as weed a bed without leaving one's own creative mark. Not that such minimal activity would have done for Bottengoms, or Guma's Valley, where I have an increasing sense of its inhabitants being kept well on the go for centuries. A closer stare at its situation tells me that the farm crouches sideways in a valley which is in a valley, that ages ago the people who worked here dug out a shallow recess in the western hill so that they could dwell in a high-rimmed saucer lowered into the natural declivity. And more digging on an heroic scale must have gone on between the front garden and the first of the front fields, where one side of the ditch is as steep as a defensive earthwork. The up-hill, down-dale of it all makes it laborious still. Nowhere can one see everything at once; it is all vistas within vistas and, from less than a mile off, even these interlocking definitions vanish and last winter, plunging back from the village along the field ridges where the snow was thinnest, I found to my amazement that Guma's half-dug, half-natural valley had utterly disappeared in a white-out and that a compass wouldn't have come amiss. On that icy day I understood an important aspect of the farm's siting where John was concerned, how its landscape was both domestic ('Back to the old homestead!' he would say as his little car, crammed with drawing-boards, bottles of milk, fishing-tackle, plants, and plenty of rubbish, jogged down the track) and dramatic. How its solid 'peace', as the visitors invariably describe its atmosphere, is for its residents shot through and fractured by sharp little threatenings which you can't actually put your finger on but which keep you on your toes. Low-lying places are supposed to be soporific but this sunken house isn't. Cunningly masked by an extravagant display of calm, it has its own uneasy system of alerts to raise the adrenalin.

It could be the valley's objection to the hubris which has unconsciously beset its most recent occupancy. All this painting and writing, it is saying, what does it amount to in my time-scale? Forty years of art as against possibly fourteen hundred years of ploughing, of centuries of feeding off those slopes which provide only your views. Even in your present house, the valley insists, men and women have been looking out of the windows since the Tudors, and seeing much the same folds and clefts in the soil, and their accompanying skies, and it is likely that not a fraction of what you say you see so much as crossed their minds. Rooms, grounds, the stream, the track, how can they be expected to run without protest to these come-lately rhythms after running for such ages in time with the great drudge of the seasons?

There scarcely exists so much as a pencil scrawl of the house itself by John. Every kind of oil, water-colour, drawing, and woodcut of everything spread out around it, of course, but not of the building itself. Its purpose for him was to be able to work away inside it at what he could see from it. Like the subjects people never mention, there is a special eloquence about this deliberate omission. What was it about the house that forbade him putting it into the picture? The barns, yes (the last tumbledown skeleton of which is being battered into the earth by tractors as I write), the basic lines of Guma's land certainly, for such patterns provided him with a kind of ultimate poetry; every tree, every cutting and, if he could have had his way, every flower, but not the old homestead, a phrase often said in a tone of cagey mockery.

It is a beautiful house, powerful, confident. It is a typical East Anglian long house which likes you to think that it is younger than it is and no more than three or four hundred, but tucked away under its artful bodging lurks its true antiquity. But it follows the traditional style of a huge rectangular oaken frame set on brick sills, and with the interstices of its half-timbering (halved or cut wood, as opposed to unshaped logs) stuffed tight with wattle screens plastered with earth. The roof is its crowning glory without a doubt. Originally thatched and dizzily steep, it has since the eighteenth century boasted one of the most generous tile slopes in the neighbourhood, for after the addition of the Georgian dairy and store-rooms its descent was carried to within four feet of the garden. These lovely hand-made tiles in their many thousands, and some still pinned to the battens with delicately whittled hawthorn pegs, do not descend with a sheer, hard linear force, but with a slightly dipping, skirt-spreading concavity which is so gentle that one doesn't notice at first that there is such a lovely tilting check in their rush towards the grass. The rooms ramble into each other with a not so much as 'by your leave' and have never heard of anything as discreet as a corridor. Here and there are fragments of generations of partitioning, shoved up and pulled down as many now unknowable births and deaths required. In the roof itself, and quite window-less, but still white- and blue-washed, are a lot of little rooms which can only be reached by ladders, and which could have been the bothy, or the unmarried labourers' quarters. Straw pallets, snow on their faces, and mouse fidgetings. Downstairs the vast open hearths still hide behind a Victorian grate and an oil-fired Rayburn respectively. The latter is very near to being the house-god, so comfort-and pleasure-giving is it. William Barnes once wrote a furious and despairing poem about the usurpation of the ancient hearths by the Rayburn's nineteenth-century ancestors.

The garden surges urgently against the walls and has to be beaten back. In summer the south wall completely vanishes behind a thirty-foot vine in which birds sleep in their scores. One hears their weary flittering and cheeping just behind the bedhead, and when there is a strong wind, the scrunch of vine boughs on the brickwork. The vine is so high that I've never managed to get at the topmost grapes and they swing just below the apex of the roof until November, when they tumble, soft and rotten, into the huge euphorbias which flourish here. Dioscorides, who was physician to Antony and Cleopatra, and who also wrote one of the first herbals, is said to have named this great spurge after Euphorbus, physician to King Juba of Mauritania. John considered it 'very handsome', an accolade he bestowed on women as well as favoured plants. Along the dairy wall and recessed between fat brick buttresses are fuchsias and, in late summer, a forest of balsam whose seed-pods explode at the merest finger-touch, communicating their own urgency to the human nervous system. *Impatiens*, the botanists call it. The saucer-shaped ground tips sharply upwards here and the garden John made loses itself in the Old Orchard, a tangled, fruitless place which is a rabbit and pheasant kingdom, and from which one bursts on the far side upon a soaring view that encompasses Bures and the land-sweep towards Aga Fen. This is East Angle – East Saxon border country where King Edmund was crowned in 855. He was fifteen and he reigned for fifteen years before the manner of his death turned him into England's St. Sebastian. I can see Cuckoo Hill, the site of his coronation, from the garden-edge, as well as the smudge of brown which is Bottengom's Farm from the spot where Edmund, Offa's adopted son, received the Saxon diadem. The Stour divides these tribal lands. Its name means 'powerful' or maybe 'worshipful stream' and perhaps there is a mystic connection between this lovely Suffolk-Essex river and the River Stura in Cisalpina Gallia which flowed near the Rubicon and into Italy to join the Po. These classical thoughts are allowable to someone living in an old valley only six miles from Colchester, the birthplace of St. Helena, mother of Constantine, the shrine of the deified Claudius – and the capital of Cymbeline. Our church tower is entirely built of Roman bricks, and as children we searched for arrow heads on the hillside below Edmund's chapel as this particular field was said to be where Boadicea skirmished, although we never found one. The harvests from Bottengom's would have floated slowly past it on the river barges which collected up produce from Harwich to Sudbury. My neighbour who has farmed the Bottengom's fields for fifty years tells me that deep in the chalk of those which rise so spectacularly to meet one's gaze as one clambers from the Old Orchard, there are seven springs. One of them has 'watered' this place ever since it was inhabited, man and creatures. The others break surface further along in ponds, a small lake, ever-running ditches, and cuts.

John loved a pond as much as anything. 'Never pass up a good pond', was his motto. The four in his garden are tiny but crammed with fish and plants. In the summer you need a machete to find them. The boggy ground near them produces an heroic vegetation, partly exotic, partly native, which totally conceals them. In the old days there would be pond-cleaning forays when the weather was hot so that we could work in them stripped except for a thin, silky covering of mud, and with the perch darting between our knees. 'It's clean mud', we told each other as we dragged up the weed. He often painted these ponds in their catholic thickets of bamboo, crab-apple, giant dock, guelders, willow, and hemlocks. Nightingales would sing there as he drew, though these have gone now.

To the east the garden is bordered by the track, the bastion-like entrenchment, and the pastures – now in the process of being ploughed for corn. Above this hill are the Horkesleys, the 'hurks' or Saxon lamb shelters, and a mysterious fortification called Pitchbury Ramparts, and below the hill on the other side lies the little wool town of Nayland whose bells and church clock can be heard in the farmhouse when the wind is right. A huge palette-shaped bed crammed to the edges with pink and yellow peonies, carpets of cyclamen, tea-roses and a lifetime's amassing of flowers of every kind is spread out here. I have sometimes seen friends or visitors attempting to formulate or diagnose what taste or impulse lay behind the creation of this garden, and I myself found it hard to say what judgement and rules made it and governed it. Until, after John's death, I began to read Dean Hole. Although in his enchanting *Book About Roses* – which I commend to anyone who is interested in pure pleasure – S. Reynolds Hole deals only with this supreme flower, I recognize both in accent and attitude a concept of gardening lust and philosophy, aesthetic and preferment which was John's to a T. It was an entirely unselfconscious, really wholly unaware Victorian standard of intellectual gardening that he introduced to Guma's midden and cabbage-patch, and maintained. Guma's garden, if such an unlikely thing existed, would certainly have been succeeded by a long list of country gardens with their matter-of-fact mixing of blooms and food, all different, all gone, save in remnants such as the great Portugal quince with its regular hundredweight of furry-skinned fruit and its not-quite-nice scent. Village folk used to add quince to an apple-pie to make it 'brisk', and they set it among their pear-trees to make them extra fruitful. It is very acid and maybe the pectin called quin is named after it. Fragments of old walls, too, circumscribe earlier garden patterns. And there is a stout holly hedge, half veiled in bryony, which was planted as a barrier against something or other long ago – though what? Lightly digging in the early spring, I now and then exhume a yard or two of the cinders and flints of Victorian paths. There remain, too, inconclusive stumps in the blond aftermath of rough scythings where fine old trees once stood, and which seem to petrify and remain, rather than rot away. John drew out the present garden above or around all this, as well as in terms which owed nothing to mid-twentieth-century taste in such matters.

He himself illustrated many excellent gardening essays by some of the best garden-makers of his time but the emotion or spirit of his own garden derives from the immediately preceding taste. And where is this taste most confidently and unaffectedly displayed – but in Dean Hole's *A Book About Roses*. Once, wandering about Falmouth, I stumbled across, as they say, the Dean's autobiography, *Then and Now*, which I triumphantly presented to John. He received it with the caution which one would show at being offered a key to what one has always privately known, and I was reduced to reading my own gift, though allowed to 'call bits out' (which he rather liked).

'Call a bit out', he'd say.

The bits I'd call out now would not be from the Dean's life, sensible and kind though it was, but from his little masterpiece, for if the essence of what occurred during the 1940s and '50s in Guma's Valley can be found on any printed page, it lies in this Victorian rosarium. John's pencil ticks against his favourite blooms in the appendix – *Charles Lefebvre, Mrs John Laing* ('a continuous bloomer'), *Prince Camille de Rohan* ('the freest flowering of all the dark roses' – he had a passion for dark roses), *Cristata, White* (Provence roses), *De Meaux* (miniature Provence or pompon), *Red Damask, Rosa Mundi*, and *Tuscany* (adored), *Boule de Neige* (dazzling white clusters), *Dundee Rambler* (Ayreshire), the creamy *Félicité Perpétué*, which is an evergreen, the *Old Blush* and *Cramoisie Supérieure* china roses, the great tea-roses *Bouquet d'Or* and, of course, *Gloire de Dijon* (his favourite flower) and the pretty little Japanese picotee-edged rose *Fimbriata*, all beloved roses of the Nineties, and most could have been found in Benjamin Cant's celebrated nursery at Colchester at this time – reveal his determination to collect those necessary for his existence, but it is the actual style and philosophy of the Dean's

363

outlook on gardening generally which is echoed at Bottengom's. How amazed the previous owner, Mr Lewis, and indeed all those centuries of farmers and their wives who 'like to see a bit of a show, like, near the house' would have been by what John Nash liked. Winding, irregular paths, particularly with plants flopping over the edges, secret dank corners, walks mown between tall grass in which a sequence of flowers appeared from February to November, everything from precious things such as fritillaries and martagon or Turk's cap lilies, to lords and ladies, and especially handsome stands of sheep's parsley, and dead trees clothed in climbers. Wildness and cultivation were lured into hob-nobbing.

The only way in which this early and this belated Victorian gardener differed entirely was in their botany. John called himself an artist-plantsman, not a gardener, the Dean a rosarian – and 'a true gardener'. John was also a brilliant botanist but the Dean, because he could not master the subject himself, doubted if one could find 'a scientific botanist and a successful florist [i.e. grower of flowers] under the same hat'. The Dean said he was like the undergraduate who, told off by a farmer for riding over his wheat, answered, 'I am no botanist'. So that while the Bottengom's garden is, in summer, knee-deep in those delights recommended by Dean Hole, it also contains a certain intellectual force which is not exactly relaxing. Except for eating his meals in it during good weather, I never saw John lying about on the grass, as I do. It kept him very much on his toes. The Dean, I fancy, would have been neither learned nor idle but would have walked about from shrub to shrub, joyful and exclaiming. Guma, should he catch sight of either one of us from his forgotten barrow on some stony hoo by the river, would be bewildered by the elaboration of it all. He who had the sheltered corn slopes, the beasts in the hurk, the running water, and the wooden hall to live in.